THE MYTHS OF MEXICO AND PERU

LEWIS SPENCE

DOVER PUBLICATIONS, INC.
NEW YORK

This Dover edition, first published in 1994, is an unabridged republication of *The Myths of Mexico & Peru*, originally published by George G. Harrap & Company Ltd., London, in 1913. Some of the illustrations have been repositioned for this edition; five were originally in color.

Library of Congress Cataloging-in-Publication Data

Spence, Lewis, 1874–1955.
    The myths of Mexico and Peru / Lewis Spence. — Dover ed.
        p.   cm.
    Originally published: London : G.G. Harrap, 1913.
    Includes bibliographical references and index.
    ISBN 0-486-28332-1 (pbk.)
        1. Indian mythology—Mexico.   2. Indian mythology—
    Peru.   3. Maya mythology.   I. Title.
    F1219.3.R38S75   1994
    398.2′089972—dc20   94-22661
                                                          CIP

Manufactured in the United States of America
Dover Publications, Inc., 31 East 2nd Street, Mineola, N.Y. 11501

PREFACE

IN recent years a reawakening has taken place in the study of American archæology and antiquities, owing chiefly to the labours of a band of scholars in the United States and a few enthusiasts in the continent of Europe. For the greater part of the nineteenth century it appeared as if the last word had been written upon Mexican archæology. The lack of excavations and exploration had cramped the outlook of scholars, and there was nothing for them to work upon save what had been done in this respect before their own time. The writers on Central America who lived in the third quarter of the last century relied on the travels of Stephens and Norman, and never appeared to consider it essential that the country or the antiquities in which they specialised should be examined anew, or that fresh expeditions should be equipped to discover whether still further monuments existed relating to the ancient peoples who raised the *teocallis* of Mexico and the *huacas* of Peru. True, the middle of the century was not altogether without its Americanist explorers, but the researches of these were performed in a manner so perfunctory that but few additions to the science resulted from their labours.

Modern Americanist archæology may be said to have been the creation of a brilliant band of scholars who, working far apart and without any attempt at co-operation, yet succeeded in accomplishing much. Among these may be mentioned the Frenchmen Charnay and de Rosny, and the Americans Brinton, H. H. Bancroft, and Squier. To these succeeded the German scholars Seler, Schellhas, and Förstemann, the Americans Winsor, Starr, Savile, and Cyrus Thomas, and the Englishmen Payne and Sir Clements Markham. These men,

PREFACE

splendidly equipped for the work they had taken in
hand, were yet hampered by the lack of reliable data
—a want later supplied partly by their own excavations and partly by the painstaking labours of
Professor Maudslay, principal of the International
College of Antiquities at Mexico, who, with his wife,
is responsible for the exact pictorial reproductions of
many of the ancient edifices in Central America and
Mexico.

Writers in the sphere of Mexican and Peruvian
myth have been few. The first to attack the subject
in the light of the modern science of comparative
religion was Daniel Garrison Brinton, professor of
American languages and archæology in the University
of Philadelphia. He has been followed by Payne,
Schellhas, Seler, and Förstemann, all of whom, however,
have confined the publication of their researches to
isolated articles in various geographical and scientific
journals. The remarks of mythologists who are not
also Americanists upon the subject of American myth
must be accepted with caution.

The question of the alphabets of ancient America
is perhaps the most acute in present-day pre-Columbian
archæology. But progress is being made in this branch
of the subject, and several scholars are working in
whole-hearted co-operation to secure final results.

What has Great Britain accomplished in this new
and fascinating field of science ? If the lifelong and
valuable labours of the late Sir Clements Markham
be excepted, almost nothing. It is earnestly hoped
that the publication of this volume may prove the
means of leading many English students to the study
and consideration of American archæology.

There remains the romance of old America. The
real interest of American mediæval history must ever

PREFACE

circle around Mexico and Peru—her golden empires, her sole exemplars of civilisation ; and it is to the books upon the character of these two nations that we must turn for a romantic interest as curious and as absorbing as that bound up in the history of Egypt or Assyria.

If human interest is craved for by any man, let him turn to the narratives of Garcilasso el Inca de la Vega and Ixtlilxochitl, representatives and last descendants of the Peruvian and Tezcucan monarchies, and read there the frightful story of the path to fortune of red-heeled Pizarro and cruel Cortés, of the horrible cruelties committed upon the red man, whose colour was "that of the devil," of the awful pageant of gold-sated pirates laden with the treasures of palaces, of the stripping of temples whose very bricks were of gold, whose very drain-pipes were of silver, of rapine and the sacrilege of high places, of porphyry gods dashed down the pyramidal sides of lofty *teocallis*, of princesses torn from the very steps of the throne—ay, read these for the most wondrous tales ever writ by the hand of man, tales by the side of which the fables of Araby seem dim —the story of a clash of worlds, the conquest of a new, of an isolated hemisphere.

It is usual to speak of America as "a continent without a history." The folly of such a statement is extreme. For centuries prior to European occupation Central America was the seat of civilisations boasting a history and a semi-historical mythology second to none in richness and interest. It is only because the sources of that history are unknown to the general reader that such assurance upon the lack of it exists.

Let us hope that this book may assist in attracting many to the head-fountain of a river whose affluents water many a plain of beauty not the less lovely because

PREFACE

bizarre, not the less fascinating because somewhat remote from modern thought.

In conclusion I have to acknowledge the courtesy of the Bureau of American Ethnology, which placed in my hands a valuable collection of illustrations and allowed me to select from these at my discretion. The pictures chosen include the drawings used as tail-pieces to chapters; others, usually half-tones, are duly acknowledged where they occur.

LEWIS SPENCE

CONTENTS

LIST OF ILLUSTRATIONS

LIST OF ILLUSTRATIONS

LIST OF ILLUSTRATIONS

THE DESCENT OF QUETZALCOATL

CHAPTER I : THE CIVILISATION OF MEXICO

The Civilisations of the New World

THERE is now no question as to the indigenous origin of the civilisations of Mexico, Central America, and Peru. Upon few subjects, however, has so much mistaken erudition been lavished. The beginnings of the races who inhabited these regions, and the cultures which they severally created, have been referred to nearly every civilised or semi-civilised nation of antiquity, and wild if fascinating theories have been advanced with the intention of showing that civilisation was initiated upon American soil by Asiatic or European influence. These speculations were for the most part put forward by persons who possessed but a merely general acquaintance with the circumstances of American aboriginal civilisation, and who were struck by the superficial resemblances which undoubtedly exist between American and Asiatic peoples, customs, and art-forms, but which cease to be apparent to the Americanist, who perceives in them only such likenesses as inevitably occur in the work of men situated in similar environments and surrounded by similar social and religious conditions.

The Maya of Yucatan may be regarded as the most highly civilised of the peoples who occupied the American continent before the advent of Europeans, and it is usually their culture which we are asked to believe had its seat of origin in Asia. It is unnecessary to refute this theory in detail, as that has already been ably accomplished.[1] But it may be remarked that the surest proof of the purely native origin of American

---

[1] By Payne in *The New World called America*, London, 1892-99.

civilisation is to be found in the unique nature of American art, the undoubted result of countless centuries of isolation. American language, arithmetic, and methods of time-reckoning, too, bear no resemblance to other systems, European or Asiatic, and we may be certain that had a civilising race entered America from Asia it would have left its indelible impress upon things so intensely associated with the life of a people as well as upon the art and architecture of the country, for they are as much the product of culture as is the ability to raise temples.

Evidence of Animal and Plant Life

It is impossible in this connection to ignore the evidence in favour of native advancement which can be adduced from the artificial production of food in America. Nearly all the domesticated animals and cultivated food-plants found on the continent at the period of the discovery were totally different from those known to the Old World. Maize, cocoa, tobacco, and the potato, with a host of useful plants, were new to the European conquerors, and the absence of such familiar animals as the horse, cow, and sheep, besides a score of lesser animals, is eloquent proof of the prolonged isolation which the American continent underwent subsequent to its original settlement by man.

Origin of American Man

An Asiatic origin is, of course, admitted for the aborigines of America, but it undoubtedly stretched back into that dim Tertiary Era when man was little more than beast, and language as yet was not, or at the best was only half formed. Later immigrants there certainly were, but these probably arrived by way of Behring

2

Strait, and not by the land-bridge connecting Asia and America by which the first-comers found entrance. At a later geological period the general level of the North American continent was higher than at present, and a broad isthmus connected it with Asia. During this prolonged elevation vast littoral plains, now submerged, extended continuously from the American to the Asiatic shore, affording an easy route of migration to a type of man from whom both the Mongolian branches may have sprung. But this type, little removed from the animal as it undoubtedly was, carried with it none of the refinements of art or civilisation ; and if any resemblances occur between the art-forms or polity of its equal descendants in Asia and America, they are due to the influence of a remote common ancestry, and not to any later influx of Asiatic civilisation to American shores.

Traditions of Intercourse with Asia

The few traditions of Asiatic intercourse with America are, alas ! easily dissipated. It is a dismal business to be compelled to refute the dreams of others. How much more fascinating would American history have been had Asia sowed the seeds of her own peculiar civilisation in the western continent, which would then have become a newer and further East, a more glowing and golden Orient ! But America possesses a fascination almost as intense when there falls to be considered the marvel of the evolution of her wondrous civilisations—the flowers of progress of a new, of an isolated world.

The idea that the " Fu-Sang " of the Chinese annals alluded to America was rendered illusory by Klaproth, who showed its identity with a Japanese island. It is not impossible that Chinese and Japanese vessels may have drifted on to the American coasts, but that they sailed thither of set purpose is highly improbable. Gomara, the Mexican historian, states that those who served with Coronado's expedition in 1542 saw off the Pacific coast certain ships having their prows decorated with gold and silver, and laden with merchandise, and these they supposed to be of Cathay or China, "because they intimated by signs that they had been thirty days on their voyage." Like most of these interesting stories, however, the tale has no foundation in fact, as the incident cannot be discovered in the original account of the expedition, published in 1838 in the travel-collection of Ternaux-Compans.

Legends of European Intercourse

We shall find the traditions, one might almost call them legends, of early European intercourse with America little more satisfactory than those which recount its ancient connection with Asia. We may dismiss the sagas of the discovery of America by the Norsemen, which are by no means mere tradition, and pass on to those in which the basis of fact is weaker and the legendary interest more strong. We are told that when the Norsemen drove forth those Irish monks who had settled in Iceland, the fugitives voyaged to "Great Ireland," by which many antiquarians of the older school imagine the author of the myth to have meant America. The Irish *Book of Lismore* recounts the voyage of St. Brandan, Abbot of Cluainfert, in Ireland, to an island in the ocean which Providence had intended as the abode of saints. It gives a glowing account of his seven years' cruise in western waters, and tells of numerous discoveries, among them a hill of fire and an endless island, which he quitted after an unavailing journey of forty days, loading his ships

4

with its fruits, and returning home. Many Norse legends exist regarding this "Greater Ireland," or "Huitramanna Land" (White Man's Land), among them one concerning a Norseman who was cast away on its shores, and who found there a race of white men who went to worship their gods bearing banners, and "shouting with a loud voice." There is, of course, the bare possibility that the roving Norsemen may have on occasions drifted or have been cast away as far south as Mexico, and such an occurrence becomes the more easy of belief when we remember that they certainly reached the shores of North America.

The Legend of Madoc

A much more interesting because more probable story is that which tells of the discovery of distant lands across the western ocean by Madoc, a princeling of North Wales, in the year 1170. It is recorded in Hakluyt's *English Voyages* and Powel's *History of Wales*. Madoc, the son of Owen Gwyneth, disgusted by the strife of his brothers for the principality of their dead father, resolved to quit such an uncongenial atmosphere, and, fitting out ships with men and munition, sought adventure by sea, sailing west, and leaving the coast of Ireland so far north that he came to a land unknown, where he saw many strange things. "This land," says Hakluyt, "must needs be some part of that country of which the Spaniards affirme themselves to be the first finders since Hanno's time," and through this allusion we are enabled to see how these legends relating to mythical lands came to be associated with the American continent. Concerning the land discovered by Madoc many tales were current in Wales in mediæval times. Madoc on his return declared that it was pleasant and fruitful, but uninhabited. He succeeded in persuading a large number of people to accompany him to this delectable region, and, as he never returned, Hakluyt concludes that the descendants of the folk he took with him composed the greater part of the population of the America of the seventeenth century, a conclusion in which he has been supported by more than one modern antiquarian. Indeed, the wildest fancies have been based upon this legend, and stories of Welsh-speaking Indians who were able to converse with Cymric immigrants to the American colonies have been received with complacency by the older school of American historians as the strongest confirmation of the saga. It is notable, however, that Henry VII of England, the son of a Welshman, may have been influenced in his patronage of the early American explorers by this legend of Madoc, as it is known that he employed one Guttyn Owen, a Welsh historiographer, to draw up his paternal pedigree, and that this same Guttyn includ_d the story in his works. Such legends as those relating to Atlantis and Antilia scarcely fall within the scope of American myth, as they undoubtedly relate to early communication with the Canaries and Azores.

American Myths of the Discovery

But what were the speculations of the Red Men on the other side of the Atlantic? Were there no rumours there, no legends of an Eastern world? Immediately prior to the discovery there was in America a widely disseminated belief that at a relatively remote period strangers from the east had visited American soil, eventually returning to their own abodes in the Land of Sunrise. Such, for example, was the Mexican legend of Quetzalcoatl, to which we shall revert later in its more essentially mythical connection. He landed with several companions at Vera Cruz, and speedily brought to bear

6

the power of a civilising agency upon native opinion. In the ancient Mexican *pinturas,* or paintings, he is represented as being habited in a long black gown, fringed with white crosses. After sojourning with the Mexicans for a number of years, during which time he initiated them into the arts of life and civilisation, he departed from their land on a magic raft, promising, however, to return. His second advent was anxiously looked for, and when Cortés and his companions arrived at Vera Cruz, the identical spot at which Quetzalcoatl was supposed to have set out on his homeward journey, the Mexicans fully believed him to be the returned hero. Of course Montezuma, their monarch, was not altogether taken by surprise at the coming of the white man, as he had been informed of the arrival of mysterious strangers in Yucatan and elsewhere in Central America ; but in the eyes of the commonalty the Spanish leader was a "hero-god" indeed. In this interesting figure several of the monkish chroniclers of New Spain saw the Apostle St. Thomas, who had journeyed to the American continent to effect its conversion to Christianity.

A Peruvian Prophecy

The Mexicans were by no means singular in their presentiments. When Hernando de Soto, on landing in Peru, first met the Inca Huascar, the latter related an ancient prophecy which his father, Huaina Ccapac, had repeated on his death-bed, that in the reign of the thirteenth Inca white men of surpassing strength and valour would come from their father the Sun, and subject the Peruvians to their rule. "I command you," said the dying king, "to yield them homage and obedience, for they will be of a nature superior to ours." [1]
But the most interesting of American legends connected

---

[1] Garcilasso el Inca de la Vega, *Hist. des Incas,* lib. ix. cap. 15.

with the discovery is that in which the prophecy of the Maya priest Chilan Balam is described. Father Lizana, a venerable Spanish author, records the prophecy, which he states was very well known throughout Yucatan, as does Villagutierre, who quotes it.

The Prophecy of Chilan Balam
Part of this strange prophecy runs as follows : " At the end of the thirteenth age, when Itza is at the height of its power, as also the city called Tancah, the signal of God will appear on the heights, and the Cross with which the world was enlightened will be manifested. There will be variance of men's will in future times, when this signal shall be brought. . . . Receive your barbarous bearded guests from the east, who bring the signal of God, who comes to us in mercy and pity. The time of our life is coming. . . ."

It would seem from the perusal of this prophecy that a genuine substratum of native tradition has been overlaid and coloured by the influence of the early Spanish missionaries. The terms of the announcement are much too exact, and the language employed is obviously Scriptural. But the native books of Chilan Balam, whence the prophecy is taken, are much less explicit, and the genuineness of their character is evinced by the idiomatic use of the Maya tongue, which, in the form they present it in, could have been written by none save those who had habitually employed it from infancy. As regards the prophetic nature of these deliverances it is known that the Chilan, or priest, was wont to utter publicly at the end of certain prolonged periods a prophecy forecasting the character of the similar period to come, and there is reason to believe that some distant rumours of the coming of the white man had reached the ears of several of the seers.

8

THE TYPE OF MEXICAN CIVILISATION

These vague intimations that the seas separated them from a great continent where dwelt beings like themselves seem to have been common to white and red men alike. And who shall say by what strange magic of telepathy they were inspired in the minds of the daring explorers and the ascetic priests who gave expression to them in act and utterance ? The discovery of America was much more than a mere scientific process, and romance rather than the cold speculations of mediæval geography urged men to tempt the dim seas of the West in quest of golden islands seen in dreams.

The Type of Mexican Civilisation

The first civilised American people with whom the discoverers came into contact were those of the Nahua or ancient Mexican race. We use the term "civilised" advisedly, for although several authorities of standing have refused to regard the Mexicans as a people who had achieved such a state of culture as would entitle them to be classed among civilised communities, there is no doubt that they had advanced nearly as far as it was possible for them to proceed when their environment and the nature of the circumstances which handicapped them are taken into consideration. In architecture they had evolved a type of building, solid yet wonderfully graceful, which, if not so massive as the Egyptian and Assyrian, was yet more highly decorative. Their artistic outlook as expressed in their painting and pottery was more versatile and less conventional than that of the ancient people of the Orient, their social system was of a more advanced type, and a less rigorous attitude was evinced by the ruling caste toward the subject classes. Yet, on the other hand, the picture is darkened by the terrible if picturesque

9

rites which attended their religious ceremonies, and the dread shadow of human sacrifice which eternally overhung their teeming populations. Nevertheless, the standard of morality was high, justice was even-handed, the forms of government were comparatively mild, and but for the fanaticism which demanded such troops of victims, we might justly compare the civilisation of ancient Mexico with that of the peoples of old China or India, if the literary activity of the Oriental states be discounted.

The Mexican Race

The race which was responsible for this varied and highly coloured civilisation was that known as the Nahua (Those who live by Rule), a title adopted by them to distinguish them from those tribes who still roamed in an unsettled condition over the contiguous plains of New Mexico and the more northerly tracts. This term was employed by them to designate the race as a whole, but it was composed of many diverse elements, the characteristics of which were rendered still more various by the adoption into one or other of the tribes which composed it of surrounding aboriginal peoples. Much controversy has raged round the question regarding the original home of the Nahua, but their migration legends consistently point to a northern origin; and when the close affinity between the art-forms and mythology of the present-day natives of British Columbia and those of the Nahua comes to be considered along with the very persistent legends of a prolonged pilgrimage from the North, where they dwelt in a place "by the water," the conclusion that the Nahua emanated from the region indicated is well-nigh irresistible.[1]

[1] See Payne, *History of the New World called America*, vol. ii. pp. 373 *et seq.*

LEGENDS OF MEXICAN MIGRATION

In Nahua tradition the name of the locality whence the race commenced its wanderings is called Aztlan (The Place of Reeds), but this place-name is of little or no value as a guide to any given region, though probably every spot betwixt Behring Strait and Mexico has been identified with it by zealous antiquarians. Other names discovered in the migration legends are Tlapallan (The Country of Bright Colours) and Chicomoztoc (The Seven Caves), and these may perhaps be identified with New Mexico or Arizona.

Legends of Mexican Migration

All early writers on the history of Mexico agree that the Toltecs were the first of the several swarms of Nahua who streamed upon the Mexican plateau in ever-widening waves. Concerning the reality of this people so little is known that many authorities of standing have regarded them as wholly mythical, while others profess to see in them a veritable race, the founders of Mexican civilisation. The author has already elaborated his theory of this difficult question elsewhere,[1] but will briefly refer to it when he comes to deal with the subject of the Toltec civilisation and the legends concerning it. For the present we must regard the Toltecs merely as a race alluded to in a migration myth as the first Nahua immigrants to the region of Mexico. Ixtlilxochitl, a native chronicler who flourished shortly after the Spanish conquest of Mexico, gives two separate accounts of the early Toltec migrations, the first of which goes back to the period of their arrival in the fabled land of Tlapallan, alluded to above. In this account Tlapallan is described as a region near the sea, which the Toltecs reached by voyaging southward, skirting the coasts of California.

[1] See Spence, *Civilisation of Ancient Mexico*, chap. ii.

This account must be received with the greatest caution. But we know that the natives of British Columbia have been expert in the use of the canoe from an early period, and that the Mexican god Quetzalcoatl, who is probably originally derived from a common source with their deity Yetl, is represented as being skilled in the management of the craft. It is, therefore, not outside the bounds of possibility that the early swarms of Nahua immigrants made their way to Mexico by sea, but it is much more probable that their migrations took place by land, following the level country at the base of the Rocky Mountains.

The Toltec Upheaval

Like nearly all legendary immigrants, the Toltecs did not set out to colonise distant countries from any impulse of their own, but were the victims of internecine dissension in the homeland, and were expelled from the community to seek their fortunes elsewhere. Thus thrust forth, they set their faces southward, and reached Tlapallan in the year 1 Tecpatl (A.D. 387). Passing the country of Xalisco, they effected a landing at Huatulco, and journeyed down the coast until they reached Tochtepec, whence they pushed inland to Tollantzinco. To enable them to make this journey they required no less than 104 years. Ixtlilxochitl furnishes another account of the Toltec migration in his *Relaciones*, a work dealing with the early history of the Mexican races. In this he recounts how the chiefs of Tlapallan, who had revolted against the royal power, were banished from that region in A.D. 439. Lingering near their ancient territory for the space of eight years, they then journeyed to Tlapallantzinco, where they halted for three years before setting out on a prolonged pilgrimage, which occupied the tribe for over a century, and in the course of which it halted at no less than thirteen different resting-places, six of which can be traced to stations on the Pacific coast, and the remainder to localities in the north of Mexico.

Artificial Nature of the Migration Myths

It is plain from internal evidence that these two legends of the Toltec migrations present an artificial aspect. But if we cannot credit them in detail, that is not to say that they do not describe in part an actual pilgrimage. They are specimens of numerous migration myths which are related concerning the various branches of the Mexican races. Few features of interest are presented in them, and they are chiefly remarkable for wearisome repetition and divergence in essential details.

Myths of the Toltecs

But we enter a much more fascinating domain when we come to peruse the myths regarding the Toltec kingdom and civilisation, for, before entering upon the origin or veritable history of the Toltec race, it will be better to consider the native legends concerning them. These exhibit an almost Oriental exuberance of imagination and colouring, and forcibly remind the reader of the gorgeous architectural and scenic descriptions in the *Arabian Nights*. The principal sources of these legends are the histories of Zumarraga and Ixtlilxochitl. The latter is by no means a satisfactory authority, but he has succeeded in investing the traditions of his native land with no inconsiderable degree of charm. The Toltecs, he says, founded the magnificent city of Tollan in the year 566 of the Incarnation. This city, the site of which is now occupied by the modern town of Tula, was situated north-west of the mountains which bound the Mexican valley. Thither were the Toltecs guided by the powerful necromancer Hueymatzin (Great Hand), and under his direction they decided to build a city upon the site of what had been their place of bivouac. For six years they toiled at the building of Tollan, and magnificent edifices, palaces, and temples arose, the whole forming a capital of a splendour unparalleled in the New World. The valley wherein it stood was known as the " Place of Fruits," in allusion to its great fertility. The surrounding rivers teemed with fish, and the hills which encircled this delectable site sheltered large herds of game. But as yet the Toltecs were without a ruler, and in the seventh year of their occupation of the city the assembled chieftains took counsel together, and resolved to surrender their power into the hands of a monarch whom the people might elect. The choice fell upon Chalchiuh Tlatonac (Shining Precious Stone), who reigned for fifty-two years.

Legends of Toltec Artistry

Happily settled in their new country, and ruled over by a king whom they could regard with reverence, the Toltecs made rapid progress in the various arts, and their city began to be celebrated far and wide for the excellence of its craftsmen and the beauty of its architecture and pottery. The name of "Toltec," in fact, came to be regarded by the surrounding peoples as synonymous with " artist," and as a kind of hall-mark which guaranteed the superiority of any article of Toltec workmanship. Everything in and about the city was eloquent of the taste and artistry of its founders. The very walls were encrusted with rare stones, and their masonry was so beautifully chiselled and laid as to resemble the choicest mosaic. One of the edifices of which the inhabitants of Tollan were most justly proud was the temple wherein their high-priest officiated. This building was a very gem of architectural art and mural decoration. It contained four apartments. The walls of the first were inlaid with gold, the second with precious stones of every description, the third with beautiful sea-shells of all conceivable hues and of the most brilliant and tender shades encrusted in bricks of silver, which sparkled in the sun in such a manner as to dazzle the eyes of beholders. The fourth apartment was formed of a brilliant red stone, ornamented with shells.

The House of Feathers

Still more fantastic and weirdly beautiful was another edifice, " The House of Feathers." This also possessed four apartments, one decorated with feathers of a brilliant yellow, another with the radiant and sparkling hues of the Blue Bird. These were woven into a kind of tapestry, and placed against the walls in graceful hangings and festoons. An apartment described as of entrancing beauty was that in which the decorative scheme consisted of plumage of the purest and most dazzling white. The remaining chamber was hung with feathers of a brilliant red, plucked from the most beautiful birds.

Huemac the Wicked

A succession of more or less able kings succeeded the founder of the Toltec monarchy, until in A.D. 994 Huemac II ascended the throne of Tollan. He ruled first with wisdom, and paid great attention to the duties of the state and religion. But later he fell from the high place he had made for himself in the regard of the people by his faithless deception of them and his intemperate and licentious habits. The provinces rose in revolt, and many signs and gloomy omens foretold the downfall of the city. Toveyo, a cunning sorcerer, collected a great concourse of people near Tollan, and by dint of beating upon a magic drum until the darkest hours of the night, forced them to dance to its sound until, exhausted by their efforts, they fell headlong over a dizzy precipice into a deep ravine, where they were turned into stone. Toveyo also maliciously destroyed a stone bridge, so that thousands of people fell into the river beneath and were drowned. The neighbouring volcanoes burst into eruption, presenting a frightful aspect, and grisly apparitions could be seen among the flames threatening the city with terrible gestures of menace.

The rulers of Tollan resolved to lose no time in placating the gods, whom they decided from the portents must have conceived the most violent wrath against their capital. They therefore ordained a great sacrifice of war-captives. But upon the first of the victims being placed upon the altar a still more terrible catastrophe occurred. In the method of sacrifice common to the Nahua race the breast of a youth was opened for the purpose of extracting the heart, but no such organ could the officiating priest perceive. Moreover the veins of the victim were bloodless. Such a deadly odour was exhaled from the corpse that a terrible pestilence arose, which caused the death of thousands of Toltecs. Huemac, the unrighteous monarch who had brought all this suffering upon his folk, was confronted in the forest by the Tlalocs, or gods of moisture, and humbly petitioned these deities to spare him, and not to take from him his wealth and rank. But the gods were disgusted at the callous selfishness displayed in his desires, and departed, threatening the Toltec race with six years of plagues.

Toveyo and the Magic Drum
William Sewell

(See page 16)

The Plagues of the Toltecs

In the next winter such a severe frost visited the land that all crops and plants were killed. A summer of torrid heat followed, so intense in its suffocating fierceness that the streams were dried up and the very rocks were melted. Then heavy rain-storms descended, which flooded the streets and ways, and terrible tempests swept through the land. Vast numbers of loathsome toads invaded the valley, consuming the refuse left by the destructive frost and heat, and entering the very houses of the people. In the following year a terrible drought caused the death of thousands from starvation, and the ensuing winter was again a marvel of severity. Locusts descended in cloud-like swarms, and hail- and thunder-storms completed the wreck. During these visitations nine-tenths of the people perished, and all artistic endeavour ceased because of the awful struggle for food.

King Acxitl

With the cessation of these inflictions the wicked Huemac resolved upon a more upright course of life, and became most assiduous for the welfare and proper government of his people. But he had announced that Acxitl, his illegitimate son, should succeed him, and had further resolved to abdicate at once in favour of this youth. With the Toltecs, as with most primitive peoples, the early kings were regarded as divine, and the attempt to place on the throne one who was not of the royal blood was looked upon as a serious offence against the gods. A revolt ensued, but its two principal leaders were bought over by promises of preferment. Acxitl ascended the throne, and for a time ruled wisely. But he soon, like his father, gave way to a life of dissipation, and succeeded in setting a bad example to the members of his court and to the priesthood, the vicious spirit communicating itself to all classes of his subjects and permeating every rank of society. The iniquities of the people of the capital and the enormities practised by the royal favourites caused such scandal in the out-lying provinces that at length they broke into open revolt, and Huehuetzin, chief of an eastern viceroyalty, joined to himself two other malcontent lords and marched upon the city of Tollan at the head of a strong force. Acxitl could not muster an army sufficiently powerful to repel the rebels, and was forced to resort to the expedient of buying them off with rich presents, thus patching up a truce. But the fate of Tollan was in the balance. Hordes of rude Chichimec savages, profiting by the civil broils in the Toltec state, in-vaded the lake region of Anahuac, or Mexico, and settled upon its fruitful soil. The end was in sight !

A Terrible Visitation

The wrath of the gods increased instead of diminish-ing, and in order to appease them a great convention of the wise men of the realm met at Teotihuacan, the sacred city of the Toltecs. But during their delibera-tions a giant of immense proportions rushed into their midst, and, seizing upon them by scores with his bony hands, hurled them to the ground, dashing their brains out. In this manner he slew great numbers, and when the panic-stricken folk imagined themselves delivered from him he returned in a different guise and slew many more. Again the grisly monster appeared, this time taking the form of a beautiful child. The people, fascinated by its loveliness, ran to observe it more closely, only to discover that its head was a mass of corruption, the stench from which was so

18

fatal that many were killed outright. The fiend who had thus plagued the Toltecs at length deigned to inform them that the gods would listen no longer to their prayers, but had fully resolved to destroy them root and branch, and he further counselled them to seek safety in flight.

Fall of the Toltec State

By this time the principal families of Tollan had deserted the country, taking refuge in neighbouring states. Once more Huehuetzin menaced Tollan, and by dint of almost superhuman efforts old King Huemac, who had left his retirement, raised a force sufficient to face the enemy. Acxitl's mother enlisted the services of the women of the city, and formed them into a regiment of Amazons. At the head of all was Acxitl, who divided his forces, despatching one portion to the front under his commander-in-chief, and forming the other into a reserve under his own leadership. During three years the king defended Tollan against the combined forces of the rebels and the semi-savage Chichimecs. At length the Toltecs, almost decimated, fled after a final desperate battle into the marshes of Lake Tezcuco and the fastnesses of the mountains. Their other cities were given over to destruction, and the Toltec empire was at an end.

The Chichimec Exodus

Meanwhile the rude Chichimecs of the north, who had for many years carried on a constant warfare with the Toltecs, were surprised that their enemies sought their borders no more, a practice which they had engaged in principally for the purpose of obtaining captives for sacrifice. In order to discover the reason for this suspicious quiet they sent out spies into Toltec territory, who returned with the amazing news that the Toltec domain for a distance of six hundred miles from the Chichimec frontier was a desert, the towns ruined and empty and their inhabitants scattered. Xolotl, the Chichimec king, summoned his chieftains to his capital, and, acquainting them with what the spies had said, proposed an expedition for the purpose of annexing the abandoned land. No less than 3,202,000 people composed this migration, and only 1,600,000 remained in the Chichimec territory.

The Chichimecs occupied most of the ruined cities, many of which they rebuilt. Those Toltecs who remained became peaceful subjects, and through their knowledge of commerce and handicrafts amassed considerable wealth. A tribute was, however, demanded from them, which was peremptorily refused by Nauhyotl, the Toltec ruler of Colhuacan ; but he was defeated and slain, and the Chichimec rule was at last supreme.

The Disappearance of the Toltecs

The transmitters of this legendary account give it as their belief, which is shared by some authorities of standing, that the Toltecs, fleeing from the civil broils of their city and the inroads of the Chichimecs, passed into Central America, where they became the founders of the civilisation of that country, and the architects of the many wonderful cities the ruins of which now litter its plains and are encountered in its forests. But it is time that we examined the claims put forward on behalf of Toltec civilisation and culture by the aid of more scientific methods.

Did the Toltecs Exist?

Some authorities have questioned the existence of the Toltecs, and have professed to see in them a race which had merely a mythical significance. They base this theory upon the circumstance that the duration of the reigns of the several Toltec monarchs is very frequently stated to have lasted for exactly fifty-two years, the duration of the great Mexican cycle of years which had been adopted so that the ritual calendar might coincide with the solar year. The circumstance is certainly suspicious, as is the fact that many of the names of the Toltec monarchs are also those of the principal Nahua deities, and this renders the whole dynastic list of very doubtful value. Dr. Brinton recognised in the Toltecs those children of the sun who, like their brethren in Peruvian mythology, were sent from heaven to civilise the human race, and his theory is by no means weakened by the circumstance that Quetzalcoatl, a deity of solar significance, is alluded to in Nahua myth as King of the Toltecs. Recent considerations and discoveries, however, have virtually forced students of the subject to admit the existence of the Toltecs as a race. The author has dealt with the question at some length elsewhere,[1] and is not of those who are free to admit the definite existence of the Toltecs from a historical point of view. The late Mr. Payne of Oxford, an authority entitled to every respect, gave it as his opinion that "the accounts of Toltec history current at the conquest contain a nucleus of substantial truth," and he writes convincingly : "To doubt that there once existed in Tollan an advancement superior to that which prevailed among the Nahuatlaca generally at the conquest, and that its people spread their advancement throughout Anahuac, and into the districts eastward and southward, would be to reject a belief universally entertained, and confirmed rather than shaken by the efforts made in later times to

[1] See *Civilisation of Ancient Mexico*, chap. ii.

construct for the Pueblo something in the nature of a history."[1]

A Persistent Tradition

The theory of the present author concerning Toltec historical existence is rather more non-committal. He admits that a most persistent body of tradition as to their existence gained general credence among the Nahua, and that the date (1055) of their alleged dispersal admits of the approximate exactness and probability of this body of tradition at the time of the conquest. He also admits that the site of Tollan contains ruins which are undoubtedly of a date earlier than that of the architecture of the Nahua as known at the conquest, and that numerous evidences of an older civilisation exist. He also believes that the early Nahua having within their racial recollection existed as savages, the time which elapsed between their barbarian condition and the more advanced state which they achieved was too brief to admit of evolution from savagery to culture. Hence they must have adopted an older civilisation, especially as through the veneer of civilisation possessed by them they exhibited every sign of gross barbarism.

A Nameless People

If this be true it would go to show that a people of comparatively high culture existed at a not very remote period on the Mexican tableland. But what their name was or their racial affinity the writer does not profess to know. Many modern American scholars of note have conferred upon them the name of "Toltecs," and speak freely of the "Toltec period" and of "Toltec art." It may appear pedantic to refuse to recognise that the

[1] Payne, *Hist. New World*, vol. ii. p. 430.

cultured people who dwelt in Mexico in pre-Nahua times were "the Toltecs." But in the face of the absence of genuine and authoritative native written records dealing with the question, the author finds himself compelled to remain unconvinced as to the exact designation of the mysterious older race which preceded the Nahua. There are not wanting authorities who appear to regard the pictorial chronicles of the Nahua as quite as worthy of credence as written records, but it must be clear that tradition or even history set down in pictorial form can never possess that degree of definiteness contained in a written account.

Toltec Art

As has been stated above, the Toltecs of tradition were chiefly remarkable for their intense love of art and their productions in its various branches. Ixtlilxochitl says that they worked in gold, silver, copper, tin, and lead, and as masons employed flint, porphyry, basalt, and obsidian. In the manufacture of jewellery and *objets d'art* they excelled, and the pottery of Cholula, of which specimens are frequently recovered, was of a high standard.

Other Aboriginal Peoples

Mexico contained other aboriginal races besides the Toltecs. Of these many and diverse peoples the most remarkable were the Otomi, who still occupy Guanajuato and Queretaro, and who, before the coming of the Nahua, probably spread over the entire valley of Mexico. In the south we find the Huasteca, a people speaking the same language as the Maya of Central America, and on the Mexican Gulf the Totonacs and Chontals. On the Pacific side of the country the Mixteca and Zapoteca were responsible for a flourishing civilisation which exhibited many original characteristics, and which in some degree was a link between the cultures of Mexico and Central America. Traces of a still older population than any of these are still to be found in the more remote parts of Mexico, and the Mixe, Zaque, Kuicatec, and Popolcan are probably the remnants of prehistoric races of vast antiquity.

The Cliff-dwellers

It is probable that a race known as "the Cliff-dwellers," occupying the plateau country of Arizona, New Mexico, Colorado, and Utah, and even extending in its ramifications to Mexico itself, was related ethnologically to the Nahua. The present-day Pueblo Indians dwelling to the north of Mexico most probably possess a leaven of Nahua blood. Ere the tribes who communicated this leaven to the whole had intermingled with others of various origin, it would appear that they occupied with others those tracts of country now inhabited by the Pueblo Indians, and in the natural recesses and shallow caverns found in the faces of the cliffs erected dwellings and fortifications, displaying an architectural ability of no mean order. These communities extended as far south as the Gila river, the most southern affluent of the Colorado, and the remains they have left there appear to be of a later date architecturally than those situated farther north. These were found in ruins by the first Spanish explorers, and it is thought that their builders were eventually driven back to rejoin their kindred in the north. Fartner to the south in the cañons of the Piedras Verdes river in Chihuahua, Mexico, are cliff-dwellings corresponding in many respects with those of the Pueblo region, and Dr. Hrdlicka has examined others so far south as the State of Jalisco, in Central Mexico. These may be the ruins of dwellings erected either by the early Nahua or by some of the peoples relatively aboriginal to them, and may display the architectural features general among the Nahua prior to their adoption of other alien forms. Or else they may be the remains of dwellings similar to those of the Tarahumare, a still existing tribe of Mexico, who, according to Lumholtz,[1] inhabit similar structures at the present day. It is clear from the architectural development of the cliff-dwellers that their civilisation developed generally from south to north, that this race was cognate to the early Nahua, and that it later withdrew to the north, or became fused with the general body of the Nahua peoples. It must not be understood, however, that the race arrived in the Mexican plateau before the Nahua, and the ruins of Jalisco and other mid-Mexican districts may merely be the remains of comparatively modern cliff-dwellings, an adaptation by mid-Mexican communities of the " Cliff-dweller " architecture, or a local development of it owing to the exigencies of early life in the district.

The Nahua Race

The Nahua peoples included all those tribes speaking the Nahuatlatolli (Nahua tongue), and occupied a sphere extending from the southern borders of New Mexico to the Isthmus of Tehuantepec on the south, or very much within the limits of the modern Republic of Mexico. But this people must not be regarded as one race of homogeneous origin. A very brief account of their racial affinities must be sufficient here. The Chichimecs were probably related to the Otomi, whom we have alluded to as among the first-comers to the

[1] *Unknown Mexico*, vol. i., 1902 ; also see Bulletin 30, Bureau of American Ethnology, p. 309.

Mexican valley. They were traditionally supposed to have entered it at a period subsequent to the Toltec occupation. Their chief towns were Tezcuco and Tenayucan, but they later allied themselves with the Nahua in a great confederacy, and adopted the Nahua language. There are circumstances which justify the assumption that on their entrance to the Mexican valley they consisted of a number of tribes loosely united, presenting in their general organisation a close resemblance to some of the composite tribes of modern American Indians.

The Aculhuaque

Next to them in point of order of tribal arrival were the Aculhuaque, or Acolhuans. The name means "tall" or "strong" men, literally "People of the Broad Shoulder," or "Pushers," who made a way for themselves. Gomara states in his *Conquista de Mexico* that they arrived in the valley from Acolhuacan about A.D. 780, and founded the towns of Tollan, Colhuacan, and Mexico itself. The Acolhuans were pure Nahua, and may well have been the much-disputed Toltecs, for the Nahua people always insisted on the fact that the Toltecs were of the same stock as themselves, and spoke an older and purer form of the Nahua tongue. From the Acolhuans sprang the Tlascalans, the inveterate enemies of the Aztecs, who so heartily assisted Cortés in his invasion of the Aztec capital, Tenochtitlan, or Mexico.

The Tecpanecs

The Tecpanecs were a confederacy of purely Nahua tribes dwelling in towns situated upon the Lake of Tezcuco, the principal of which were Tlacopan and Azcapozalco. The name Tecpanec signifies that each settlement possessed its own chief's house, or *tecpan*.

THE AZTEC CHARACTER

This tribe were almost certainly later Nahua immigrants who arrived in Mexico after the Acolhuans, and were great rivals to the Chichimec branch of the race.

The Aztecs

The Aztecâ, or Aztecs, were a nomad tribe of doubtful origin, but probably of Nahua blood. Wandering over the Mexican plateau for generations, they at length settled in the marshlands near the Lake of Tezcuco, hard by Tlacopan. The name Aztecâ means "Crane People," and was bestowed upon the tribe by the Tecpanecs, probably because of the fact that, like cranes, they dwelt in a marshy neighbourhood. They founded the town of Tenochtitlan, or Mexico, and for a while paid tribute to the Tecpanecs. But later they became the most powerful allies of that people, whom they finally surpassed entirely in power and splendour.

The Aztec Character

The features of the Aztecs as represented in the various Mexican paintings are typically Indian, and argue a northern origin. The race was, and is, of average height, and the skin is of a dark brown hue. The Mexican is grave, taciturn, and melancholic, with a deeply rooted love of the mysterious, slow to anger, yet almost inhuman in the violence of his passions when aroused. He is usually gifted with a logical mind, quickness of apprehension, and an ability to regard the subtle side of things with great nicety. Patient and imitative, the ancient Mexican excelled in those arts which demanded such qualities in their execution. He had a real affection for the beautiful in nature and a passion for flowers, but the Aztec music lacked gaiety, and the national amusements were too often of a gloomy and ferocious character. The women are more vivacious than the men, but were in the days before the conquest very subservient to the wills of their husbands. We have already very briefly outlined the trend of Nahua civilisation, but it will be advisable to examine it a little more closely, for if the myths of this people are to be understood some knowledge of its life and general culture is essential.

Legends of the Foundation of Mexico

At the period of the conquest of Mexico by Cortés the city presented an imposing appearance. Led to its neighbourhood by Huitzilopochtli, a traditional chief, afterwards deified as the god of war, there are several legends which account for the choice of its site by the Mexicans. The most popular of these relates how the nomadic Nahua beheld perched upon a cactus plant an eagle of great size and majesty, grasping in its talons a huge serpent, and spreading its wings to catch the rays of the rising sun. The soothsayers or medicine-men of the tribe, reading a good omen in the spectacle, advised the leaders of the people to settle on the spot, and, hearkening to the voice of what they considered divine authority, they proceeded to drive piles into the marshy ground, and thus laid the foundation of the great city of Mexico.

An elaboration of this legend tells how the Aztecs had about the year 1325 sought refuge upon the western shore of the Lake of Tezcuco, in an island among the marshes on which they found a stone on which forty years before one of their priests had sacrificed a prince of the name of Copal, whom they had made prisoner. A nopal plant had sprung from an earth-filled crevice in this rude altar, and upon this the royal eagle alluded to in the former account had alighted, grasping the serpent in his talons. Beholding in this a good omen, and urged by a supernatural impulse which he could not explain, a priest of high rank dived into a pool close at hand, where he found himself face to face with Tlaloc, the god of waters. After an interview with the deity the priest obtained permission from him to found a city on the site, from the humble beginnings of which arose the metropolis of Mexico-Tenochtitlan.

Mexico at the Conquest

At the period of the conquest the city of Mexico had a circumference of no less than twelve miles, or nearly that of modern Berlin without its suburbs. It contained 60,000 houses, and its inhabitants were computed to number 300,000. Many other towns, most of them nearly half as large, were grouped on the islands or on the margin of Lake Tezcuco, so that the population of what might almost be called "Greater Mexico" must have amounted to several millions. The city was intersected by four great roadways or avenues built at right angles to one another, and laid four-square with the cardinal points. Situated as it was in the midst of a lake, it was traversed by numerous canals, which were used as thoroughfares for traffic. The four principal ways described above were extended across the lake as dykes or viaducts until they met its shores. The dwellings of the poorer classes were chiefly composed of adobes, but those of the nobility were built of a red porous stone quarried close by. They were usually of one story only, but occupied a goodly piece of ground and had flat roofs, many of which were covered with flowers. In general they were coated with a hard, white cement, which gave them an added resemblance to the Oriental type of building.

Towering high among these, and a little apart from the vast squares and market-places, were the *teocallis*, or temples. These were in reality not temples or covered-in buildings, but "high places," great pyramids of stone, built platform on platform, around which a staircase led to the summit, on which was usually erected a small shrine containing the tutelar deity to whom the *teocalli* had been raised. The great temple of Huitzilopochtli, the war-god, built by King Ahuizotl, was, besides being typical of all, by far the greatest of these votive piles. The enclosing walls of the building were 4800 feet in circumference, and strikingly decorated by carvings representing festoons of intertwined reptiles, from which circumstance they were called *coetpantli* (walls of serpents). A kind of gate-house on each side gave access to the enclosure. The *teocalli*, or great temple, inside the court was in the shape of a parallelogram, measuring 375 feet by 300 feet, and was built in six platforms, growing smaller in area as they descended. The mass of this structure was composed of a mixture of rubble, clay, and earth, covered with carefully worked stone slabs, cemented together with infinite care, and coated with a hard gypsum. A flight of 340 steps circled round the terraces and led to the upper platform, on which were raised two three-storied towers 56 feet in height, in which stood the great statues of the tutelar deities and the jasper stones of sacrifice. These sanctuaries, say the old Conquistadores who entered them, had the appearance and odour of shambles, and human blood was bespattered everywhere. In this weird chapel of horrors burned a fire the extinction of which it was supposed would have brought about the end of the Nahua power. It was

The Guardian of the Sacred Fire

Gilbert James

(See page 30)

(See page 31)

The Altar of Skulls

In the National Museum, Mexico

Photo C. B. Waite, Mexico

tended with a care as scrupulous as that with which the Roman Vestals guarded their sacred flame. No less than 600 of these sacred braziers were kept alight in the city of Mexico alone.

A Pyramid of Skulls

The principal fane of Huitzilopochtli was surrounded by upwards of forty inferior *teocallis* and shrines. In the Tzompantli (Pyramid of Skulls) were collected the grisly relics of the countless victims to the implacable war-god of the Aztecs, and in this horrid structure the Spanish conquerors counted no less than 136,000 human skulls. In the court or *teopan* which surrounded the temple were the dwellings of thousands of priests, whose duties included the scrupulous care of the temple precincts, and whose labours were minutely apportioned.

Nahua Architecture and Ruins

As we shall see later, Mexico is by no means so rich in architectural antiquities as Guatemala or Yucatan, the reason being that the growth of tropical forests has to a great extent protected ancient stone edifices in the latter countries from destruction. The ruins discovered in the northern regions of the republic are of a ruder type than those which approach more nearly to the sphere of Maya influence, as, for example, those of Mitla, built by the Zapotecs, which exhibit such unmistakable signs of Maya influence that we prefer to describe them when dealing with the antiquities of that people.

Cyclopean Remains

In the mountains of Chihuahua, one of the most northerly provinces, is a celebrated group called the

Casas Grandes (Large Houses), the walls of which are still about 30 feet in height. These approximate in general appearance to the buildings of more modern tribes in New Mexico and Arizona, and may be referred to such peoples rather than to the Nahua. At Quemada, in Zacatecas, massive ruins of Cyclopean appearance have been discovered. These consist of extensive terraces and broad stone causeways, *teocallis* which have weathered many centuries, and gigantic pillars, 18 feet in height and 17 feet in circumference. Walls 12 feet in thickness rise above the heaps of rubbish which litter the ground. These remains exhibit little connection with Nahua architecture to the north or south of them. They are more massive than either, and must have been constructed by some race which had made considerable strides in the art of building.

Teotihuacan

In the district of the Totonacs, to the north of Vera Cruz, we find many architectural remains of a highly interesting character. Here the *teocalli* or pyramidal type of building is occasionally crowned by a covered-in temple with the massive roof characteristic of Maya architecture. The most striking examples found in this region are the remains of Teotihuacan and Xochicalco. The former was the religious Mecca of the Nahua races, and in its proximity are still to be seen the *teocallis* of the sun and moon, surrounded by extensive burying-grounds where the devout of Anahuac were laid in the sure hope that if interred they would find entrance into the paradise of the sun. The *teocalli* of the moon has a base covering 426 feet and a height of 137 feet. That of the sun is of greater dimensions, with a base of 735 feet and a height of 203 feet. These

Pyramid of the Moon, San Juan Teotihuacan
Photo C. B. Waite, Mexico

Pyramid of the Sun, San Juan Teotihuacan
Photo C. B. Waite, Mexico

(See page 32)

(See page 33)

Ruins of the Pyramid of Xochicalco
Photo C. B. Waite, Mexico

pyramids were divided into four stories, three of which remain. On the summit of that of the sun stood a temple containing a great image of that luminary carved from a rough block of stone. In the breast was inlaid a star of the purest gold, seized afterwards as loot by the insatiable followers of Cortés. From the *teocalli* of the moon a path runs to where a little rivulet flanks the " Citadel." This path is known as " The Path of the Dead," from the circumstance that it is surrounded by some nine square miles of tombs and tumuli, and, indeed, forms a road through the great cemetery. The Citadel, thinks Charnay, was a vast tennis or *tlachtli* court, where thousands flocked to gaze at the national sport of the Nahua with a zest equal to that of the modern devotees of football. Teotihuacan was a flourishing centre contemporary with Tollan. It was destroyed, but was rebuilt by the Chichimec king Xolotl, and preserved thenceforth its traditional sway as the focus of the Nahua national religion. Charnay identifies the architectural types discovered there with those of Tollan. The result of his labours in the vicinity included the unearthing of richly decorated pottery, vases, masks, and terra-cotta figures. He also excavated several large houses or palaces, some with chambers more than 730 feet in circumference, with walls over $7\frac{1}{2}$ feet thick, into which were built rings and slabs to support torches and candles. The floors were tessellated in various rich designs, " like an Aubusson carpet." Charnay concluded that the monuments of Teotihuacan were partly standing at the time of the conquest.

The Hill of Flowers

Near Tezcuco is Xochicalco (The Hill of Flowers), a *teocalli* the sculpture of which is both beautiful

and luxuriant in design. The porphyry quarries from
which the great blocks, 12 feet in length, were cut lie
many miles away. As late as 1755 the structure
towered to a height of five stories, but the vandal has
done his work only too well, and a few fragmentary
carvings of exquisite design are all that to-day remain
of one of Mexico's most magnificent pyramids.

Tollan

We have already indicated that on the site of the
"Toltec" city of Tollan ruins have been discovered
which prove that it was the centre of a civilisation of
a type distinctly advanced. Charnay unearthed there
gigantic fragments of caryatides, each some 7 feet high.
He also found columns of two pieces, which were fitted
together by means of mortise and tenon, bas-reliefs of
archaic figures of undoubted Nahua type, and many
fragments of great antiquity. On the hill of Palpan,
above Tollan, he found the ground-plans of several
houses with numerous apartments, frescoed, columned,
and having benches and cisterns recalling the *implu-
vium* of a Roman villa. Water-pipes were also actually
unearthed, and a wealth of pottery, many pieces of
which were like old Japanese china. The ground-plan
or foundations of the houses unearthed at Palpan
showed that they had been designed by practical
architects, and had not been built in any merely hap-
hazard fashion. The cement which covered the walls
and floors was of excellent quality, and recalled that
discovered in ancient Italian excavations. The roofs
had been of wood, supported by pillars.

Picture-Writing

The Aztecs, and indeed the entire Nahua race,
employed a system of writing of the type scientifically

INTERPRETATION OF THE HIEROGLYPHS

described as "pictographic," in which events, persons, and ideas were recorded by means of drawings and coloured sketches. These were executed on paper made from the agave plant, or were painted on the skins of animals. By these means not only history and the principles of the Nahua mythology were communicated from generation to generation, but the transactions of daily life, the accountings of merchants, and the purchase and ownership of land were placed on record. That a phonetic system was rapidly being approached is manifest from the method by which the Nahua scribes depicted the names of individuals or cities. These were represented by means of several objects, the names of which resembled that of the person for which they stood. The name of King Ixcoatl, for example, is represented by the drawing of a serpent (*coatl*) pierced by flint knives (*iztli*), and that of Motequauhzoma (Montezuma) by a mouse-trap (*montli*), an eagle (*quauhtli*), a lancet (*zo*), and a hand (*maitl*). The phonetic values employed by the scribes varied exceedingly, so that at times an entire syllable would be expressed by the painting of an object the name of which commenced with it. At other times only a letter would be represented by the same drawing. But the general intention of the scribes was undoubtedly more ideographic than phonetic ; that is, they desired to convey their thoughts more by sketch than by sound.

Interpretation of the Hieroglyphs

These *pinturas*, as the Spanish conquerors designated them, offer no very great difficulty in their elucidation to modern experts, at least so far as the general trend of their contents is concerned. In this they are unlike the manuscripts of the Maya of Central America with which we shall make acquaintance further on. Their interpretation was largely traditional, and was learned by rote, being passed on by one generation of *amamatini* (readers) to another, and was by no means capable of elucidation by all and sundry.

Native Manuscripts

The *pinturas* or native manuscripts which remain to us are but few in number. Priestly fanaticism, which ordained their wholesale destruction, and the still more potent passage of time have so reduced them that each separate example is known to bibliophiles and Americanists the world over. In such as still exist we can observe great fullness of detail, representing for the most part festivals, sacrifices, tributes, and natural phenomena, such as eclipses and floods, and the death and accession of monarchs. These events, and the supernatural beings who were supposed to control them, were depicted in brilliant colours, executed by means of a brush of feathers.

The Interpretative Codices

Luckily for future students of Mexican history, the blind zeal which destroyed the majority of the Mexican manuscripts was frustrated by the enlightenment of certain European scholars, who regarded the wholesale destruction of the native records as little short of a calamity, and who took steps to seek out the few remaining native artists, from whom they procured copies of the more important paintings, the details of which were, of course, quite familiar to them. To those were added interpretations taken down from the lips of the native scribes themselves, so that no doubt might remain regarding the contents of the manuscripts. These are known as the "Interpretative Codices," and are of considerable assistance to the student of Mexican

history and customs. Three only are in existence.
The Oxford Codex, treasured in the Bodleian Library,
is of a historical nature, and contains a full list of the
lesser cities which were subservient to Mexico in its
palmy days. The Paris or Tellerio-Remensis Codex,
so called from having once been the property of
Le Tellier, Archbishop of Rheims, embodies many
facts concerning the early settlement of the various
Nahua city-states. The Vatican MSS. deal chiefly
with mythology and the intricacies of the Mexican
calendar system. Such Mexican paintings as were
unassisted by an interpretation are naturally of less
value to present-day students of the lore of the Nahua.
They are principally concerned with calendric matter,
ritualistic data, and astrological computations or horo-
scopes.

The Mexican "Book of the Dead"

Perhaps the most remarkable and interesting manuscript in the Vatican collection is one the last pages of
which represent the journey of the soul after death
through the gloomy dangers of the Other-world. This
has been called the Mexican "Book of the Dead."
The corpse is depicted dressed for burial, the soul escaping from its earthly tenement by way of the mouth. The
spirit is ushered into the presence of Tezcatlipoca, the
Jupiter of the Aztec pantheon, by an attendant dressed
in an ocelot skin, and stands naked with a wooden yoke
round the neck before the deity, to receive sentence.
The dead person is given over to the tests which pre-
cede entrance to the abode of the dead, the realm of
Mictlan, and so that he may not have to meet the
perils of the journey in a defenceless condition a sheaf
of javelins is bestowed upon him. He first passes
between two lofty peaks, which may fall and crush him

if he cannot skilfully escape them. A terrible serpent then intercepts his path, and, if he succeeds in defeating this monster, the fierce alligator Xochitonal awaits him. Eight deserts and a corresponding number of mountains have then to be negotiated by the hapless spirit, and a whirlwind sharp as a sword, which cuts even through solid rocks, must be withstood. Accompanied by the shade of his favourite dog, the harassed ghost at length encounters the fierce Izpuzteque, a demon with the backward-bent legs of a cock, the evil Nextepehua, the fiend who scatters clouds of ashes, and many another grisly foe, until at last he wins to the gates of the Lord of Hell, before whom he does reverence, after which he is free to greet his friends who have gone before.

The Calendar System

As has been said, the calendar system was the source of all Mexican science, and regulated the recurrence of all religious rites and festivals. In fact, the entire mechanism of Nahua life was resident in its provisions. The type of time-division and computation exemplified in the Nahua calendar was also found among the Maya peoples of Yucatan and Guatemala and the Zapotec people of the boundary between the Nahua and Maya races. By which of these races it was first employed is unknown. But the Zapotec calendar exhibits signs of both Nahua and Maya influence, and from this it has been inferred that the calendar systems of these races have been evolved from it. It might with equal probability be argued that both Nahua and Maya art were offshoots of Zapotec art, because the characteristics of both are discovered in it, whereas the circumstance merely illustrates the very natural acceptance by a border people, who settled down to civilisation at a

The Spirit of the dead Aztec is attacked by an Evil Spirit
who scatters Clouds of Ashes

Gilbert James

(See page 38)

The Aztec Calendar Stone

Photo C. B. Waite, Mexico

(See page 38)

relatively later date, of the artistic tenets of the two greater peoples who environed them. The Nahua and Maya calendars were in all likelihood evolved from the calendar system of that civilised race which undoubtedly existed on the Mexican plateau prior to the coming of the later Nahua swarms, and which in general is loosely alluded to as the "Toltec."

The Mexican Year

The Mexican year was a cycle of 365 days, without any intercalary addition or other correction. In course of time it almost lost its seasonal significance because of the omission of the extra hours included in the solar year, and furthermore many of its festivals and occasions were altered by high-priests and rulers to suit their convenience. The Mexican *nexiuhilpilitztli* (binding of years) contained fifty-two years, and ran in two separate cycles—one of fifty-two years of 365 days each, and another of seventy-three groups of 260 days each. The first was of course the solar year, and embraced eighteen periods of twenty days each, called "months" by the old Spanish chroniclers, with five *nemontemi* (unlucky days) over and above. These days were not intercalated, but were included in the year, and merely overflowed the division of the year into periods of twenty days. The cycle of seventy-three groups of 260 days, subdivided into groups of thirteen days, was called the "birth-cycle."

Lunar Reckoning

People in a barbarous condition almost invariably reckon time by the period between the waxing and waning of the moon as distinct from the entire passage of a lunar revolution, and this period of twenty days will be found to be the basis in the time-reckoning of the Mexicans, who designated it *cempohualli*. Each day included in it was denoted by a sign, as " house," " snake," " wind," and so forth. Each *cempohualli* was subdivided into four periods of five days each, sometimes alluded to as " weeks" by the early Spanish writers, and these were known by the sign of their middle or third day. These day-names ran on without reference to the length of the year. The year itself was designated by the name of the middle day of the week in which it began. Out of twenty day-names in the Mexican " month" it was inevitable that the four *calli* (house), *tochtli* (rabbit), *acatl* (reed), and *tecpati* (flint) should always recur in sequence because of the incidence of these days in the Mexican solar year. Four years made up a year of the sun. During the *nemontemi* (unlucky days) no work was done, as they were regarded as ominous and unwholesome.

We have seen that the civil year permitted the day-names to run on continuously from one year to another. The ecclesiastical authorities, however, had a reckoning of their own, and made the year begin always on the first day of their calendar, no matter what sign denominated that day in the civil system.

Groups of Years

As has been indicated, the years were formed into groups. Thirteen years constituted a *xiumalpilli* (bundle), and four of these a *nexiuhilpilitztli* (complete binding of the years). Each year had thus a double aspect, first as an individual period of time, and secondly as a portion of the " year of the sun," and these were so numbered and named that each year in the series of fifty-two possessed a different description.

THE BIRTH-CYCLE

The Dread of the Last Day

With the conclusion of each period of fifty-two years a terrible dread came upon the Mexicans that the world would come to an end. A stated period of time had expired, a period which was regarded as fixed by divine command, and it had been ordained that on the completion of one of those series of fifty-two years earthly time would cease and the universe be demolished. For some time before the ceremony of *toxilmolpilia* (the binding up of the years) the Mexicans abandoned themselves to the utmost prostration, and the wicked went about in terrible fear. As the first day of the fifty-third year dawned the people narrowly observed the Pleiades, for if they passed the zenith time would proceed and the world would be respited. The gods were placated or refreshed by the slaughter of the human victim, on whose still living breast a fire of wood was kindled by friction, the heart and body being consumed by the flames so lighted. As the planets of hope crossed the zenith loud acclamations resounded from the people, and the domestic hearths, which had been left cold and dead, were rekindled from the sacred fire which had consumed the sacrifice. Mankind was safe for another period.

The Birth-Cycle

The birth-cycle, as we have said, consisted of 260 days. It had originally been a lunar cycle of thirteen days, and once bore the names of thirteen moons. It formed part of the civil calendar, with which, however, it had nothing in common, as it was used for ecclesiastical purposes only. The lunar names were abandoned later, and the numbers one to thirteen adopted in their places.

Language of the Nahua

The Nahua language represented a very low state of culture. Speech is the general measure of the standard of thought of a people, and if we judged the civilisation of the Nahua by theirs, we should be justified in concluding that they had not yet emerged from barbarism. But we must recollect that the Nahua of the conquest period had speedily adopted the older civilisation which they had found awaiting them on their entrance to Mexico, and had retained their own primitive tongue. The older and more cultured people who had preceded them probably spoke a more polished dialect of the same language, but its influence had evidently but little effect upon the rude Chichimecs and Aztecs. The Mexican tongue, like most American languages, belongs to the "incorporative" type, the genius of which is to unite all the related words in a sentence into one conglomerate term or word, merging the separate words of which it is composed one into another by altering their forms, and so welding them together as to express the whole in one word. It will be at once apparent that such a system was clumsy in the extreme, and led to the creation of words and names of the most barbarous appearance and sound. In a narrative of the Spanish discovery written by Chimalpahin, the native chronicler of Chalco, born in 1579, we have, for example, such a passage as the following: *Oc chiucnauhxihuitl inic onen quilantimanca España camo niman ic yuh ca omacoc ihuelitiliztli inic niman ye chiuhcnauhxiuhtica, in oncan ohualla.* This passage is chosen quite at random, and is an average specimen of literary Mexican of the sixteenth century. Its purport is, freely translated: "For nine years he [Columbus] remained in vain in Spain. Yea, for nine years there he waited for influence." The clumsy and cumbrous nature of the language could scarcely be better illustrated tnan by pointing out that *chiucnauhxihuitl* signifies "nine years"; *quilantimanca*, "he below remained"; and *omacoc ihuelitiliztli*, "he has got his powerfulness." It must be recollected that this specimen of Mexican was composed by a person who had had the benefit of a Spanish education, and is cast in literary form. What the spoken Mexican of pre-conquest times was like can be contemplated with misgiving in the grammars of the old Spanish missionaries, whose greatest glory is that they mastered such a language in the interests of their faith.

Aztec Science

The science of the Aztecs was, perhaps, one of the most picturesque sides of their civilisation. As with all peoples in a semi-barbarous state, it consisted chiefly in astrology and divination. Of the former the wonderful calendar system was the basis, and by its aid the priests, or those of them who were set apart for the study of the heavenly bodies, pretended to be able to tell the future of new-born infants and the progress of the dead in the other world. This they accomplished by weighing the influence of the planets and other luminaries one against another, and extracting the net result. Their art of divination consisted in drawing omens from the song and flight of birds, the appearance of grains of seed, feathers, and the entrails of animals, by which means they confidently predicted both public and private events.

Nahua Government

The limits of the Aztec Empire may be defined, if its tributary states are included, as extending over the territory comprised in the modern states of Mexico, Southern Vera Cruz, and Guerrero. Among the civilised peoples of this extensive tract the prevailing form of government was an absolute monarchy, although several of the smaller communities were republics. The law of succession, as with the Celts of Scotland, prescribed that the eldest surviving brother of the deceased monarch should be elected to his throne, and, failing him, the eldest nephew. But incompetent persons were almost invariably ignored by the elective body, although the choice was limited to one family. The ruler was generally selected both because of his military prowess and his ecclesiastical and political knowledge. Indeed, a Mexican monarch was nearly always a man of the highest culture and artistic refinement, and the ill-fated Montezuma was an example of the true type of Nahua sovereign. The council of the monarch was composed of the electors and other personages of importance in the realm. It undertook the government of the provinces, the financial affairs of the country, and other matters of national import. The nobility held all the highest military, judicial, and ecclesiastical offices. To each city and province judges were delegated who exercised criminal and civil jurisdiction, and whose opinion superseded even that of the Crown itself. Petty cases were settled by lesser officials, and a still inferior grade of officers acted as a species of police in the supervision of families.

Domestic Life

The domestic life of the Nahua was a peculiar admixture of simplicity and display. The mass of the people led a life of strenuous labour in the fields, and in the cities they wrought hard at many trades, among which may be specified building, metal-working, making

A MYSTERIOUS TOLTEC BOOK

robes and other articles of bright featherwork and
quilted suits of armour, jewellery, and small wares.
Vendors of flowers, fruit, fish, and vegetables swarmed
in the markets. The use of tobacco was general among
the men of all classes. At banquets the women attended,
although they were seated at separate tables. The enter-
tainments of the upper class were marked by much
magnificence, and the variety of dishes was considerable, including venison, turkey, many smaller birds,
fish, a profusion of vegetables, and pastry, accompanied
by sauces of delicate flavour. These were served in
dishes of gold and silver. *Pulque*, a fermented drink
brewed from the agave, was the universal beverage.
Cannibalism was indulged in usually on ceremonial
occasions, and was surrounded by such refinements of
the table as served only to render it the more repulsive
in the eyes of Europeans. It has been stated that this
revolting practice was engaged in owing solely to
the tenets of the Nahua religion, which enjoined the
slaughter of slaves or captives in the name of a deity,
and their consumption with the idea that the con-
sumers attained unity with that deity in the flesh. But
there is good reason to suspect that the Nahua, deprived
of the flesh of the larger domestic animals, practised
deliberate cannibalism. It would appear that the older
race which preceded them in the country were innocent
of these horrible repasts.

A Mysterious Toltec Book

A piece of Nahua literature, the disappearance of
which is surrounded by circumstances of the deepest
mystery, is the *Teo-Amoxtli* (Divine Book), which
is alleged by certain chroniclers to have been the work
of the ancient Toltecs. Ixtlilxochitl, a native Mexican
author, states that it was written by a Tezcucan wise

man, one Huematzin, about the end of the seventh
century, and that it described the pilgrimage of the
Nahua from Asia, their laws, manners, and customs,
and their religious tenets, science, and arts. In 1838
the Baron de Waldeck stated in his *Voyage Pit-
toresque* that he had it in his possession, and the
Abbé Brasseur de Bourbourg identified it with the
Maya Dresden Codex and other native manuscripts.
Bustamante also states that the *amamatini* (chroniclers)
of Tezcuco had a copy in their possession at the time of
the taking of their city. But these appear to be mere
surmises, and if the *Teo-Amoxtli* ever existed, which
on the whole is not unlikely, it has probably never
been seen by a European.

A Native Historian

One of the most interesting of the Mexican historians is Don Fernando de Alva Ixtlilxochitl, a half-
breed of royal Tezcucan descent. He was responsible
for two notable works, entitled *Historia Chichimeca*
(The History of the Chichimecs) and the *Relaciones*,
a compilation of historical and semi-historical incidents.
He was cursed, or blessed, however, by a strong leaning
toward the marvellous, and has coloured his narratives
so highly that he would have us regard the Toltec or
ancient Nahua civilisations as by far the most splendid
and magnificent that ever existed. His descriptions of
Tezcuco, if picturesque in the extreme, are manifestly
the outpourings of a romantic and idealistic mind,
which in its patriotic enthusiasm desired to vindicate
the country of his birth from the stigma of savagery and
to prove its equality with the great nations of antiquity. For this we have not the heart to quarrel with
him. But we must be on our guard against accepting
any of his statements unless we find strong corro-

boration of it in the pages of a more trustworthy
and less biased author.

Nahua Topography

The geography of Mexico is by no means as familiar
to Europeans as is that of the various countries of our
own continent, and it is extremely easy for the reader
who is unacquainted with Mexico and the puzzling
orthography of its place-names to flounder among them,
and during the perusal of such a volume as this to find
himself in a hopeless maze of surmise as to the exact
locality of the more famous centres of Mexican history.
A few moments' study of this paragraph will enlighten
him in this respect, and will save him much confusion
further on. He will see from the map (p. 330) that
the city of Mexico, or Tenochtitlan, its native name,
was situated upon an island in the Lake of Tezcuco.
This lake has now partially dried up, and the modern
city of Mexico is situated at a considerable distance
from it. Tezcuco, the city second in importance, lies
to the north-east of the lake, and is somewhat more
isolated, the other *pueblos* (towns) clustering round
the southern or western shores. To the north of
Tezcuco is Teotihuacan, the sacred city of the gods. To
the south-east of Mexico is Tlaxcallan, or Tlascala, the
city which assisted Cortés against the Mexicans, and the
inhabitants of which were the deadliest foes of the
central Nahua power. To the north lie the sacred city
of Cholula and Tula, or Tollan.

Distribution of the Nahua Tribes

Having become acquainted with the relative position
of the Nahua cities, we may now consult for a moment
the map which exhibits the geographical distribution

of the various Nahua tribes, and which is self-explanatory (p. 331).

Nahua History

A brief historical sketch or epitome of what is known of Nahua history as apart from mere tradition will further assist the reader in the comprehension of Mexican mythology. From the period of the settlement of the Nahua on an agricultural basis a system of feudal government had evolved, and at various epochs in the history of the country certain cities or groups of cities held a paramount sway. Subsequent to the "Toltec" period, which we have already described and discussed, we find the Acolhuans in supreme power, and ruling from their cities of Tollantzinco and Cholula a considerable tract of country. Later Cholula maintained an alliance with Tlascala and Huexotzinco.

Bloodless Battles

The maxim "Other climes, other manners" is nowhere better exemplified than by the curious annual strife betwixt the warriors of Mexico and Tlascala. Once a year they met on a prearranged battle-ground and engaged in combat, not with the intention of killing one another, but with the object of taking prisoners for sacrifice on the altars of their respective war-gods. The warrior seized his opponent and attempted to bear him off, the various groups pulling and tugging desperately at each other in the endeavour to seize the limbs of the unfortunate who had been first struck down, with the object of dragging him into durance or effecting his rescue. Once secured, the Tlascaltec warrior was brought to Mexico in a cage, and first placed upon a stone slab, to which one of his feet was secured by a chain or

48

A Prisoner Fighting for his Life
He was painted white and tufts of cotton-wool were put on his head
Gilbert James
(See page 48)

Priest making an Incantation over an Aztec Lady
Gilbert James
(See page 54)

thong. He was then given light weapons, more like playthings than warrior's gear, and confronted by one of the most celebrated Mexican warriors. Should he succeed in defeating six of these formidable antagonists, he was set free. But no sooner was he wounded than he was hurried to the altar of sacrifice, and his heart was torn out and offered to Huitzilopochtli, the implacable god of war.

The Tlascaltecs, having finally secured their position by a defeat of the Tecpanecs of Huexotzinco about A.D. 1384, sank into comparative obscurity save for their annual bout with the Mexicans.

The Lake Cities

The communities grouped round the various lakes in the valley of Mexico now command our attention. More than two score of these thriving communities flourished at the time of the conquest of Mexico, the most notable being those which occupied the borders of the Lake of Tezcuco. These cities grouped themselves round two nuclei, Azcapozalco and Tezcuco, between whom a fierce rivalry sprang up, which finally ended in the entire discomfiture of Azcapozalco. From this event the real history of Mexico may be said to commence. Those cities which had allied themselves to Tezcuco finally overran the entire territory of Mexico from the Mexican Gulf to the Pacific.

Tezcuco

If, as some authorities declare, Tezcuco was originally Otomi in affinity, it was in later years the most typically Nahuan of all the lacustrine powers. But several other communities, the power of which was very

49

nearly as great as that of Tezcuco, had assisted that city to supremacy. Among these was Xaltocan, a city-state of unquestionable Otomi origin, situated at the northern extremity of the lake. As we have seen from the statements of Ixtlilxochitl, a Tezcucan writer, his native city was in the forefront of Nahua civilisation at the time of the coming of the Spaniards, and if it was practically subservient to Mexico (Tenochtitlan) at that period it was by no means its inferior in the arts.

The Tecpanecs

The Tecpanecs, who dwelt in Tlacopan, Coyohuacan, and Huitzilopocho, were also typical Nahua. The name, as we have already explained, indicates that each settlement possessed its own *tecpan* (chief's house), and has no racial significance. Their state was probably founded about the twelfth century, although a chronology of no less than fifteen hundred years was claimed for it. This people composed a sort of buffer-state betwixt the Otomi on the north and other Nahua on the south.

The Aztecs

The menace of these northern Otomi had become acute when the Tecpanecs received reinforcements in the shape of the Aztecâ, or Aztecs, a people of Nahua blood, who came, according to their own accounts, from Aztlan (Crane Land). The name Aztecâ signifies "Crane People," and this has led to the assumption that they came from Chihuahua, where cranes abound. Doubts have been cast upon the Nahua origin of the Aztecâ. But these are by no means well founded, as the names of the early Aztec chieftains and kings are unquestionably Nahuan. This people on their arrival in Mexico were in a very inferior state of culture, and

50

were probably little better than savages. We have already outlined some of the legends concerning the coming of the Aztecs to the land of Anahuac, or the valley of Mexico, but their true origin is uncertain, and it is likely that they wandered down from the north as other Nahua immigrants did before them, and as the Apache Indians still do to this day. By their own showing they had sojourned at several points *en route*, and were reduced to slavery by the chiefs of Colhuacan. They proved so truculent in their bondage, however, that they were released, and journeyed to Chapoultepec, which they quitted because of their dissensions with the Xaltocanecs. On their arrival in the district inhabited by the Tecpanecs a tribute was levied upon them, but nevertheless they flourished so exceedingly that the swamp villages which the Tecpanecs had permitted them to raise on the borders of the lake soon grew into thriving communities, and chiefs were provided for them from among the nobility of the Tecpanecs.

The Aztecs as Allies

By the aid of the Aztecs the Tecpanecs greatly extended their territorial possessions. City after city was added to their empire, and the allies finally invaded the Otomi country, which they speedily subdued. Those cities which had been founded by the Acolhuans on the fringes of Tezcuco also allied themselves with the Tecpanecs with the intention of freeing themselves from the yoke of the Chichimecs, whose hand was heavy upon them. The Chichimecs or Tezcucans made a stern resistance, and for a time the sovereignty of the Tecpanecs hung in the balance. But eventually they conquered, and Tezcuco was overthrown and given as a spoil to the Aztecs.

New Powers

Up to this time the Aztecs had paid a tribute to Azcapozalco, but now, strengthened by the successes of the late conflict, they withheld it, and requested permission to build an aqueduct from the shore for the purpose of carrying a supply of water into their city. This was refused by the Tecpanecs, and a policy of isolation was brought to bear upon Mexico, an embargo being placed upon its goods and intercourse with its people being forbidden. War followed, in which the Tecpanecs were defeated with great slaughter. After this event, which may be placed about the year 1428, the Aztecs gained ground rapidly, and their march to the supremacy of the entire Mexican valley was almost undisputed. Allying themselves with Tezcuco and Tlacopan, the Mexicans overran many states far beyond the confines of the valley, and by the time of Montezuma I had extended their boundaries almost to the limits of the present republic. The Mexican merchant followed in the footsteps of the Mexican warrior, and the commercial expansion of the Aztecs rivalled their military fame. Clever traders, they were merciless in their exactions of tribute from the states they conquered, manufacturing the raw material paid to them by the subject cities into goods which they afterwards sold again to the tribes under their sway. Mexico became the chief market of the empire, as well as its political nucleus. Such was the condition of affairs when the Spaniards arrived in Anahuac. Their coming has been deplored by certain historians as hastening the destruction of a Western Eden. But bad as was their rule, it was probably mild when compared with the cruel and insatiable sway of the Aztecs over their unhappy dependents.

NEW POWERS

The Spaniards found a tyrannical despotism in the conquered provinces, and a faith the accessories of which were so fiendish that it cast a gloom over the entire national life. These they replaced by a milder vassalage and the earnest ministrations of a more enlightened priesthood.

COMBAT BETWEEN MEXICAN AND BILIMEC
WARRIORS
From the Aubin-Goupil MS.

CHAPTER II : MEXICAN MYTHOLOGY

Nahua Religion

THE religion of the ancient Mexicans was a polytheism or worship of a pantheon of deities, the general aspect of which presented similarities to the systems of Greece and Egypt. Original influences, however, were strong, and they are especially discernible in the institutions of ritualistic cannibalism and human sacrifice. Strange resemblances to Christian practice were observed in the Aztec mythology by the Spanish Conquistadores, who piously condemned the native customs of baptism, consubstantiation, and confession as frauds founded and perpetuated by diabolic agency.

A superficial examination of the Nahua religion might lead to the inference that within its scope and system no definite theological views were embraced and no ethical principles propounded, and that the entire mythology presents only the fantastic attitude of the barbarian mind toward the eternal verities. Such a conclusion would be both erroneous and unjust to a human intelligence of a type by no means debased. As a matter of fact, the Nahua displayed a theological advancement greatly superior to that of the Greeks or Romans, and quite on a level with that expressed by the Egyptians and Assyrians. Toward the period of the Spanish occupation the Mexican priesthood was undoubtedly advancing to the contemplation of the exaltation of one god, whose worship was fast excluding that of similar deities, and if our data are too imperfect to allow us to speak very fully in regard to this phase of religious advancement, we know at least that much of the Nahua ritual and many of the prayers preserved by the labours of the Spanish fathers are unquestionably genuine, and display the attainment of a high religious level.

Cosmology

Aztec theology postulated an eternity which, however, was not without its epochs. It was thought to be broken up into a number of æons, each of which depended upon the period of duration of a separate "sun." No agreement is noticeable among authorities on Mexican mythology as to the number of these "suns," but it would appear as probable that the favourite tradition stipulated for four "suns" or epochs, each of which concluded with a national disaster—flood, famine, tempest, or fire. The present æon, they feared, might conclude upon the completion of every "sheaf" of fifty-two years, the "sheaf" being a merely arbitrary portion of an æon. The period of time from the first creation to the current æon was variously computed as 15,228, 2386, or 1404 solar years, the discrepancy and doubt arising because of the equivocal nature of the numeral signs expressing the period in the *pinturas* or native paintings. As regards the sequence of "suns" there is no more agreement than there is regarding their number. The Codex Vaticanus states it to have been water, wind, fire, and famine. Humboldt gives it as hunger, fire, wind, and water; Boturini as water, famine, wind, and fire; and Gama as hunger, wind, fire, and water.

In all likelihood the adoption of four ages arose from the sacred nature of that number. The myth doubtless shaped itself upon the *tonalamatl* (Mexican native calendar), the great repository of the wisdom of the Nahua race, which the priestly class regarded as its *vade mecum*, and which was closely consulted by it on every occasion, civil or religious.

The Sources of Mexican Mythology

Our knowledge of the mythology of the Mexicans is chiefly gained through the works of those Spaniards, lay and cleric, who entered the country along with or immediately subsequent to the Spanish Conquistadores. From several of these we have what might be called first-hand accounts of the theogony and ritual of the Nahua people. The most valuable compendium is that of Father Bernardino Sahagun, entitled *A General History of the Affairs of New Spain,* which was published from manuscript only in the middle of last century, though written in the first half of the sixteenth century. Sahagun arrived in Mexico eight years after the country had been reduced by the Spaniards to a condition of servitude. He obtained a thorough mastery of the Nahuatl tongue, and conceived a warm admiration for the native mind and a deep interest in the antiquities of the conquered people. His method of collecting facts concerning their mythology and history was as effective as it was ingenious. He held daily conferences with reliable Indians, and placed questions before them, to which they replied by symbolical paintings detailing the answers which he required. These he submitted to scholars who had been trained under his own supervision, and who, after consultation among themselves, rendered him a criticism in Nahuatl of the hieroglyphical paintings he had placed at their disposal. Not content with this process, he subjected these replies to the criticism of a third body, after which the matter was included in his work. But ecclesiastical intolerance was destined to keep the work from publication for a couple of centuries. Afraid that such a volume would be successful in keeping alight the fires of paganism in Mexico, Sahagun's brethren refused him the assistance he required for its publication. But on his appealing to the Council of the Indies in Spain he was met with encouragement, and was ordered to translate his great work into Spanish, a task he undertook when over eighty years of age. He transmitted the work to Spain, and for three hundred years nothing more was heard of it.

The Romance of the Lost "Sahagun"

For generations antiquarians interested in the lore or ancient Mexico bemoaned its loss, until at length one Muñoz, more indefatigable than the rest, chanced to visit the crumbling library of the ancient convent of Tolosi, in Navarre. There, among time-worn manuscripts and tomes relating to the early fathers and the intricacies of canon law, he discovered the lost Sahagun ! It was printed separately by Bustamante at Mexico and by Lord Kingsborough in his collection in 1830, and has been translated into French by M. Jourdanet. Thus the manuscript commenced in or after 1530 was given to the public after a lapse of no less than three hundred years !

Torquemada

Father Torquemada arrived in the New World about the middle of the sixteenth century, at which period he was still enabled to take from the lips of such of the Conquistadores as remained much curious information regarding the circumstances of their advent. His *Monarchia Indiana* was first published at Seville in 1615, and in it he made much use of the manuscript of Sahagun, not then published. At the same time his observations upon matters pertaining to the native religion are often illuminating and exhaustive.

In his *Storia Antica del Messico* the Abbé Clavigero,

who published his work in 1780, did much to disperse the clouds of tradition which hung over Mexican history and mythology. The clarity of his style and the exactness of his information render his work exceedingly useful.

Antonio Gama, in his *Descripcion Historica y Cronologica de las dos Piedras*, poured a flood of light on Mexican antiquities. His work was published in 1832. With him may be said to have ceased the line of Mexican archæologists of the older school. Others worthy of being mentioned among the older writers on Mexican mythology (we are not here concerned with history) are Boturini, who, in his *Idea de una Nueva Historia General de la America Septentrional,* gives a vivid picture of native life and tradition, culled from first-hand communication with the people ; Ixtlilxochitl, a half-breed, whose mendacious works, the *Relaciones* and *Historia Chichimeca,* are yet valuable repositories of tradition ; José de Acosta, whose *Historia Natural y Moral de las Yndias* was published at Seville in 1580 ; and Gomara, who, in his *Historia General de las Indias* (Madrid, 1749), rested upon the authority of the Conquistadores. Tezozomoc's *Chronica Mexicana,* reproduced in Lord Kingsborough's great work, is valuable as giving unique facts regarding the Aztec mythology, as is the *Teatro Mexicana* of Vetancurt, published at Mexico in 1697–98.

The Worship of One God

The ritual of this dead faith of another hemisphere abounds in expressions concerning the unity of the deity approaching very nearly to many of those we ourselves employ regarding God's attributes. The various classes of the priesthood were in the habit of addressing the several gods to whom they ministered as " omnipotent," " endless." " invisible," " the one god complete in perfection and unity," and " the Maker and Moulder of All." These appellations they applied not to one supreme being, but to the individual deities to whose service they were attached. It may be thought that such a practice would be fatal to the evolution of a single and universal god. But there is every reason to believe that Tezcatlipoca, the great god of the air, like the Hebrew Jahveh, also an air-god, was fast gaining precedence of all other deities, when the coming of the white man put an end to his chances of sovereignty.

Tezcatlipoca

Tezcatlipoca (Fiery Mirror) was undoubtedly the Jupiter of the Nahua pantheon. He carried a mirror or shield, from which he took his name, and in which he was supposed to see reflected the actions and deeds of mankind. The evolution of this god from the status of a spirit of wind or air to that of the supreme deity of the Aztec people presents many points of deep interest to students of mythology. Originally the personification of the air, the source both of the breath of life and of the tempest, Tezcatlipoca possessed all the attributes of a god who presided over these phenomena. As the tribal god of the Tezcucans who had led them into the Land of Promise, and had been instrumental in the defeat of both the gods and men of the elder race they dispossessed, Tezcatlipoca naturally advanced so speedily in popularity and public honour that it was little wonder that within a comparatively short space of time he came to be regarded as a god of fate and fortune, and as inseparably connected with the national destinies. Thus, from being the peculiar deity of a small band of Nahua immigrants, the prestige accruing from the rapid conquest made under his tutelary direction and the speedily disseminated tales of the

59

prowess of those who worshipped him seemed to render him at once the most popular and the best feared god in Anahuac, therefore the one whose cult quickly overshadowed that of other and similar gods.

Tezcatlipoca, Overthrower of the Toltecs

We find Tezcatlipoca intimately associated with the legends which recount the overthrow of Tollan, the capital of the Toltecs. His chief adversary on the Toltec side is the god-king Quetzalcoatl, whose nature and reign we will consider later, but whom we will now merely regard as the enemy of Tezcatlipoca. The rivalry between these gods symbolises that which existed between the civilised Toltecs and the barbarian Nahua, and is well exemplified in the following myths.

Myths of Quetzalcoatl and Tezcatlipoca

In the days of Quetzalcoatl there was abundance of everything necessary for subsistence. The maize was plentiful, the calabashes were as thick as one's arm, and cotton grew in all colours without having to be dyed. A variety of birds of rich plumage filled the air with their songs, and gold, silver, and precious stones were abundant. In the reign of Quetzalcoatl there was peace and plenty for all men.

But this blissful state was too fortunate, too happy to endure. Envious of the calm enjoyment of the god and his people the Toltecs, three wicked " necromancers " plotted their downfall. The reference is of course to the gods of the invading Nahua tribes, the deities Huitzilopochtli, Titlacahuan or Tezcatlipoca, and Tlacahuepan. These laid evil enchantments upon the city of Tollan, and Tezcatlipoca in particular took the lead in these envious conspiracies. Disguised as an aged man with white hair, he presented himself at the palace of Quetzalcoatl, where he said to the pages-in-waiting : " Pray present me to your master the king I desire to speak with him."

The pages advised him to retire, as Quetzalcoatl was indisposed and could see no one. He requested them, however, to tell the god that he was waiting outside. They did so, and procured his admittance.

On entering the chamber of Quetzalcoatl the wily Tezcatlipoca simulated much sympathy with the suffering god-king. " How are you, my son ?" he asked. " I have brought you a drug which you should drink, and which will put an end to the course of your malady."

" You are welcome, old man," replied Quetzalcoatl. " I have known for many days that you would come. I am exceedingly indisposed. The malady affects my entire system, and I can use neither my hands nor feet."

Tezcatlipoca assured him that if he partook of the medicine which he had brought him he would immediately experience a great improvement in health. Quetzalcoatl drank the potion, and at once felt much revived. The cunning Tezcatlipoca pressed another and still another cup of the potion upon him, and as it was nothing but *pulque,* the wine of the country, he speedily became intoxicated, and was as wax in the hands of his adversary.

Tezcatlipoca and the Toltecs

Tezcatlipoca, in pursuance of his policy inimical to the Toltec state, took the form of an Indian of the name of Toueyo (Toveyo), and bent his steps to the palace of Uemac, chief of the Toltecs in temporal matters. This worthy had a daughter so fair that she was desired in marriage by many of the Toltecs, but all to no purpose, as her father refused her hand to one and all. The princess, beholding the false Toueyo passing her father's palace, fell deeply in love with him, and so tumultuous was her passion that she became seriously ill because of her longing for him. Uemac, hearing of her indisposition, bent his steps to her apartments, and inquired of her women the cause of her illness. They told him that it was occasioned by the sudden passion which had seized her for the Indian who had recently come that way. Uemac at once gave orders for the arrest of Toueyo, and he was haled before the temporal chief of Tollan.

"Whence come you?" inquired Uemac of his prisoner, who was very scantily attired.

"Lord, I am a stranger, and I have come to these parts to sell green paint," replied Tezcatlipoca.

"Why are you dressed in this fashion? Why do you not wear a cloak?" asked the chief.

"My lord, I follow the custom of my country," replied Tezcatlipoca.

"You have inspired a passion in the breast of my daughter," said Uemac. "What should be done to you for thus disgracing me?"

"Slay me; I care not," said the cunning Tezcatlipoca.

"Nay," replied Uemac, "for if I slay you my daughter will perish. Go to her and say that she may wed you and be happy."

Now the marriage of Toueyo to the daughter of Uemac aroused much discontent among the Toltecs; and they murmured among themselves, and said: "Wherefore did Uemac give his daughter to this Toueyo?" Uemac, having got wind of these murmurings, resolved to distract the attention of the Toltecs by making war upon the neighbouring state of Coatepec.

TEZCATLIPOCA AND THE TOLTECS

The Toltecs assembled armed for the fray, and having arrived at the country of the men of Coatepec they placed Toueyo in ambush with his body-servants, hoping that he would be slain by their adversaries. But Toueyo and his men killed a large number of the enemy and put them to flight. His triumph was celebrated by Uemac with much pomp. The knightly plumes were placed upon his head, and his body was painted with red and yellow—an honour reserved for those who distinguished themselves in battle.

Tezcatlipoca's next step was to announce a great feast in Tollan, to which all the people for miles around were invited. Great crowds assembled, and danced and sang in the city to the sound of the drum. Tezcatlipoca sang to them and forced them to accompany the rhythm of his song with their feet. Faster and faster the people danced, until the pace became so furious that they were driven to madness, lost their footing, and tumbled pell-mell down a deep ravine, where they were changed into rocks. Others in attempting to cross a stone bridge precipitated themselves into the water below, and were changed into stones.

On another occasion Tezcatlipoca presented himself as a valiant warrior named Tequiua, and invited all the inhabitants of Tollan and its environs to come to the flower-garden called Xochitla. When assembled there he attacked them with a hoe, and slew a great number, and others in panic crushed their comrades to death.

Tezcatlipoca and Tlacahuepan on another occasion repaired to the market-place of Tollan, the former displaying upon the palm of his hand a small infant whom he caused to dance and to cut the most amusing capers. This infant was in reality Huitzilopochtli, the Nahua god of war. At this sight the Toltecs crowded upon one another for the purpose of getting a better view, and their eagerness resulted in many being crushed to death. So enraged were the Toltecs at this that upon the advice of Tlacahuepan they slew both Tezcatlipoca and Huitzilopochtli. When this had been done the bodies of the slain gods gave forth such a pernicious effluvia that thousands of the Toltecs died of the pestilence. The god Tlacahuepan then advised them to cast out the bodies lest worse befell them, but on their attempting to do so they discovered their weight to be so great that they could not move them. Hundreds wound cords round the corpses, but the strands broke, and those who pulled upon them fell and died suddenly, tumbling one upon the other, and suffocating those upon whom they collapsed.

The Departure of Quetzalcoatl

The Toltecs were so tormented by the enchantments of Tezcatlipoca that it was soon apparent to them that their fortunes were on the wane and that the end of their empire was at hand. Quetzalcoatl, chagrined at the turn things had taken, resolved to quit Tollan and go to the country of Tlapallan, whence he had come on his civilising mission to Mexico. He burned all the houses which he had built, and buried his treasure of gold and precious stones in the deep valleys between the mountains. He changed the cacao-trees into mezquites, and he ordered all the birds of rich plumage and song to quit the valley of Anahuac and to follow him to a distance of more than a hundred leagues. On the road from Tollan he discovered a great tree at a point called Quauhtitlan. There he rested, and requested his pages to hand him a mirror. Regarding himself in the polished surface, he exclaimed, "I am old," and from that circumstance the spot was named Huehuequauhtit-

64

lan (Old Quauhtitlan). Proceeding on his way accompanied by musicians who played the flute, he walked until fatigue arrested his steps, and he seated himself upon a stone, on which he left the imprint of his hands. This place is called Temacpalco (The Impress of the Hands). At Coaapan he was met by the Nahua gods, who were inimical to him and to the Toltecs.

"Where do you go?" they asked him. "Why do you leave your capital?"

"I go to Tlapallan," replied Quetzalcoatl, "whence I came."

"For what reason?" persisted the enchanters.

"My father the Sun has called me thence," replied Quetzalcoatl.

"Go, then, happily," they said, "but leave us the secret of your art, the secret of founding in silver, of working in precious stones and woods, of painting, and of feather-working, and other matters."

But Quetzalcoatl refused, and cast all his treasures into the fountain of Cozcaapa (Water of Precious Stones). At Cochtan he was met by another enchanter, who asked him whither he was bound, and on learning his destination proffered him a draught of wine. On tasting the vintage Quetzalcoatl was overcome with sleep. Continuing his journey in the morning, the god passed between a volcano and the Sierra Nevada (Mountain of Snow), where all the pages who accompanied him died of cold. He regretted this misfortune exceedingly, and wept, lamenting their fate with most bitter tears and mournful songs. On reaching the summit of Mount Poyauhtecatl he slid to the base. Arriving at the sea-shore, he embarked upon a raft of serpents, and was wafted away toward the land of Tlapallan.

It is obvious that these legends bear some resemblance

to those of Ixtlilxochitl which recount the fall of the Toltecs. They are taken from Sahagun's work, *Historia General de Nueva España*, and are included as well for the sake of comparison as for their own intrinsic value.

Tezcatlipoca as Doomster

Tezcatlipoca was much more than a mere personification of wind, and if he was regarded as a life-giver he had also the power of destroying existence. In fact on occasion he appears as an inexorable death-dealer, and as such was styled Nezahualpilli (The Hungry Chief) and Yaotzin (The Enemy). Perhaps one of the names by which he was best known was Telpochtli (The Youthful Warrior), from the fact that his reserve of strength, his vital force, never diminished, and that his youthful and boisterous vigour was apparent in the tempest.

Tezcatlipoca was usually depicted as holding in his right hand a dart placed in an *atlatl* (spear-thrower), and his mirror-shield with four spare darts in his left. This shield is the symbol of his power as judge of mankind and upholder of human justice.

The Aztecs pictured Tezcatlipoca as rioting along the highways in search of persons on whom to wreak his vengeance, as the wind of night rushes along the deserted roads with more seeming violence than it does by day. Indeed one of his names, Yoalli Ehecatl, signifies " Night Wind." Benches of stone, shaped like those made for the dignitaries of the Mexican towns, were distributed along the highways for his especial use, that on these he might rest after his boisterous journeyings. These seats were concealed by green boughs, beneath which the god was supposed to lurk in wait for his victims. But if one of the persons

Tezcatlipoca, Lord of the Night Winds
Gilbert James
(See page 66)

he seized overcame him in the struggle he might ask whatever boon he desired, secure in the promise of the deity that it should be granted forthwith.

It was supposed that Tezcatlipoca had guided the Nahua, and especially the people of Tezcuco, from a more northerly clime to the valley of Mexico. But he was not a mere local deity of Tezcuco, his worship being widely celebrated throughout the country. His exalted position in the Mexican pantheon seems to have won for him especial reverence as a god of fate and fortune. The place he took as the head of the Nahua pantheon brought him many attributes which were quite foreign to his original character. Fear and a desire to exalt their tutelar deity will impel the devotees of a powerful god to credit him with any or every quality, so that there is nothing remarkable in the spectacle of the heaping of every possible attribute, human or divine, upon Tezcatlipoca when we recall the supreme position he occupied in Mexican mythology. His priestly caste far surpassed in power and in the breadth and activity of its propaganda the priesthoods of the other Mexican deities. To it is credited the invention of many of the usages of civilisation, and that it all but succeeded in making his worship universal is pretty clear, as has been shown. The other gods were worshipped for some special purpose, but the worship of Tezcatlipoca was regarded as compulsory, and to some extent as a safeguard against the destruction of the universe, a calamity the Nahua had been led to believe might occur through his agency. He was known as Moneneque (The Claimer of Prayer), and in some of the representations of him an ear of gold was shown suspended from his hair, toward which small tongues of gold strained upward in appeal of prayer. In times of national danger, plague, or famine universal prayer was made to Tezcatlipoca. The heads of the community repaired to his *teocalli* (temple) accompanied by the people *en masse*, and all prayed earnestly together for his speedy intervention. The prayers to Tezcatlipoca still extant prove that the ancient Mexicans fully believed that he possessed the power of life and death, and many of them are couched in the most piteous terms.

The Teotleco Festival

The supreme position occupied by Tezcatlipoca in the Mexican religion is well exemplified in the festival of the Teotleco (Coming of the Gods), which is fully described in Sahagun's account of the Mexican festivals. Another peculiarity connected with his worship was that he was one of the few Mexican deities who had any relation to the expiation of sin. Sin was symbolised by the Nahua as excrement, and in various manuscripts Tezcatlipoca is represented as a turkey-cock to which ordure is being offered up.

Of the festival of the Teotleco Sahagun says : " In the twelfth month a festival was celebrated in honour of all the gods, who were said to have gone to some country I know not where. On the last day of the month a greater one was held, because the gods had returned. On the fifteenth day of this month the young boys and the servitors decked all the altars or oratories of the gods with boughs, as well as those which were in the houses, and the images which were set up by the wayside and at the cross-roads. This work was paid for in maize. Some received a basketful, and others only a few ears. On the eighteenth day the ever-youthful god Tlamatzincatl or Titlacahuan arrived. It was said that he marched better and arrived the first because he was strong and young. Food was offered

68

him in his temple on that night. Every one drank, ate, and made merry. The old people especially celebrated the arrival of the god by drinking wine, and it was alleged that his feet were washed by these rejoicings. The last day of the month was marked by a great festival, on account of the belief that the whole of the gods arrived at that time. On the preceding night a quantity of flour was kneaded on a carpet into the shape of a cheese, it being supposed that the gods would leave a footprint thereon as a sign of their return. The chief attendant watched all night, going to and fro to see if the impression appeared. When he at last saw it he called out, 'The master has arrived,' and at once the priests of the temple began to sound the horns, trumpets, and other musical instruments used by them. Upon hearing this noise every one set forth to offer food in all the temples." The next day the aged gods were supposed to arrive, and young men disguised as monsters hurled victims into a huge sacrificial fire.

The Toxcatl Festival

The most remarkable festival in connection with Tezcatlipoca was the Toxcatl, held in the fifth month. On the day of this festival a youth was slain who for an entire year previously had been carefully instructed in the *rôle* of victim. He was selected from among the best war captives of the year, and must be without spot or blemish. He assumed the name, garb, and attributes of Tezcatlipoca himself, and was regarded with awe by the entire populace, who imagined him to be the earthly representative of the deity. He rested during the day, and ventured forth at night only, armed with the dart and shield of the god, to scour the roads. This practice was, of course, symbolical of the wind-god's progress over the night-bound highways. He carried also the whistle symbolical of the deity, and made with it a noise such as the weird wind of night makes when it hurries through the streets. To his arms and legs small bells were attached. He was followed by a retinue of pages, and at intervals rested upon the stone seats which were placed upon the highways for the convenience of Tezcatlipoca. Later in the year he was mated to four beautiful maidens of high birth, with whom he passed the time in amusement of every description. He was entertained at the tables of the nobility as the earthly representative of Tezcatlipoca, and his latter days were one constant round of feasting and excitement. At last the fatal day upon which he must be sacrificed arrived. He took a tearful farewell of the maidens whom he had espoused, and was carried to the *teocalli* of sacrifice, upon the sides of which he broke the musical instruments with which he had beguiled the time of his captivity. When he reached the summit he was received by the high-priest, who speedily made him one with the god whom he represented by tearing his heart out on the stone of sacrifice.

Huitzilopochtli, the War-God

Huitzilopochtli occupied in the Aztec pantheon a place similar to that of Mars in the Roman. His origin is obscure, but the myth relating to it is distinctly original in character. It recounts how, under the shadow of the mountain of Coatepec, near the Toltec city of Tollan, there dwelt a pious widow called Coatlicue, the mother of a tribe of Indians called Centzonuitznaua, who had a daughter called Coyolxauhqui, and who daily repaired to a small hill with the intention of offering up prayers to the gods in a penitent spirit of piety. Whilst occupied in her devotions one day she was surprised by a small ball of brilliantly coloured feathers falling upon her from on high. She was pleased by the bright variety of its hues, and placed it in her bosom, intending to offer it up to the sun-god. Some time afterwards she learnt that she was to become the mother of another child. Her sons, hearing of this, rained abuse upon her, being incited to humiliate her in every possible way by their sister Coyolxauhqui.

Coatlicue went about in fear and anxiety ; but the spirit of her unborn infant came and spoke to her and gave her words of encouragement, soothing her troubled heart. Her sons, however, were resolved to wipe out what they considered an insult to their race by the death of their mother, and took counsel with one another to slay her. They attired themselves in their war-gear, and arranged their hair after the manner of warriors going to battle. But one of their number, Quauitlicac, relented, and confessed the perfidy of his brothers to the still unborn Huitzilopochtli, who replied to him : " O brother, hearken attentively to what I have to say to you. I am fully informed of what is about to happen." With the intention of slaying their mother, the Indians went in search of her. At their head marched their sister, Coyolxauhqui. They were armed to the teeth, and carried bundles of darts with which they intended to kill the luckless Coatlicue.

Quauitlicac climbed the mountain to acquaint Huitzilopochtli with the news that his brothers were approaching to kill their mother.

" Mark well where they are at," replied the infant god. " To what place have they advanced ? "

" To Tzompantitlan," responded Quauitlicac.

Later on Huitzilopochtli asked : " Where may they be now ? "

" At Coaxalco," was the reply.

Once more Huitzilopochtli asked to what point his enemies had advanced.

" They are now at Petlac," Quauitlicac replied.

After a little while Quauitlicac informed Huitzilopochtli that the Centzonuitznaua were at hand under the leadership of Coyolxauhqui. At the moment of the enemy's arrival Huitzilopochtli was born, flourishing a shield and spear of a blue colour. He was painted, his head was surmounted by a panache, and his left leg was covered with feathers. He shattered Coyolxauhqui with a flash of serpentine lightning, and then gave chase to the Centzonuitznaua, whom he pursued four times round the mountain. They did not attempt to defend themselves, but fled incontinently. Many perished in the waters of the adjoining lake, to which they had rushed in their despair. All were slain save a few who escaped to a place called Uitzlampa, where they surrendered to Huitzilopochtli and gave up their arms.

The name Huitzilopochtli signifies "Humming-bird to the left," from the circumstance that the god wore the feathers of the humming-bird, or *colibri*, on his left leg. From this it has been inferred that he was a humming-bird totem. The explanation of Huitzilopochtli's origin is a little deeper than this, however. Among the American tribes, especially those of the northern continent, the serpent is regarded with the deepest veneration as the symbol of wisdom and magic. From these sources come success in war. The serpent also typifies the lightning, the symbol of the divine spear, the apotheosis of warlike might. Fragments of serpents are regarded as powerful war-physic among many tribes. Atatarho, a mythical wizard-king of the Iroquois, was clothed with living serpents as with a robe, and his myth throws light on one of the names of Huitzilopochtli's mother, Coatlantona (Robe of Serpents). Huitzilopochtli's image was surrounded by serpents, and rested on serpent-shaped supporters. His sceptre was a single snake, and his great drum was of serpent-skin.

In American mythology the serpent is closely associated with the bird. Thus the name of the god Quetzalcoatl is translatable as " Feathered Serpent," and many similar cases where the conception of bird and serpent have been unified could be adduced. Huitzilopochtli is undoubtedly one of these. We may regard him as a god the primary conception of whom arose from the idea of the serpent, the symbol of warlike wisdom and might, the symbol of the warrior's dart or spear, and the humming-bird, the harbinger of summer, type of the season when the snake or lightning god has power over the crops.

Huitzilopochtli was usually represented as wearing on his head a waving panache or plume of humming-birds' feathers. His face and limbs were striped with bars of blue, and in his right hand he carried four spears. His left hand bore his shield, on the surface of which were displayed five tufts of down, arranged in the form of a quincunx. The shield was made with reeds, covered with eagle's down. The spear he brandished was also tipped with tufts of down instead of flint. These weapons were placed in the hands of those who as captives engaged in the sacrificial fight, for in the Aztec mind Huitzilopochtli symbolised the warrior's death on the gladiatorial stone of combat. As has been said, Huitzilopochtli was war-god of the Aztecs, and was supposed to have led them to the site of Mexico from their original home in the north. The city of Mexico took its name from one of its districts, which was designated by a title of Huitzilopochtli's, Mexitli (Hare of the Aloes).

The War-God as Fertiliser

But Huitzilopochtli was not a war-god alone. As the serpent-god of lightning he had a connection with summer, the season of lightning, and therefore had dominion to some extent over the crops and fruits of the earth. The Algonquian Indians of North America believed that the rattlesnake could raise ruinous storms or grant favourable breezes. They alluded to it also as the symbol of life, for the serpent has a phallic significance because of its similarity to the symbol of generation and fructification. With some American tribes also, notably the Pueblo Indians of Arizona, the serpent has a solar significance, and with tail in mouth symbolises the annual round of the sun. The Nahua believed that Huitzilopochtli could grant them fair weather for the fructification of their crops, and they placed an image of Tlaloc, the rain-god, near him, so that, if necessary, the war-god could compel the rain-maker to exert his pluvial powers or to abstain from the creation of floods. We must, in considering the nature of this deity, bear well in mind the connection in the Nahua consciousness between the pantheon, war, and the food-supply. If war was not waged annually the gods must go without flesh food and perish, and if the gods succumbed the crops would fail, and famine would destroy the race. So it was small wonder that Huitzilopochtli was one of the chief gods of Mexico.

Huitzilopochtli's principal festival was the Toxcatl, celebrated immediately after the Toxcatl festival of Tezcatlipoca, to which it bore a strong resemblance. Festivals of the god were held in May and December, at the latter of which an image of him, moulded in dough kneaded with the blood of sacrificed children, was pierced by the presiding priest with an arrow—an act significant of the death of Huitzilopochtli until his resurrection in the next year.

Strangely enough, when the absolute supremacy of Tezcatlipoca is remembered, the high-priest of Huitzilopochtli, the Mexicatl Teohuatzin, was considered to be the religious head of the Mexican priesthood. The priests of Huitzilopochtli held office by right of descent, and their primate exacted absolute obedience from the priesthoods of all the other deities, being regarded as next to the monarch himself in power and dominion.

Tlaloc, the Rain-God

Tlaloc was the god of rain and moisture. In a country such as Mexico, where the success or failure of the crops depends entirely upon the plentiful nature or otherwise of the rainfall, he was, it will be readily granted, a deity of high importance. It was believed that he made his home in the mountains which surround the valley of Mexico, as these were the source of the local rainfall, and his popularity is vouched for by the fact that sculptured representations of him occur more often than those of any other of the Mexican deities. He is generally represented in a semi-recumbent attitude, with the upper part of the body raised upon the elbows, and the knees half drawn up, probably to represent the mountainous character of the country whence comes the rain. He was espoused to Chalchihuitlicue (Emerald Lady), who bore him a numerous progeny, the Tlalocs (Clouds). Many of the figures which represented him were carved from the green stone called *chalchiuitl* (jadeite), to typify the colour of water, and in some of these he was shown holding a serpent of gold to typify the lightning, for water-gods are often closely identified with the thunder, which hangs over the hills and accompanies heavy rains. Tlaloc, like his prototype, the Kiche god Hurakan, manifested himself in three forms, as the lightning-flash, the thunderbolt, and the thunder. Although his image faced the east, where he was supposed to have originated, he was worshipped as inhabiting the four cardinal points and every mountain-top. The colours of the four points of the compass, yellow, green, red, and blue, whence came the rain-bearing winds, entered into the composition of his costume, which was further crossed with streaks of silver, typifying the mountain torrents. A vase containing every description of grain was usually placed before his idol, an offering of the growth which it was hoped he would fructify. He dwelt in a many-watered paradise called Tlalocan (The Country of Tlaloc), a place of plenty and fruitfulness, where those who had been drowned or struck by lightning or had died from dropsical diseases enjoyed eternal bliss. Those of the common people who did not die such deaths went to the dark abode of Mictlan, the all-devouring and gloomy Lord of Death.

In the native manuscripts Tlaloc is usually portrayed as having a dark complexion, a large round eye, a row of tusks, and over the lips an angular blue stripe curved downward and rolled up at the ends. The latter character is supposed to have been evolved originally from the coils of two snakes, their mouths with long fangs in the upper jaw meeting in the middle of the upper lip. The snake, besides being symbolised by lightning in many American mythologies, is also symbolical of water, which is well typified in its sinuous movements.

Many maidens and children were annually sacrificed to Tlaloc. If the children wept it was regarded as a

(See page 75)

Statue of Tlaloc, the Rain-God

In the National Museum, Mexico

It is averred without any substantial evidence that the Maya called this deity Chac-Mool

Photo C. B. Waite, Mexico

happy omen for a rainy season. The Etzalqualiztli
(When they eat Bean Food) was his chief festival, and
was held on a day approximating to May 13, about
which date the rainy season usually commenced.
Another festival in his honour, the Quauitleua, commenced the Mexican year on February 2. At the
former festival the priests of Tlaloc plunged into a
lake, imitating the sounds and movements of frogs,
which, as denizens of water, were under the special
protection of the god. Chalchihuitlicue, his wife, was
often symbolised by the small image of a frog.

Sacrifices to Tlaloc

Human sacrifices also took place at certain points in
the mountains where artificial ponds were consecrated
to Tlaloc. Cemeteries were situated in their vicinity,
and offerings to the god interred near the burial-place
of the bodies of the victims slain in his service. His
statue was placed on the highest mountain of Tezcuco,
and an old writer mentions that five or six young
children were annually offered to the god at various
points, their hearts torn out, and their remains interred.
The mountains Popocatepetl and Teocuinani were regarded as his special high places, and on the heights
of the latter was built his temple, in which stood his
image carved in green stone.

The Nahua believed that the constant production of
food and rain induced a condition of senility in those
deities whose duty it was to provide them. This they
attempted to stave off, fearing that if they failed in so
doing the gods would perish. They afforded them,
accordingly, a period of rest and recuperation, and once
in eight years a festival called the Atamalqualiztli (Fast
of Porridge-balls and Water) was held, during which
every one in the Nahua community returned for the time

being to the conditions of savage life. Dressed in costumes representing all forms of animal and bird life, and mimicking the sounds made by the various creatures they typified, the people danced round the *teocalli* of Tlaloc for the purpose of diverting and entertaining him after his labours in producing the fertilising rains of the past eight years. A lake was filled with water-snakes and frogs, and into this the people plunged, catching the reptiles in their mouths and devouring them alive. The only grain food which might be partaken during this season of rest was thin water-porridge of maize.

Should one of the more prosperous peasants or yeomen deem a rainfall necessary to the growth of his crops, or should he fear a drought, he sought out one of the professional makers of dough or paste idols, whom he desired to mould one of Tlaloc. To this image offerings of maize-porridge and *pulque* were made. Throughout the night the farmer and his neighbours danced, shrieking and howling round the figure for the purpose of rousing Tlaloc from his drought-bringing slumbers. Next day was spent in quaffing huge libations of *pulque*, and in much-needed rest from the exertions of the previous night.

In Tlaloc it is easy to trace resemblances to a mythological conception widely prevalent among the indigenous American peoples. He is similar to such deities as the Hurakan of the Kiche of Guatemala, the Pillan of the aborigines of Chile, and Con, the thunder-god of the Collao of Peru. Only his thunderous powers are not so apparent as his rain-making abilities, and in this he differs somewhat from the gods alluded to.

Quetzalcoatl

It is highly probable that Quetzalcoatl was a deity of the pre-Nahua people of Mexico. He was regarded by the Aztec race as a god of somewhat alien character, and had but a limited following in Mexico, the city of Huitzilopochtli. In Cholula, however, and others of the older towns his worship flourished exceedingly. He was regarded as " The Father of the Toltecs," and, legend says, was the seventh and youngest son of the Toltec Abraham, Iztacmixcohuatl. Quetzalcoatl (whose name means " Feathered Serpent " or "Feathered Staff") became, at a relatively early period, ruler of Tollan, and by his enlightened sway and his encouragement of the liberal arts did much to further the advancement of his people. His reign had lasted for a period sufficient to permit of his placing the cultivated arts upon a satisfactory basis when the country was visited by the cunning magicians Tezcatlipoca and Coyotl inaual, god of the Amantecas. Disentangled from its terms of myth, this statement may be taken to imply that bands of invading Nahua first began to appear within the Toltec territories. Tezcatlipoca, descending from the sky in the shape of a spider by way of a fine web, proffered him a draught of *pulque*, which so intoxicated him that the curse of lust descended upon him, and he forgot his chastity with Quetzalpetlatl. The doom pronounced upon him was the hard one of banishment, and he was compelled to forsake Anahuac. His exile wrought peculiar changes upon the face of the country. He secreted his treasures of gold and silver, burned his palaces, transformed the cacao-trees into mezquites, and banished all the birds from the neighbourhood of Tollan. The magicians, nonplussed at these unexpected happenings, begged him to return, but he refused on the ground that the sun required his presence. He proceeded to Tabasco, the fabled land of Tlapallan, and, embarking upon a raft made of serpents, floated away to the east. A slightly different version of this myth has already been given. Other accounts state that the king cast himself upon a funeral pyre and was consumed, and that the ashes arising from the conflagration flew upward, and were changed into birds of brilliant plumage. His heart also soared into the sky, and became the morning star. The Mexicans averred that Quetzalcoatl died when the star became visible, and thus they bestowed upon him the title " Lord of the Dawn." They further said that when he died he was invisible for four days, and that for eight days he wandered in the underworld, after which time the morning star appeared, when he achieved resurrection, and ascended his throne as a god.

It is the contention of some authorities that the myth of Quetzalcoatl points to his status as god of the sun. That luminary, they say, begins his diurnal journey in the east, whence Quetzalcoatl returned as to his native home. It will be recalled that Montezuma and his subjects imagined that Cortés was no other than Quetzalcoatl, returned to his dominions, as an old prophecy declared he would do. But that he stood for the sun itself is highly improbable, as will be shown. First of all, however, it will be well to pay some attention to other theories concerning his origin.

Perhaps the most important of these is that which regards Quetzalcoatl as a god of the air. He is connected, say some, with the cardinal points, and wears the insignia of the cross, which symbolises them. Dr. Seler says of him : " He has a protruding, trumpet-like mouth, for the wind-god blows. . . . His figure suggests whirls and circles. Hence his temples were built in circular form. . . . The head of the wind-god stands for the second of the twenty day signs, which was called Ehecatl (Wind)." The same authority, however, in his essay on Mexican chronology, gives to Quetzalcoatl a dual nature, " the dual nature which seems to

The Aged Quetzalcoatl leaves Mexico on a Raft of Serpents
Gilbert James
(See page 79)

Statue of a Male Divinity
Probably Centeotl the Son

(See page 90)

THE MAN OF THE SUN

belong to the wind-god Quetzalcoatl, who now appears simply a wind-god, and again seems to show the true characters of the old god of fire and light." [1]

Dr. Brinton perceived in Quetzalcoatl a similar dual nature. "He is both lord of the eastern light and of the winds," he writes (*Myths of the New World*, p. 214). "Like all the dawn heroes, he too was represented as of white complexion, clothed in long, white robes, and, as many of the Aztec gods, with a full and flowing beard. . . . He had been overcome by Tezcatlipoca, the wind or spirit of night, who had descended from heaven by a spider's web, and presented his rival with a draught supposed to confer immortality, but in fact producing an intolerable longing for home. For the wind and the light both depart when the gloaming draws near, or when the clouds spread their dark and shadowy webs along the mountains, and pour the vivifying rain upon the fields."

The theory which derives Quetzalcoatl from a "culture-hero" who once actually existed is scarcely reconcilable with probability. It is more than likely that, as in the case of other mythical paladins, the legend of a mighty hero arose from the somewhat weakened idea of a great deity. Some of the early Spanish missionaries professed to see in Quetzalcoatl the Apostle St. Thomas, who had journeyed to America to effect its conversion!

The Man of the Sun

A more probable explanation of the origin of Quetzalcoatl and a more likely elucidation of his nature is that which would regard him as the Man of the Sun, who has quitted his abode for a season for the purpose of inculcating in mankind those arts which represent

[1] Bulletin 28 of the U.S. Bureau of Ethnology.

the first steps in civilisation, who fulfils his mission, and who, at a late period, is displaced by the deities of an invading race. Quetzalcoatl was represented as a traveller with staff in hand, and this is proof of his solar character, as is the statement that under his rule the fruits of the earth flourished more abundantly than at any subsequent period. The abundance of gold said to have been accumulated in his reign assists the theory, the precious metal being invariably associated with the sun by most barbarous peoples. In the native *pinturas* it is noticeable that the solar disc and semi-disc are almost invariably found in connection with the feathered serpent as the symbolical attributes of Quetzal-coatl. The Hopi Indians of Mexico at the present day symbolise the sun as a serpent, tail in mouth, and the ancient Mexicans introduced the solar disc in connection with small images of Quetzalcoatl, which they attached to the head-dress. In still other examples Quetzalcoatl is pictured as if emerging or stepping from the luminary, which is represented as his dwelling-place.

Several tribes tributary to the Aztecs were in the habit of imploring Quetzalcoatl in prayer to return and free them from the intolerable bondage of the conqueror. Notable among them were the Totonacs, who passionately believed that the sun, their father, would send a god who would free them from the Aztec yoke. On the coming of the Spaniards the European conquerors were hailed as the servants of Quetzalcoatl, thus in the eyes of the natives fulfilling the tradition that he would return.

Various Forms of Quetzalcoatl
Various conceptions of Quetzalcoatl are noticeable in the mythology of the territories which extended from the north of Mexico to the marshes of Nicaragua. In

Guatemala the Kiches recognised him as Gucumatz, and in Yucatan proper he was worshipped as Kukulcan, both of which names are but literal translations of his Mexican title of " Feathered Serpent " into Kiche and Mayan. That the three deities are one and the same there can be no shadow of doubt. Several authorities have seen in Kukulcan a " serpent-and-rain god." He can only be such in so far as he is a solar god also. The cult of the feathered snake in Yucatan was unquestionably a branch of sun-worship. In tropical latitudes the sun draws the clouds round him at noon. The rain falls from the clouds accompanied by thunder and lightning—the symbols of the divine serpent. Therefore the manifestations of the heavenly serpent were directly associated with the sun, and no statement that Kukulcan is a mere serpent-and-water god satisfactorily elucidates his characteristics.

Quetzalcoatl's Northern Origin

It is by no means improbable that Quetzalcoatl was of northern origin, and that on his adoption by southern peoples and tribes dwelling in tropical countries his characteristics were gradually and unconsciously altered in order to meet the exigencies of his environment. The mythology of the Indians of British Columbia, whence in all likelihood the Nahua originally came, is possessed of a central figure bearing a strong resemblance to Quetzalcoatl. Thus the Thlingit tribe worship Yetl ; the Quaquiutl Indians, Kanikilak ; the Salish people of the coast, Kumsnöotl, Quäaqua, or Släalekam. It is noticeable that these divine beings are worshipped as the Man of the Sun, and totally apart from the luminary himself, as was Quetzalcoatl in Mexico. The Quaquiutl believe that before his settlement among them for the purpose of inculcating in the tribe the arts of life, the sun descended as a bird, and assumed a human shape. Kanikilak is his son, who, as his emissary, spreads the arts of civilisation over the world. So the Mexicans believed that Quetzalcoatl descended first of all in the form of a bird, and was ensnared in the fowler's net of the Toltec hero Hueymatzin.

The titles bestowed upon Quetzalcoatl by the Nahua show that in his solar significance he was god of the vault of the heavens, as well as merely son of the sun. He was alluded to as Ehecatl (The Air), Yolcuat (The Rattlesnake), Tohil (The Rumbler), Nanihehecatl (Lord of the Four Winds), Tlauizcalpantecutli (Lord of the Light of the Dawn). The whole heavenly vault was his, together with all its phenomena. This would seem to be in direct opposition to the theory that Tezcatlipoca was the supreme god of the Mexicans. But it must be borne in mind that Tezcatlipoca was the god of a later age, and of a fresh body of Nahua immigrants, and as such inimical to Quetzalcoatl, who was probably in a similar state of opposition to Itzamna, a Maya deity of Yucatan.

The Worship of Quetzalcoatl

The worship of Quetzalcoatl was in some degree antipathetic to that of the other Mexican deities, and his priests were a separate caste. Although human sacrifice was by no means so prevalent among his devotees, it is a mistake to aver, as some authorities have done, that it did not exist in connection with his worship. A more acceptable sacrifice to Quetzalcoatl appears to have been the blood of the celebrant or worshipper, shed by himself. When we come to consider the mythology of the Zapotecs, a people whose customs and beliefs appear to have formed a species of link between the Mexican and Mayan civilisations, we

84

shall find that their high-priests occasionally enacted the legend of Quetzalcoatl in their own persons, and that their worship, which appears to have been based upon that of Quetzalcoatl, had as one of its most pronounced characteristics the shedding of blood. The celebrant or devotee drew blood from the vessels lying under the tongue or behind the ear by drawing across those tender parts a cord made from the thorn-covered fibres of the agave. The blood was smeared over the mouths of the idols. In this practice we can perceive an act analogous to the sacrificial substitution of the part for the whole, as obtaining in early Palestine and many other countries—a certain sign that tribal or racial opinion has contracted a disgust for human sacrifice, and has sought to evade the anger of the gods by yielding to them a portion of the blood of each worshipper, instead of sacrificing the life of one for the general weal.

The Maize-Gods of Mexico

A special group of deities called Centeotl presided over the agriculture of Mexico, each of whom personified one or other of the various aspects of the maize-plant. The chief goddess of maize, however, was Chicomecohuatl (Seven-serpent), her name being an allusion to the fertilising power of water, which element the Mexicans symbolised by the serpent. As Xilonen she typified the *xilote*, or green ear of the maize. But it is probable that Chicomecohuatl was the creation of an older race, and that the Nahua new-comers adopted or brought with them another growth-spirit, the "Earth-mother," Teteoinnan (Mother of the Gods), or Tocitzin (Our Grandmother). This goddess had a son, Centeotl, a male maize-spirit. Sometimes the mother was also known as Centeotl, the generic name for the entire group, and this fact has led to some confusion in the minds of Americanists. But this does not mean that Chicomecohuatl was by any means neglected. Her spring festival, held on April 5, was known as Hueytozoztli (The Great Watch), and was accompanied by a general fast, when the dwellings of the Mexicans were decorated with bulrushes which had been sprinkled with blood drawn from the extremities of the inmates. The statues of the little *tepitoton* (household gods) were also decorated. The worshippers then proceeded to the maize-fields, where they pulled the tender stalks of the growing maize, and, having decorated them with flowers, placed them in the *calpulli* (the common house of the village). A mock combat then took place before the altar of Chicomecohuatl. The girls of the village presented the goddess with bundles of maize of the previous season's harvesting, later restoring them to the granaries in order that they might be utilised for seed for the coming year. Chicomecohuatl was always represented among the household deities of the Mexicans, and on the occasion of her festival the family placed before the image a basket of provisions surmounted by a cooked frog, bearing on its back a piece of cornstalk stuffed with pounded maize and vegetables. This frog was symbolic of Chalchihuitlicue, wife of Tlaloc, the rain-god, who assisted Chicomecohuatl in providing a bountiful harvest. In order that the soil might further benefit, a frog, the symbol of water, was sacrificed, so that its vitality should recuperate that of the weary and much-burdened earth.

The Sacrifice of the Dancer

A more important festival of Chicomecohuatl, however, was the Xalaquia, which lasted from June 28 to July 14, commencing when the maize plant had attained

its full growth. The women of the *pueblo* (village)
wore their hair unbound, and shook and tossed it so
that by sympathetic magic the maize might take the
hint and grow correspondingly long. *Chian pinolli*
was consumed in immense quantities, and maize-
porridge was eaten. Hilarious dances were nightly
performed in the *teopan* (temple), the central figure
in which was the Xalaquia, a female captive or slave,
with face painted red and yellow to represent the
colours of the maize-plant. She had previously undergone a long course of training in the dancing-school,
and now, all unaware of the horrible fate awaiting
her, she danced and pirouetted gaily among the rest.
Throughout the duration of the festival she danced,
and on its expiring night she was accompanied in the
dance by the women of the community, who circled
round her, chanting the deeds of Chicomecohuatl.
When daybreak appeared the company was joined by
the chiefs and headmen, who, along with the exhausted
and half-fainting victim, danced the solemn death-dance.
The entire community then approached the *teocalli*
(pyramid of sacrifice), and, its summit reached, the victim
was stripped to a nude condition, the priest plunged a
knife of flint into her bosom, and, tearing out the still palpitating heart, offered it up to Chicomecohuatl. In this
manner the venerable goddess, weary with the labours
of inducing growth in the maize-plant, was supposed
to be revivified and refreshed. Hence the name
Xalaquia, which signifies "She who is clothed with
the Sand." Until the death of the victim it was not
lawful to partake of the new corn.

The general appearance of Chicomecohuatl was none
too pleasing. Her image rests in the National Museum
in Mexico, and is girdled with snakes. On the under-
side the symbolic frog is carved. The Americanists

of the eighteenth and early nineteenth centuries were
unequal to the task of elucidating the origin of the
figure, which they designated Teoyaominqui. The
first to point out the error was Payne, in his *History
of the New World called America*, vol. i. p. 424. The
passage in which he announces his discovery is of such
real interest that it is worth transcribing fully.

An Antiquarian Mare's-Nest

" All the great idols of Mexico were thought to
have been destroyed until this was disinterred among
other relics in the course of making new drains in the
Plaza Mayor of Mexico in August 1790. The discovery produced an immense sensation. The idol was
dragged to the court of the University, and there set
up ; the Indians began to worship it and deck it with
flowers ; the antiquaries, with about the same degree
of intelligence, to speculate about it. What most
puzzled them was that the face and some other parts
of the goddess are found in duplicate at the back or
the figure ; hence they concluded it to represent two
gods in one, the principal of whom they further concluded to be a female, the other, indicated by the back,
a male. The standard author on Mexican antiquities
at that time was the Italian *dilettante* Boturini, of
whom it may be said that he is better, but not much
better, than nothing at all. From page 27 of his work
the antiquaries learned that Huitzilopochtli was accompanied by the goddess Teoyaominqui, who was charged
with collecting the souls of those slain in war and
sacrifice. This was enough. The figure was at once
named Teoyaominqui or Huitzilopochtli (The One plus
the Other), and has been so called ever since. The
antiquaries next elevated this imaginary goddess to
the rank of the war-god's wife. 'A soldier,' says

Bardolph, 'is better accommodated than with a wife':
a fortiori, so is a war-god. Besides, as Torquemada
(vol. ii. p. 47) says with perfect truth, the Mexicans
did not think so grossly of the divinity as to have
married gods or goddesses at all. The figure is
undoubtedly a female. It has no vestige of any
weapon about it, nor has it any limbs. It differs in
every particular from the war-god Huitzilopochtli,
every detail of which is perfectly well known. There
never was any goddess called Teoyaominqui. This
may be plausibly inferred from the fact that such a
goddess is unknown not merely to Sahagun, Torquemada, Acosta, Tezozomoc, Duran, and Clavigero, but
to all other writers except Boturini. The blunder of
the last-named writer is easily explained. Antonio
Leon y Gama, a Mexican astronomer, wrote an account
of the discoveries of 1790, in which, evidently puzzled
by the name of Teoyaominqui, he quotes a manuscript
in Mexican, said to have been written by an Indian of
Tezcuco, who was born in 1528, to the effect that
Teoyaotlatohua and Teoyaominqui were spirits who
presided over the fifteenth of the twenty signs of the
fortune-tellers' calendar, and that those born in this
sign would be brave warriors, but would soon die.
(As the fifteenth sign was *quauhtli*, this is likely
enough.) When their hour had come the former spirit
scented them out, the latter killed them. The rubbish
printed about Huitzilopochtli, Teoyaominqui, and
Mictlantecutli in connection with this statue would fill a
respectable volume. The reason why the features were
duplicated is obvious. The figure was carried in the
midst of a large crowd. Probably it was considered to
be an evil omen if the idol turned away its face from
its worshippers ; this the duplicate obviated. So when
the dance was performed round the figure (*cf.* Janus).

This duplication of the features, a characteristic of the very oldest gods, appears to be indicated when the numeral *ome* (two) is prefixed to the title of the deity. Thus the two ancestors and preservers of the race were called Ometecuhtli and Omecihuatl (two-chief, two-woman), ancient Toltec gods, who at the conquest become less prominent in the theology of Mexico, and who are best represented in that of the Mexican colony of Nicaragua."

The Offering to Centeotl

During her last hours the victim sacrificed at the Xalaquia wore a ritual dress made from the fibres of the aloe, and with this garment the maize-god Centeotl was clothed. Robed in this he temporarily represented the earth-goddess, so that he might receive her sacrifice. The blood of victims was offered up to him in a vessel decorated with that brilliant and artistic feather-work which excited such admiration in the breasts of the connoisseurs and æsthetes of the Europe of the sixteenth century. Upon partaking of this blood-offering the deity emitted a groan so intense and terrifying that it has been left on record that such Spaniards as were present became panic-stricken. This ceremony was followed by another, the *nitiçapoloa* (tasting of the soil), which consisted in raising a little earth on one finger to the mouth and eating it.

As has been said, Centeotl the son has been confounded with Centeotl the mother, who is in reality the earth-mother Teteoinnan. Each of these deities had a *teopan* (temple) of his or her own, but they were closely allied as parent and child. But of the two, Centeotl the son was the more important. On the death of the sacrificed victim her skin was conveyed to the temple of Centeotl the son, and worn there in the succeeding ritual by the officiating priests. This gruesome dress is frequently depicted in the Aztec *pinturas*, where the skin of the hands, and in some instances the feet, of the victims can be seen dangling from the wrists and ankles of the priest.

Importance of the Food-Gods

To the Mexicans the deities of most importance to the community as a whole were undoubtedly the food-gods. In their emergence from the hunting to the agricultural state of life, when they began to exist almost solely upon the fruits of the earth, the Mexicans were quick to recognise that the old deities of the chase, such as Mixcoatl, could not now avail them or succour them in the same manner as the guardians of the crops and fertilisers of the soil. Gradually we see these gods, then, advance in power and influence until at the time of the Spanish invasion we find them paramount. Even the terrible war-god himself had an agricultural significance, as we have pointed out. A distinct bargain with the food-gods can be clearly traced, and is none the less obvious because it was never written or codified. The covenant was as binding to the native mind as any made betwixt god and man in ancient Palestine, and included mutual assistance as well as provision for mere alimentary supply. In no mythology is the understanding between god and man so clearly defined as in the Nahuan, and in none is its operation better exemplified.

Xipe

Xipe (The Flayed) was widely worshipped throughout Mexico, and is usually depicted in the *pinturas* as being attired in a flayed human skin. At his special festival, the " Man-flaying," the skins were removed from the victims and worn by the devotees of the god for the succeeding twenty days. He is usually represented as of a red colour. In the later days of the Aztec monarchy the kings and leaders of Mexico assumed the dress or classical garments of Xipe. This dress consisted of a crown made of feathers of the roseate spoonbill, the gilt timbrel, the jacket of spoonbill feathers, and an apron of green feathers lapping over one another in a tile-like pattern. In the Cozcatzin Codex we see a picture of King Axayacatl dressed as Xipe in a feather skirt, and having a tiger-skin scabbard to his sword. The hands of a flayed human skin also dangle over the monarch's wrists, and the feet fall over his feet like gaiters.

Xipe's shield is a round target covered with the rose-coloured feathers of the spoonbill, with concentric circles of a darker hue on the surface. There are examples of it divided into an upper and lower part, the former showing an emerald on a blue field, and the latter a tiger-skin design. Xipe was imagined as possessing three forms, the first that of the roseate spoonbill, the second that of the blue cotinga, and the last that of a tiger, the three shapes perhaps corresponding to the regions of heaven, earth, and hell, or to the three elements, fire, earth, and water. The deities of many North American Indian tribes show similar variations in form and colour, which are supposed to follow as the divinity changes his dwelling to north, south, east, or west. But Xipe is seldom depicted in the *pinturas* in any other form but that of the red god, the form in which the Mexicans adopted him from the Yopi tribe of the Pacific slope. He is the god of human sacrifice *par excellence*, and may be regarded as a Yopi equivalent of Tezcatlipoca.

XOLOTL

Nanahuatl, or Nanauatzin

Nanahuatl (Poor Leper) presided over skin diseases, such as leprosy. It was thought that persons afflicted with these complaints were set apart by the moon for his service. In the Nahua tongue the words for "leprous" and "eczematous" also mean "divine." The myth of Nanahuatl tells how before the sun was created humanity dwelt in sable and horrid gloom. Only a human sacrifice could hasten the appearance of the luminary. Metztli (The Moon) led forth Nanahuatl as a sacrifice, and he was cast upon a funeral pyre, in the flames of which he was consumed. Metztli also cast herself upon the mass of flame, and with her death the sun rose above the horizon. There can be no doubt that the myth refers to the consuming of the starry or spotted night, and incidentally to the nightly death of the moon at the flaming hour of dawn.

Xolotl

Xolotl is of southern, possibly Zapotec, origin. He represents either fire rushing down from the heavens or light flaming upward. It is noticeable that in the *vinturas* the picture of the setting sun being devoured by the earth is nearly always placed opposite his image. He is probably identical with Nanahuatl, and appears as the representative of human sacrifice. He has also affinities with Xipe. On the whole Xolotl may be best described as a sun-god of the more southerly tribes. His head (*quaxolotl*) was one of the most famous devices for warriors' use, as sacrifice among the Nahua was, as we have seen, closely associated with warfare.

Xolotl was a mythical figure quite foreign to the peoples of Anahuac or Mexico, who regarded him as something strange and monstrous. He is alluded to as the "God of Monstrosities," and, thinks Dr. Seler, the

93

word "monstrosity" may suitably translate his name. He is depicted with empty eye-sockets, which circumstance is explained by the myth that when the gods determined to sacrifice themselves in order to give life and strength to the newly created sun, Xolotl withdrew, and wept so much that his eyes fell out of their sockets. This was the Mexican explanation of a Zapotec attribute. Xolotl was originally the "Lightning Beast" of the Maya

XOLOTL

or some other southern folk, and was represented by them as a dog, since that animal appeared to them to be the creature which he most resembled. But he was by no means a "natural" dog, hence their conception of him as unnatural. Dr. Seler is inclined to identify him with the tapir, and indeed Sahagun speaks of a strange animal-being, *tlaca-xolotl*, which has " a large snout, large teeth, hoofs like an ox, a thick hide, and reddish hair "—not a bad description of the tapir of Central America. Of course to the Mexicans the god Xolotl was no longer an animal, although he had evolved from one, and was imagined by them to have the form shown in the accompanying illustration.

MICTLAN

The Fire-God

This deity was known in Mexico under various names, notably Tata (Our Father), Huehueteotl (Oldest of Gods), and Xiuhtecutli (Lord of the Year). He was represented as of the colour of fire, with a black face, a headdress of green feathers, and bearing on his back a yellow serpent, to typify the serpentine nature of fire. He also bore a mirror of gold to show his connection with the sun, from which all heat emanates. On rising in the morning all Mexican families made Xiuhtecutli an offering of a piece of bread and a drink. He was thus not only, like Vulcan, the god of thunderbolts and conflagrations, but also the milder deity of the domestic hearth. Once a year the fire in every Mexican house was extinguished, and rekindled by friction before the idol of Xiuhtecutli. When a Mexican baby was born it passed through a baptism of fire on the fourth day, up to which time a fire, lighted at the time of its birth, was kept burning in order to nourish its existence.

Mictlan

Mictlantecutli (Lord of Hades) was God of the Dead and of the grim and shadowy realm to which the souls of men repair after their mortal sojourn. He is represented in the *pinturas* as a grisly monster with capacious mouth, into which fall the spirits of the dead. His terrible abode was sometimes alluded to as Tlalxicco (Navel of the Earth), but the Mexicans in general seem to have thought that it was situated in the far north, which they regarded as a place of famine, desolation, and death. Here those who by the circumstances of their demise were unfitted to enter the paradise of Tlaloc—namely, those who had not been drowned or had not died a warrior's death, or, in the case of women,

95

had not died in childbed—passed a dreary and meaningless existence. Mictlan was surrounded by a species of demons called *tzitzimimes*, and had a spouse, Mictecaciuatl. When we come to discuss the analogous deity of the Maya we shall see that in all probability Mictlan was represented by the bat, the animal typical of the underworld. In a preceding paragraph dealing with the funerary customs we have described the journey of the soul to the abode of Mictlan, and the ordeals through which the spirit of the defunct had to pass ere entering his realm (see p. 37).

Worship of the Planet Venus

The Mexicans designated the planet Venus Citlalpol (The Great Star) and Tlauizcalpantecutli (Lord of the Dawn). It seems to have been the only star worshipped by them, and was regarded with considerable veneration. Upon its rising they stopped up the chimneys of their houses, so that no harm of any kind might enter with its light. A column called Ilhuicatlan, meaning "In the Sky," stood in the court of the great temple of Mexico, and upon this a symbol of the planet was painted. On its reappearance during its usual circuit, captives were taken before this representation and sacrificed to it. It will be remembered that the myth of Quetzalcoatl states that the heart of that deity flew upward from the funeral pyre on which he was consumed and became the planet Venus. It is not easy to say whether or not this myth is anterior to the adoption of the worship of the planet by the Nahua, for it may be a tale of pre- or post-Nahuan growth. In the *tonalamatl* Tlauizcalpantecutli is represented as lord of the ninth division of thirteen days, beginning with Ce Coatl (the sign of " One Serpent "). In several of the *pinturas* he is represented as having a

96

white body with long red stripes, while round his eyes is a deep black painting like a domino mask, bordered with small white circles. His lips are a bright vermilion. The red stripes are probably introduced to accentuate the whiteness of his body, which is understood to symbolise the peculiar half-light which emanates from the planet. The black paint on the face, surrounding the eye, typifies the dark sky of night. In Mexican and Central American symbolism the eye often represents light, and here, surrounded by blackness as it is, it is perhaps almost hieroglyphic. As the star of evening, Tlauizcalpantecutli is sometimes shown with the face of a skull, to signify his descent into the underworld, whither he follows the sun. That the Mexicans and Maya carefully and accurately observed his periods of revolution is witnessed by the *pinturas*.

Sun-Worship

The sun was regarded by the Nahua, and indeed by all the Mexican and Central American peoples, as the supreme deity, or rather the principal source of subsistence and life. He was always alluded to as *the teotl, the* god, and his worship formed as it were a background to that of all the other gods. His Mexican name, Ipalnemohuani (He by whom Men Live) shows that the Mexicans regarded him as the primal source of being, and the heart, the symbol of life, was looked upon as his special sacrifice. Those who rose at sunrise to prepare food for the day held up to him on his appearance the hearts of animals they had slain for cooking, and even the hearts of the victims to Tezcatlipoca and Huitzilopochtli were first held up to the sun, as if he had a primary right to the sacrifice, before being cast into the bowl of copal which lay at the feet

97

of the idol. It was supposed that the luminary rejoiced in offerings of blood, and that it constituted the only food which would render him sufficiently vigorous to undertake his daily journey through the heavens. He is often depicted in the *pinturas* as licking up the gore of the sacrificial victims with his long tongue-like rays. The sun must fare well if he was to continue to give life, light, and heat to mankind.

The Mexicans, as we have already seen, believed that the luminary they knew had been preceded by others, each of which had been quenched by some awful cataclysm of nature. Eternity had, in fact, been broken up into epochs, marked by the destruction of successive suns. In the period preceding that in which they lived, a mighty deluge had deprived the sun of life, and some such catastrophe was apprehended at the end of every " sheaf " of fifty-two years. The old suns were dead, and the current sun was no more immortal than they. At the end of one of the " sheaves " he too would succumb.

Sustaining the Sun

It was therefore necessary to sustain the sun by the daily food of human sacrifice, for by a tithe of human life alone would he be satisfied. Naturally a people holding such a belief would look elsewhere than within their own borders for the material wherewith to placate their deity. This could be most suitably found among the inhabitants of a neighbouring state. It thus became the business of the warrior class in the Aztec state to furnish forth the altars of the gods with human victims. The most suitable district of supply was the *pueblo* of Tlaxcallan, or Tlascala, the people of which were of cognate origin to the Aztecs. The communities had, although related, been separated for so many genera-

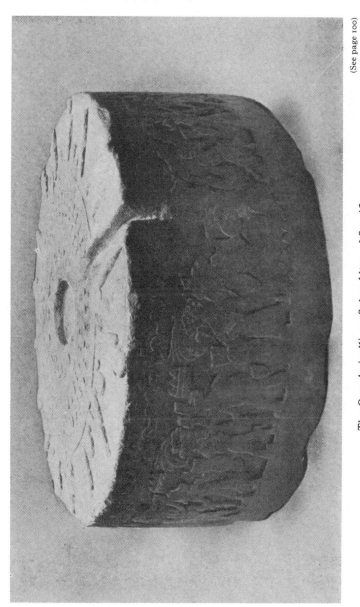

(See page 100)

The Quauhxicalli, or Solar Altar of Sacrifice
In the National Museum, Mexico
Photo C. B. Waite, Mexico

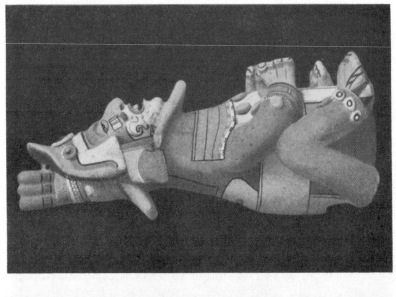

Macuilxochitl

By permission of the Bureau of American Ethnology

(See page 103)

tions that they had begun to regard each other as traditional enemies, and on a given day in the year their forces met at an appointed spot for the purpose of engaging in a strife which should furnish one side or the other with a sufficiency of victims for the purpose of sacrifice. The warrior who captured the largest number of opponents alive was regarded as the champion of the day, and was awarded the chief honours of the combat. The sun was therefore the god of warriors, as he would give them victory in battle in order that they might supply him with food. The rites of this military worship of the luminary were held in the Quauhquauhtinchan (House of the Eagles), an armoury set apart for the regiment of that name. On March 17 and December 1 and 2, at the ceremonies known as Nauhollin (The Four Motions—alluding to the quivering appearance of the sun's rays), the warriors gathered in this hall for the purpose of despatching a messenger to their lord the sun. High up on the wall of the principal court was a great symbolic representation of the orb, painted upon a brightly coloured cotton hanging. Before this copal and other fragrant gums and spices were burned four times a day. The victim, a war-captive, was placed at the foot of a long staircase leading up to the Quauhxicalli (Cup of the Eagles), the name of the stone on which he was to be sacrificed. He was clothed in red striped with white and wore white plumes in his hair—colours symbolical of the sun—while he bore a staff decorated with feathers and a shield covered with tufts of cotton. He also carried a bundle of eagle's feathers and some paint on his shoulders, to enable the sun, to whom he was the emissary, to paint his face. He was then addressed by the officiating priest in the following terms : " Sir, we pray you go to our god the sun, and greet him on our behalf; tell him that his sons and warriors and chiefs and those who remain here beg of him to remember them and to favour them from that place where he is, and to receive this small offering which we send him. Give him this staff to help him on his journey, and this shield for his defence, and all the rest that you have in this bundle." The victim, having undertaken to carry the message to the sun-god, was then despatched upon his long journey.

A Quauhxicalli is preserved in the National Museum of Mexico. It consists of a basaltic mass, circular in form, on which are shown in sculpture a series of groups representing Mexican warriors receiving the submission of war-captives. The prisoner tenders a flower to his captor, symbolical of the life he is about to offer up, for lives were the "flowers" offered to the gods, and the campaign in which these "blossoms" were captured was called Xochiyayotl (The War of Flowers). The warriors who receive the submission of the captives are represented in the act of tearing the plumes from their heads. These bas-reliefs occupy the sides of the stone. The face of it is covered by a great solar disc having eight rays, and the surface is hollowed out in the middle to form a receptacle for blood—the "cup" alluded to in the name of the stone. The Quauhxicalli must not be confounded with the *temalacatl* (spindle stone), to which the alien warrior who received a chance of life was secured. The gladiatorial combat gave the war-captive an opportunity to escape through superior address in arms. The *temalacatl* was somewhat higher than a man, and was provided with a platform at the top, in the middle of which was placed a great stone with a hole in it through which a rope was passed. To this the war-captive was secured, and if he could vanquish seven of his captors he was released. If he failed to do so he was at once sacrificed.

THE FEAST OF TOTEC

A Mexican Valhalla

The Mexican warriors believed that they continued in the service of the sun after death, and, like the Scandinavian heroes in Valhalla, that they were admitted to the dwelling of the god, where they shared all the delights of his diurnal round. The Mexican warrior dreaded to die in his bed, and craved an end on the field of battle. This explains the desperate nature of their resistance to the Spaniards under Cortés, whose officers stated that the Mexicans seemed to desire to die fighting. After death they believed that they would partake of the cannibal feasts offered up to the sun and imbibe the juice of flowers.

The Feast of Totec

The chief of the festivals to the sun was that held in spring at the vernal equinox, before the representation of a deity known as Totec (Our Great Chief). Although Totec was a solar deity he had been adopted from the people of an alien state, the Zapotecs of Zalisco, and is therefore scarcely to be regarded as the principal sun-god. His festival was celebrated by the symbolical slaughter of all the other gods for the purpose of providing sustenance to the sun, each of the gods being figuratively slain in the person of a victim. Totec was attired in the same manner as the warrior despatched twice a year to assure the sun of the loyalty of the Mexicans. The festival appears to have been primarily a seasonal one, as bunches of dried maize were offered to Totec. But its larger meaning is obvious. It was, indeed, a commemoration of the creation of the sun. This is proved by the description of the image of Totec, which was robed and equipped as the solar traveller, by the solar disc and tables of the sun's progress carved on the altar employed in the ceremony, and by the robes of the victims, who were dressed to represent dwellers in the sun-god's halls. Perhaps Totec, although of alien origin, was the only deity possessed by the Mexicans who directly represented the sun. As a borrowed god he would have but a minor position in the Mexican pantheon, but again as the only sun-god whom it was necessary to bring into prominence during a strictly solar festival he would be for the time, of course, a very important deity indeed.

Tepeyollotl

Tepeyollotl means Heart of the Mountain, and evidently alludes to a deity whom the Nahua connected with seismic disturbances and earthquakes. By the interpreter of the Codex Telleriano-Remensis he is called Tepeolotlec, an obvious distortion of his real name. The interpreter of the codex states that his name "refers to the condition of the earth after the flood. The sacrifices of these thirteen days were not good, and the literal translation of their name is 'dirt sacrifices.' They caused palsy and bad humours. . . . This Tepeolotlec was lord of these thirteen days. In them were celebrated the feast to the jaguar, and the last four preceding days were days of fasting. . . . Tepeolotlec means the 'Lord of Beasts.' The four feast days were in honour of the Suchiquezal, who was the man that remained behind on the earth upon which we now live. This Tepeolotlec was the same as the echo of the voice when it re-echoes in a valley from one mountain to another. This name 'jaguar' is given to the earth because the jaguar is the boldest animal, and the echo which the voice awakens in the mountains is a survival of the flood, it is said."

From this we can see that Tepeyollotl is a deity of the earth pure and simple, a god of desert places. It is certain that he was not a Mexican god, or at least was not of Nahua origin, as he is mentioned by none of those writers who deal with Nahua traditions, and we must look for him among the Mixtecs and Zapotecs.

Macuilxochitl, or Xochipilli

This deity, whose names mean Five-Flower and Source of Flowers, was regarded as the patron of luck in gaming. He may have been adopted by the Nahua from the Zapotecs, but the converse may be equally true. The Zapotecs represented him with a design resembling a butterfly about the mouth, and a many-coloured face which looks out of the open jaws of a bird with a tall and erect crest. The worship of this god appears to have been very widespread. Sahagun says of him that a *fête* was held in his honour, which was preceded by a rigorous fast. The people covered themselves with ornaments and jewels symbolic of the deity, as if they desired to represent him, and dancing and singing proceeded gaily to the sound of the drum. Offerings of the blood of various animals followed, and specially prepared cakes were submitted to the god. This simple fare, however, was later followed by human sacrifices, rendered by the notables, who brought certain of their slaves for immolation. This completed the festival.

Father and Mother Gods

The Nahua believed that Ometecutli and Omeciuatl were the father and mother of the human species. The names signify Lords of Duality or Lords of the Two Sexes. They were also called Tonacatecutli and Tonacaciuatl (Lord and Lady of Our Flesh, or of Subsistence). They were in fact regarded as the sexual essence of the creative deity, or perhaps more correctly of deity in general. They occupied the first place in the Nahua calendar, to signify that they had existed from the beginning, and they are usually represented as being clothed in rich attire. Ometecutli (a literal translation of his name is Two-Lord) is sometimes identified with the sky and the fire-god, the female deity representing the earth or water—conceptions similar to those respecting Kronos and Gæa. We refer again to these supreme divinities in the following chapter (see p. 118).

The Pulque-Gods

When a man was intoxicated with the native Mexican drink of *pulque*, a liquor made from the juice of the *Agave Americana*, he was believed to be under the influence of a god or spirit. The commonest form under which the drink-god was worshipped was the rabbit, that animal being considered to be utterly devoid of sense. This particular divinity was known as Ometochtli. The scale of debauchery which it was desired to reach was indicated by the number of rabbits worshipped, the highest number, four hundred, representing the most extreme degree of intoxication. The chief *pulque*-gods apart from these were Patecatl and Tequechmecauiani. If the drunkard desired to escape the perils of accidental hanging during intoxication, it was necessary to sacrifice to the latter, but if death by drowning was apprehended Teatlahuiani, the deity who harried drunkards to a watery grave, was placated. If the debauchee wished his punishment not to exceed a headache, Quatlapanqui (The Head-splitter) was sacrificed to, or else Papaztac (The Nerveless). Each trade or profession had its own Ometochtli, but for the aristocracy there was only one of these gods, Cohuatzincatl, a name signifying " He who has Grand-parents." Several of these drink-gods had names which connected them with various localities ; for example, Tepoxtecatl was the *pulque*-god of Tepoztlan. The calendar day Ometochtli, which means "Two-Rabbit," because of the symbol which accompanied it, was under the special protection of these gods, and the Mexicans believed that any one born on that day was almost inevitably doomed to become a drunkard. All the *pulque*-gods were closely associated with the soil, and with the earth-goddess. They wore the golden Huaxtec nose-ornament, the *yaca-metztli*, of crescent shape, which characterised the latter, and indeed this ornament was inscribed upon all articles sacred to the *pulque*-gods. Their faces were painted red and black, as were objects consecrated to them, their blankets and shields. After the Indians had harvested their maize they drank to intoxication, and invoked one or other of these gods. On the whole it is safe to infer that they were originally deities of local husbandry who imparted virtue to the soil as *pulque* imparted strength and courage to the warrior. The accompanying sketch of the god Tepoxtecatl (see p. 117) well illustrates the distinguish-ing characteristics of the *pulque*-god class. Here we can observe the face painted in two colours, the crescent-shaped nose-ornament, the bicoloured shield, the long necklace made from the *malinalli* herb, and the ear-pendants.

It is of course clear that the drink-gods were of the same class as the food-gods—patrons of the fruitful soil—but it is strange that they should be male whilst the food-gods are mostly female.

The Goddesses of Mexico: Metztli

Metztli, or Yohualticitl (The Lady of Night), was the Mexican goddess of the moon. She had in reality two phases, one that of a beneficent protectress of harvests and promoter of growth in general, and the other that of a bringer of dampness, cold, and miasmic airs, ghosts, mysterious shapes of the dim half-light of night and its oppressive silence.

To a people in the agricultural stage of civilisation the moon appears as the great recorder of harvests. But she has also supremacy over water, which is always connected by primitive peoples with the moon. Citatli (Moon) and Atl (Water) are constantly confounded in Nahua myth, and in many ways their characteristics were blended. It was Metztli who led forth Nanahuatl the Leprous to the pyre whereon he perished—a reference to the dawn, in which the starry sky of night is consumed in the fires of the rising sun.

Tlazolteotl

Tlazolteotl (God of Ordure), or Tlaelquani (Filth-eater), was called by the Mexicans the earth-goddess because she was the eradicator of sins, to whose priests the people went to make confession so that they might be absolved from their misdeeds. Sin was symbolised by the Mexicans as excrement. Confession covered only the sins of immorality. But if Tlazolteotl was the goddess of confession, she was also the patroness of desire and luxury. It was, however, as a deity whose chief office was the eradication of human sin that she was pre-eminent. The process by which this was supposed to be effected is quaintly described by Sahagun in the twelfth chapter of his first book. The penitent addressed the confessor as follows : " Sir, I desire to

Mexican Goddess
Photo C. B. Waite, Mexico
(See page 106)

The Penitent addressing the Fire
William Sewell

(See page 106)

approach that most powerful god, the protector of all, that is to say, Tezcatlipoca. I desire to tell him my sins in secret." The confessor replied : "Be happy, my son : that which thou wishest to do will be to thy good and advantage." The confessor then opened the divinatory book known as the Tonalamatl (that is, the Book of the Calendar) and acquainted the applicant with the day which appeared the most suitable for his confession. The day having arrived, the penitent provided himself with a mat, copal gum to burn as incense, and wood whereon to burn it. If he was a person high in office the priest repaired to his house, but in the case of lesser people the confession took place in the dwelling of the priest. Having lighted the fire and burned the incense, the penitent addressed the fire in the following terms : "Thou, lord, who art the father and mother of the gods, and the most ancient of them all, thy servant, thy slave bows before thee. Weeping, he approaches thee in great distress. He comes plunged in grief, because he has been buried in sin, having backslidden, and partaken of those vices and evil delights which merit death. O master most compassionate, who art the upholder and defence of all, receive the penitence and anguish of thy slave and vassal."

This prayer having concluded, the confessor then turned to the penitent and thus addressed him : "My son, thou art come into the presence of that god who is the protector and upholder of all ; thou art come to him to confess thy evil vices and thy hidden uncleannesses ; thou art come to him to unbosom the secrets of thy heart. Take care that thou omit nothing from the catalogue of thy sins in the presence of our lord who is called Tezcatlipoca. It is certain that thou art before him who is invisible and impalpable, thou who art not worthy to be seen before him, or to speak with him. . . ."

The allusions to Tezcatlipoca are, of course, to him in the shape of Tlazolteotl. Having listened to a sermon by the confessor, the penitent then confessed his misdeeds, after which the confessor said : " My son, thou hast before our lord god confessed in his presence thy evil actions. I wish to say in his name that thou hast an obligation to make. At the time when the goddesses called Ciuapipiltin descend to earth during the celebration of the feast of the goddesses of carnal things, whom they name Ixcuiname, thou shalt fast during four days, punishing thy stomach and thy mouth. When the day of the feast of the Ixcuiname arrives thou shalt scarify thy tongue with the small thorns of the osier [called *teocalcacatl* or *tlazotl*], and if that is not sufficient thou shalt do likewise to thine ears, the whole for penitence, for the remission of thy sin, and as a meritorious act. Thou wilt apply to thy tongue the middle of a spine of maguey, and thou wilt scarify thy shoulders. . . . That done, thy sins will be pardoned."

If the sins of the penitent were not very grave the priest would enjoin upon him a fast of a more or less prolonged nature. Only old men confessed crimes *in veneribus*, as the punishment for such was death, and younger men had no desire to risk the penalty involved, although the priests were enjoined to strict secrecy.

Father Burgoa describes very fully a ceremony of this kind which came under his notice in 1652 in the Zapotec village of San Francisco de Cajonos. He encountered on a tour of inspection an old native *cacique*, or chief, of great refinement of manners and of a stately presence, who dressed in costly garments after the Spanish fashion, and who was regarded by the Indians with much veneration. This man came to the priest for the purpose of reporting upon the progress in things spiritual and temporal in his village. Burgoa recognised his urbanity and wonderful command of the Spanish language, but perceived by certain signs that he had been taught to look for by long experience that the man was a pagan. He communicated his suspicions to the vicar of the village, but met with such assurances of the *cacique's* soundness of faith that he believed himself to be in error for once. Shortly afterwards, however, a wandering Spaniard perceived the chief in a retired place in the mountains performing idolatrous ceremonies, and aroused the monks, two of whom accompanied him to the spot where the *cacique* had been seen indulging in his heathenish practices. They found on the altar " feathers of many colours, sprinkled with blood which the Indians had drawn from the veins under their tongues and behind their ears, incense spoons and remains of copal, and in the middle a horrible stone figure, which was the god to whom they had offered this sacrifice in expiation of their sins, while they made their confessions to the blasphemous priests, and cast off their sins in the following manner : they had woven a kind of dish out of a strong herb, specially gathered for this purpose, and casting this before the priest, said to him that they came to beg mercy of their god, and pardon for their sins that they had committed during that year, and that they brought them all carefully enumerated. They then drew out of a cloth pairs of thin threads made of dry maize husks, that they had tied two by two in the middle with a knot, by which they represented their sins. They laid these threads on the dishes of grass, and over them pierced their veins, and let the blood trickle upon them, and the priest took these offerings to the idol, and in a long speech he begged the god to forgive these, his sons, their sins which were brought to him, and to permit them to be joyful and hold feasts to him as their god and lord. Then the priest came back to those who had confessed, delivered a long discourse on the ceremonies they had still to perform, and told them that the god had pardoned them and that they might be glad again and sin anew."

Chalchihuitlicue

This goddess was the wife of Tlaloc, the god of rain and moisture. The name means Lady of the Emerald Robe, in allusion to the colour of the element over which the deity partly presided. She was specially worshipped by the water-carriers of Mexico, and all those whose avocation brought them into contact with water. Her costume was peculiar and interesting. Round her neck she wore a wonderful collar of precious stones, from which hung a gold pendant. She was crowned with a coronet of blue paper, decorated with green feathers. Her eyebrows were of turquoise, set in as mosaic, and her garment was a nebulous blue-green in hue, recalling the tint of sea-water in the tropics. The resemblance was heightened by a border of sea-flowers or water-plants, one of which she also carried in her left hand, whilst in her right she bore a vase surmounted by a cross, emblematic of the four points of the compass whence comes the rain.

Mixcoatl

Mixcoatl was the Aztec god of the chase, and was probably a deity of the Otomi aborigines of Mexico. The name means Cloud Serpent, and this originated the idea that Mixcoatl was a representation of the tropical whirlwind. This is scarcely correct, however, as the hunter-god is identified with the tempest and thunder-cloud, and the lightning is supposed to represent his arrows. Like many other gods of the chase, he is figured as having the characteristics of a deer or rabbit. He is usually depicted as carrying a sheaf of arrows, to typify thunderbolts. It may be that Mixcoatl was an air and thunder deity of the Otomi, older in origin than either Quetzalcoatl or Tezcatlipoca, and that his inclusion in the Nahua pantheon becoming necessary in order to quieten Nahua susceptibilities, he received the status of god of the chase. But, on the other hand, the Mexicans, unlike the Peruvians, who adopted many foreign gods for political purposes, had little regard for the feelings of other races, and only accepted an alien deity into the native circle for some good reason, most probably because they noted the omission of the figure in their own divine system. Or, again, dread of a certain foreign god might force them to adopt him as their own in the hope of placating him. Their worship of Quetzalcoatl is perhaps an instance of this.

Camaxtli

This deity was the war-god of the Tlascalans, who were constantly in opposition to the Aztecs of Mexico. He was to the warriors of Tlascala practically what Huitzilopochtli was to those of Mexico. He was closely identified with Mixcoatl, and with the god of the morning star, whose colours are depicted on his face and body. But in all probability Camaxtli was a god of the chase, who in later times was adopted as a god of war because of his possession of the lightning dart, the symbol of divine warlike prowess. In the mythologies of North America we find similar hunter-gods, who sometimes evolve into gods of war for a like reason, and again gods of the chase who have all the appearance and attributes of the creatures hunted.

Ixtlilton

Ixtlilton (The Little Black One) was the Mexican god of medicine and healing, and therefore was often alluded to as the brother of Macuilxochitl, the god of well-being or good luck. From the account of the general appearance of his temple—an edifice of painted boards—it would seem to have evolved from the primitive tent or lodge of the medicine-man, or *shaman*. It contained several water-jars called *tlilatl* (black water), the contents of which were administered to children in bad health. The parents of children who benefited from the treatment bestowed a feast on the deity, whose idol was carried to the residence of the grateful father, where ceremonial dances and oblations were made before it. It was then thought that Ixtlilton descended to the courtyard to open fresh jars of *pulque* liquor provided for the feasters, and the entertainment concluded by an examination by the Aztec Æsculapius of such of the *pulque* jars dedicated to his service as stood in the courtyard for everyday use. Should these be found in an unclean condition, it was understood that the master of the house was a man of evil life, and he was presented by the priest with a mask to hide his face from his scoffing friends.

Omacatl

Omacatl was the Mexican god of festivity and joy. The name signifies Two Reeds. He was worshipped chiefly by bon-vivants and the rich, who celebrated him in splendid feasts and orgies. The idol of the deity was invariably placed in the chamber where these functions were to take place, and the Aztecs were known to regard it as a heinous offence if anything derogatory to the god were performed during the convivial ceremony, or if any omission were made from the prescribed form which these gatherings usually took. It was thought that if the host had been in any way remiss Omacatl would appear to the startled guests, and in tones of great severity upbraid him who had given the feast, intimating that he would regard him no longer as a worshipper and would henceforth abandon him. A terrible malady, the symptoms of which were akin to those of falling-sickness, would shortly afterwards seize the guests ; but as such symptoms are not unlike those connected with acute indigestion and other gastric troubles, it is probable that the gourmets who paid homage to the god of good cheer may have been suffering from a too strenuous instead of a lukewarm worship of him. But the idea of communion which underlay so many of the Mexican rites undoubtedly entered into the worship of Omacatl, for prior to a banquet in his honour those who took part in it formed a great bone out of maize paste, pretending that it was one of the bones of the deity whose merry rites they were about to engage in. This they devoured, washing it down with great draughts of *pulque.* The idol of Omacatl was provided with a recess in the region of the stomach, and into this provisions were stuffed. He was represented as a squatting figure, painted black and white, crowned with a paper coronet, and hung with coloured paper. A flower-fringed cloak and sceptre were the other symbols of royalty worn by this Mexican Dionysus.

Opochtli

Opochtli (The Left-handed) was the god sacred to fishers and bird-catchers. At one period of Aztec history he must have been a deity of considerable consequence, since for generations the Aztecs were marsh-dwellers and depended for their daily food on the fish netted in the lakes and the birds snared in the reeds. They credited the god with the invention of the harpoon or trident for spearing fish and the fishing-rod and bird-net. The fishermen and bird-catchers of Mexico held on occasion a special feast in honour of Opochtli, at which a certain liquor called *octli* was consumed. A procession was afterwards formed, in which marched old people who had dedicated themselves to the worship of the god, probably because they could obtain no other means of subsistence than that afforded by the vocation of which he was tutelar and patron. He was represented as a man painted black, his head decorated with the plumes of native wild birds, and crowned by a paper coronet in the shape of a rose. He was clad in green paper which fell to the knee, and was shod with white sandals. In his left hand he held a shield painted red, having in the centre a white flower with four petals placed crosswise, and in his right hand he held a sceptre in the form of a cup.

Yacatecutli

Yacatecutli was the patron of travellers of the merchant class, who worshipped him by piling their staves together and sprinkling on the heap blood from their noses and ears. The staff of the traveller was his symbol, to which prayer was made and offerings of flowers and incense tendered.

The Aztec Priesthood

The Aztec priesthood was a hierarchy in whose hands resided a goodly portion of the power of the upper classes, especially that connected with education and endowment. The mere fact that its members possessed the power of selecting victims for sacrifice must have been sufficient to place them in an almost unassailable position, and their prophetic utterances, founded upon the art of divination—so great a feature in the life of the Aztec people, who depended upon it from the cradle to the grave—probably assisted them in maintaining their hold upon the popular imagination. But withal the evidence of unbiased Spanish ecclesiastics, such as Sahagun, tends to show that they utilised their influence for good, and soundly instructed the people under their charge in the cardinal virtues ; "in short," says the venerable friar, "to perform the duties plainly pointed out by natural religion."

Priestly Revenues

The establishment of the national religion was, as in the case of the mediæval Church in Europe, based upon a land tenure from which the priestly class derived a substantial though, considering their numbers, by no means inordinate revenue. The principal temples possessed lands which sufficed for the maintenance of the priests attached to them. There was, besides, a system of first-fruits fixed by law for the priesthood, the surplusage therefrom being distributed among the poor.

Education

Education was entirely conducted by the priesthood, which undertook the task in a manner highly creditable to it, when consideration is given to surrounding conditions. Education was, indeed, highly organised. It was divided into primary and secondary grades. Boys were instructed by priests, girls by holy women or "nuns." The secondary schools were called *calmecac*, and were devoted to the higher branches of education, the curriculum including the deciphering of the *pinturas*, or manuscripts, astrology and divination, with a wealth of religious instruction.

Orders of the Priesthood

At the head of the Aztec priesthood stood the Mexicatl Teohuatzin (Mexican Lord of Divine Matters). He had a seat on the emperor's council, and possessed power which was second only to the royal authority. Next in rank to him was the high-priest of Quetzalcoatl, who dwelt in almost entire seclusion, and who had authority over his own caste only. This office was in all probability a relic from "Toltec" times. The priests of Quetzalcoatl were called by name after their tutelar deity. The lesser grades included the Tlenamacac (Ordinary Priests), who were habited in black, and wore their hair long, covering it with a kind of mantilla. The lowest order was that of the Lamacazton (Little Priests), youths who were graduating in the priestly office.

An Exacting Ritual

The priesthood enjoyed no easy existence, but led an austere life of fasting, penance, and prayer, with constant observance of an arduous and exacting ritual, which embraced sacrifice, the upkeep of perpetual fires, the chanting of holy songs to the gods, dances, and the superintend-ence of the ever-recurring festivals. They were required to rise during the night to render praise, and to maintain themselves in a condition of absolute cleanli-ness by means of constant ablutions. We have seen that blood-offering—the substitution of the part for the whole—was a common method of sacrifice, and in this the priests engaged personally on frequent occasions. If the caste did not spare the people it certainly did not spare itself, and its outlook was perhaps only a shade more gloomy and fanatical than that of the Spanish hierarchy which succeeded it in the land.

TEPOXTECATL.

CHAPTER III : MYTHS AND LEGENDS OF THE ANCIENT MEXICANS

The Mexican Idea of the Creation

" IN the year and in the day of the clouds," writes Garcia in his *Origin de los Indias*, professing to furnish the reader with a translation of an original Mixtec picture-manuscript, "before ever were years or days, the world lay in darkness. All things were orderless, and a water covered the slime and ooze that the earth then was." This picture is common to almost all American creation-stories.[1] The red man in general believed the habitable globe to have been created from the slime which arose above the primeval waters, and there can be no doubt that the Nahua shared this belief. We encounter in Nahua myth two beings of a bisexual nature, known to the Aztecs as Ometecutli-Omeciuatl (Lords of Duality), who were represented as the deities dominating the genesis of things, the beginning of the world. We have already become acquainted with them in Chapter II (see p. 104), but we may recapitulate. These beings, whose individual names were Tonacatecutli and Tonacaciuatl (Lord and Lady of our Flesh), occupy the first place in the calendar, a circumstance which makes it plain that they were regarded as responsible for the origin of all created things. They were invariably represented as being clothed in rich, variegated garments, symbolical of light. Tonacatecutli, the male principle of creation or world-generation, is often identified with the sun- or fire-god, but there is no reason to consider him as symbolical of anything but the sky. The firmament is almost universally regarded by American

[1] See the author's article on "American Creation-Myths" in the *Encyclopædia of Religion and Ethics*, vol. iv.

aboriginal peoples as the male principle of the cosmos, in contradistinction to the earth, which they think of as possessing feminine attributes, and which is undoubtedly personified in this instance by Tonacaciuatl. In North American Indian myths we find the Father Sky brooding upon the Mother Earth, just as in early Greek creation-story we see the elements uniting, the firmament impregnating the soil and rendering it fruitful. To the savage mind the growth of crops and vegetation proceeds as much from the sky as from the earth. Untutored man beholds the fecundation of the soil by rain, and, seeing in everything the expression of an individual and personal impulse, regards the genesis of vegetable growth as analogous to human origin. To him, then, the sky is the life-giving male principle, the fertilising seed of which descends in rain. The earth is the receptive element which hatches that with which the sky has impregnated her.

Ixtlilxochitl's Legend of the Creation

One of the most complete creation-stories in Mexican mythology is that given by the half-blood Indian author Ixtlilxochitl, who, we cannot doubt, received it directly from native sources. He states that the Toltecs credited a certain Tloque Nahuaque (Lord of All Existence) with the creation of the universe, the stars, mountains, and animals. At the same time he made the first man and woman, from whom all the inhabitants of the earth are descended. This "first earth" was destroyed by the "water-sun." At the commencement of the next epoch the Toltecs appeared, and after many wanderings settled in Huehue Tlapallan (Very Old Tlapallan). Then followed the second catastrophe, that of the "wind-sun." The remainder of the legend recounts how mighty earthquakes shook the world and destroyed the earth-giants. These earth-giants (Quinames) were analogous to the Greek Titans, and were a source of great uneasiness to the Toltecs. In the opinion of the old historians they were descended from the races who inhabited the more northerly portion of Mexico.

Creation-Story of the Mixtecs

It will be well to return for a moment to the creation-story of the Mixtecs, which, if emanating from a some-what isolated people in the extreme south of the Mexican Empire, at least affords us a vivid picture of what a folk closely related to the Nahua race regarded as a veritable account of the creative process. When the earth had arisen from the primeval waters, one day the deer-god, who bore the surname Puma-Snake, and the beautiful deer-goddess, or Jaguar-Snake, appeared. They had human form, and with their great knowledge (that is, with their magic) they raised a high cliff over the water, and built on it fine palaces for their dwelling. On the summit of this cliff they laid a copper axe with the edge upward, and on this edge the heavens rested. The palaces stood in Upper Mixteca, close to Apoala, and the cliff was called Place where the Heavens Stood. The gods lived happily together for many centuries, when it chanced that two little boys were born to them, beautiful of form, and skilled and experienced in the arts. From the days of their birth they were named Wind-Nine-Snake (Viento de Neuve Culebras) and Wind-Nine-Cave (Viento de Neuve Cavernas). Much care was given to their education, and they possessed the knowledge of how to change themselves into an eagle or a snake, to make themselves invisible, and even to pass through solid bodies.

After a time these youthful gods decided to make

" Place where the Heavens Stood "
William Sewell
(See page 120)

A Flood-Myth of the Nahua
William Sewell
(See page 122)

an offering and a sacrifice to their ancestors. Taking incense vessels made of clay, they filled them with tobacco, to which they set fire, allowing it to smoulder. The smoke rose heavenward, and that was the first offering (to the gods). Then they made a garden with shrubs and flowers, trees and fruit-bearing plants, and sweet-scented herbs. Adjoining this they made a grass-grown level place (*un prado*), and equipped it with everything necessary for sacrifice. The pious brothers lived contentedly on this piece of ground, tilled it, burned tobacco, and with prayers, vows, and promises they supplicated their ancestors to let the light appear, to let the water collect in certain places and the earth be freed from its covering (water), for they had no more than that little garden for their subsistence. In order to strengthen their prayer they pierced their ears and their tongues with pointed knives of flint, and sprinkled the blood on the trees and plants with a brush of willow twigs.

The deer-gods had more sons and daughters, but there came a flood in which many of these perished. After the catastrophe was over the god who is called the Creator of All Things formed the heavens and the earth, and restored the human race.

Zapotec Creation-Myth

Among the Zapotecs, a people related to the Mixtecs, we find a similar conception of the creative process. Cozaana is mentioned as the creator and maker of all beasts in the valuable Zapotec dictionary of Father Juan de Cordova, and Huichaana as the creator of men and fishes. Thus we have two separate creations for men and animals. Cozaana would appear to apply to the sun as the creator of all beasts, but, strangely enough, is alluded to in Cordova's dictionary as "procreatrix," whilst he is undoubtedly a male deity. Huichaana, the creator of men and fishes, is, on the other hand, alluded to as "water," or "the element of water," and "goddess of generation." She is certainly the Zapotec female part of the creative agency. In the Mixtec creation-myth we can see the actual creator and the first pair of tribal gods, who were also considered the progenitors of animals—to the savage equal inhabitants of the world with himself. The names of the brothers Nine-Snake and Nine-Cave undoubtedly allude to light and darkness, day and night. It may be that these deities are the same as Quetzalcoatl and Xolotl (the latter a Zapotec deity), who were regarded as twins. In some ways Quetzalcoatl was looked upon as a creator, and in the Mexican calendar followed the Father and Mother, or original sexual deities, being placed in the second section as the creator of the world and man.

The Mexican Noah

Flood-myths, curiously enough, are of more common occurrence among the Nahua and kindred peoples than creation-myths. The Abbé Brasseur de Bourbourg has translated one from the Codex Chimalpopoca, a work in Nahuatl dating from the latter part of the sixteenth century. It recounts the doings of the Mexican Noah and his wife as follows :

"And this year was that of Ce-calli, and on the first day all was lost. The mountain itself was submerged in the water, and the water remained tranquil for fifty-two springs.

"Now toward the close of the year Titlacahuan had forewarned the man named Nata and his wife Nena, saying, 'Make no more *pulque*, but straightway hollow out a large cypress, and enter it when in the month Tozoztli the water shall approach the sky.' They entered it, and when Titlacahuan had closed the door he said, ' Thou shalt eat but a single ear of maize, and thy wife but one also.'

" As soon as they had finished eating, they went forth, and the water was tranquil ; for the log did not move any more ; and opening it they saw many fish.

" Then they built a fire, rubbing together pieces of wood, and they roasted fish. The gods Citallinicue and Citallatonac, looking below, exclaimed, 'Divine Lord, what means that fire below ? Why do they thus smoke the heavens ? '

" Straightway descended Titlacahuan - Tezcatlipoca, and commenced to scold, saying, ' What is this fire doing here ? ' And seizing the fishes he moulded their hinder parts and changed their heads, and they were at once transformed into dogs."

The Myth of the Seven Caverns

But other legends apart from the creation-stories of the world pure and simple deal with the origin of mankind. The Aztecs believed that the first men emerged from a place known as Chicomoztoc (The Seven Caverns), located north of Mexico. Various writers have seen in these mythic recesses the fabulous " seven cities of Cibola " and the Casas Grandes, ruins of extensive character in the valley of the river Gila, and so forth. But the allusion to the magical number seven in the myth demonstrates that the entire story is purely imaginary and possesses no basis of fact. A similar story occurs among the myths of the Kiche of Guatemala and the Peruvians.

The Sacrificed Princess

Coming to semi-historical times, we find a variety of legends connected with the early story of the city of

Mexico. These for the most part are of a weird and gloomy character, and throw much light on the dark fanaticism of a people which could immolate its children on the altars of implacable gods. It is told how after the Aztecs had built the city of Mexico they raised an altar to their war-god Huitzilopochtli. In general the lives rendered to this most sanguinary of deities were those of prisoners of war, but in times of public calamity he demanded the sacrifice of the noblest in the land. On one occasion his oracle required that a royal princess should be offered on the high altar. The Aztec king, either possessing no daughters of his own or hesitating to sacrifice them, sent an embassy to the monarch of Colhuacan to ask for one of his daughters to become the symbolical mother of Huitzilopochtli. The King of Colhuacan, suspecting nothing amiss, and highly flattered at the distinction, delivered up the girl, who was escorted to Mexico, where she was sacrificed with much pomp, her skin being flayed off to clothe the priest who represented the deity in the festival. The unhappy father was invited to this hideous orgy, ostensibly to witness his daughter's deification. In the gloomy chambers of the war-god's temple he was at first unable to mark the trend of the horrid ritual. But, given a torch of copal-gum, he saw the officiating priest clothed in his daughter's skin, receiving the homage of the worshippers. Recognising her features, and demented with grief and horror, he fled from the temple, a broken man, to spend the remainder of his days in mourning for his murdered child.

The Fugitive Prince

One turns with relief from such a sanguinary tale to the consideration of the pleasing semi-legendary accounts of Ixtlilxochitl regarding the civilisation of Tezcuco, Mexico's neighbour and ally. We have seen in the sketch of Nahua history which has been given how the Tecpanecs overcame the Acolhuans of Tezcuco and slew their king about the year 1418. Nezahualcoyotl (Fasting Coyote), the heir to the Tezcucan throne, beheld the butchery of his royal father from the shelter of a tree close by, and succeeded in making his escape from the invaders. His subsequent thrilling adventures have been compared with those of the Young Pretender after the collapse of the " Forty-five " resistance. He had not enjoyed many days of freedom when he was captured by those who had set out in pursuit of him, and, being haled back to his native city, was cast into prison. He found a friend in the governor of the place, who owed his position to the prince's late father, and by means of his assistance he succeeded in once more escaping from the hostile Tecpanecs. For aiding Nezahualcoyotl, however, the governor promptly paid the penalty of death. The royal family of Mexico interceded for the hunted youth, and he was permitted to find an asylum at the Aztec court, whence he later proceeded to his own city of Tezcuco, occupying apartments in the palace where his father had once dwelt. For eight years he remained there, existing unnoticed on the bounty of the Tecpanec chief who had usurped the throne of his ancestors.

Maxtla the Fierce

In course of time the original Tecpanec conqueror was gathered to his fathers, and was succeeded by his son Maxtla, a ruler who could ill brook the studious prince, who had journeyed to the capital of the Tecpanecs to do him homage. He refused Nezahualcoyotl's advances of friendship, and the latter was warned by a favourably disposed courtier to take refuge in flight. This advice he adopted, and returned to Tezcuco, where, however, Maxtla set a snare for his life. A function which took place in the evening afforded the tyrant his chance. But the prince's preceptor frustrated the conspiracy, by means of substituting for his charge a youth who strikingly resembled him. This second failure exasperated Maxtla so much that he sent a military force to Tezcuco, with orders to despatch Nezahualcoyotl without delay. But the same vigilant person who had guarded the prince so well before became apprised of his danger and advised him to fly. To this advice, however, Nezahualcoyotl refused to listen, and resolved to await the approach of his enemies.

A Romantic Escape

When they arrived he was engaged in the Mexican ball-game of *tlachtli*. With great politeness he requested them to enter and to partake of food. Whilst they refreshed themselves he betook himself to another room, but his action excited no surprise, as he could be seen through the open doorway by which the apartments communicated with each other. A huge censer, however, stood in the vestibule, and the clouds of incense which arose from it hid his movements from those who had been sent to slay him. Thus obscured, he succeeded in entering a subterranean passage which led to a large disused water-pipe, through which he crawled and made his escape.

A Thrilling Pursuit

For a season Nezahualcoyotl evaded capture by hiding in the hut of a zealous adherent. The hut was searched, but the pursuers neglected to look below a heap of maguey fibre used for making cloth, under which he lay concealed. Furious at his enemy's escape, Maxtla now ordered a rigorous search, and a regular battue of the country round Tezcuco was arranged. A large reward was offered for the capture of Nezahual-coyotl dead or alive, along with a fair estate and the hand of a noble lady, and the unhappy prince was forced to seek safety in the mountainous country between Tezcuco and Tlascala. He became a wretched outcast, a pariah lurking in caves and woods, prowling about after nightfall in order to satisfy his hunger, and seldom having a whole night's rest, because of the vigilance of his enemies. Hotly pursued by them, he was compelled to seek some curious places of concealment in order to save himself. On one occasion he was hidden by some friendly soldiers inside a large drum, and on another he was concealed beneath some *chia* stalks by a girl who was engaged in reaping them. The loyalty of the Tezcucan peasantry to their hunted prince was extra-ordinary, and rather than betray his whereabouts to the creatures of Maxtla they on many occasions suffered torture, and even death itself. At a time when his affairs appeared most gloomy, however, Nezahualcoyotl experienced a change of fortune. The tyrannous Maxtla had rendered himself highly unpopular by his many oppressions, and the people in the territories he had annexed were by no means contented under his rule.

The Defeat of Maxtla

These malcontents decided to band themselves together to defy the tyrant, and offered the command of the force thus raised to Nezahualcoyotl. This he accepted, and the Tecpanec usurper was totally defeated in a general engagement. Restored to the throne of his fathers, Nezahualcoyotl allied himself with Mexico, and with the assistance of its monarch completely routed the remaining force of Maxtla, who was seized in the baths of Azcapozalco, haled forth and sacrificed, and his city destroyed.

The Solon of Anahuac

Nezahualcoyotl profited by the hard experiences he had undergone, and proved a wise and just ruler. The code of laws framed by him was an exceedingly drastic one, but so wise and enlightened was his rule that on the whole he deserves the title which has been conferred upon him of " the Solon of Anahuac." He generously encouraged the arts, and established a Council of Music, the purpose of which was to supervise artistic endeavour of every description. In Nezahualcoyotl Mexico found, in all probability, her greatest native poet. An ode of his on the mutability of life displays much nobility of thought, and strikingly recalls the sentiments expressed in the verses of Omar Khayyám.

Nezahualcoyotl's Theology

Nezahualcoyotl is said to have erected a temple to the Unknown God, and to have shown a marked preference for the worship of one deity. In one of his poems he is credited with expressing the following exalted sentiments : " Let us aspire to that heaven where all is eternal, and corruption cannot come. The horrors of the tomb are the cradle of the sun, and the dark shadows of death are brilliant lights for the stars." Unfortunately these ideas cannot be verified as the undoubted sentiments of the royal bard of Tezcuco, and we are regretfully forced to regard the attribution as spurious. We must come to such a conclusion with very real disappointment, as to discover an untutored

and spontaneous belief in one god in the midst of surroundings so little congenial to its growth would have
been exceedingly valuable from several points of view.

The Poet Prince

We find Nezahualcoyotl's later days stained by an
act which was unworthy of such a great monarch and
wise man. His eldest son, the heir to the crown,
entered into an intrigue with one of his father's wives,
and dedicated many passionate poems to her, to which
she replied with equal ardour. The poetical correspond-
ence was brought before the king, who prized the
lady highly because of her beauty. Outraged in his
most sacred feelings, Nezahualcoyotl had the youth
arraigned before the High Court, which passed sentence
of death upon him—a sentence which his father permitted to be carried out. After his son's execution he
shut himself up in his palace for some months, and
gave orders that the doors and windows of the unhappy young man's residence should be built up so
that never again might its walls echo to the sound of
a human voice.

The Queen with a Hundred Lovers

In his *History of the Chichimeca* Ixtlilxochitl tells the
following gruesome tale regarding the dreadful fate of
a favourite wife of Nezahualpilli, the son of Nezahualcoyotl : When Axaiacatzin, King of Mexico, and other
lords sent their daughters to King Nezahualpilli, for
him to choose one to be his queen and lawful wife,
whose son might succeed to the inheritance, she who
had the highest claims among them, for nobility of
birth and rank, was Chachiuhnenetzin, the young
daughter of the Mexican king. She had been brought
up by the monarch in a separate palace, with great

pomp, and with numerous attendants, as became the daughter of so great a monarch. The number of servants attached to her household exceeded two thousand. Young as she was, she was exceedingly artful and vicious ; so that, finding herself alone, and seeing that her people feared her on account of her rank and importance, she began to give way to an unlimited indulgence of her power. Whenever she saw a young man who pleased her fancy she gave secret orders that he should be brought to her, and shortly afterwards he would be put to death. She would then order a statue or effigy of his person to be made, and, adorning it with rich clothing, gold, and jewellery, place it in the apartment in which she lived. The number of statues of those whom she thus sacrificed was so great as to almost fill the room. When the king came to visit her, and inquired respecting these statues, she answered that they were her gods ; and he, knowing how strict the Mexicans were in the worship of their false deities, believed her. But, as no iniquity can be long committed with entire secrecy, she was finally found out in this manner : Three of the young men, for some reason or other, she had left alive. Their names were Chicuhcoatl, Huitzilimitzin, and Maxtla, one of whom was lord of Tesoyucan and one of the grandees of the kingdom, and the other two nobles of high rank. It happened that one day the king recognised on the apparel of one of these a very precious jewel which he had given to the queen ; and although he had no fear of treason on her part it gave him some uneasiness. Proceeding to visit her that night, her attendants told him she was asleep, supposing that the king would then return, as he had done at other times. But the affair of the jewel made him insist on entering the chamber in

The Princess and the Statues
Gilbert James
(See page 130)

which she slept ; and, going to wake her, he found
only a statue in the bed, adorned with her hair, and
closely resembling her. Seeing this, and noticing
that the attendants around were in much trepidation
and alarm, the king called his guards, and, assembling
all the people of the house, made a general search for
the queen, who was shortly found at an entertainment with the three young lords, who were arrested
with her. The king referred the case to the judges
of his court, in order that they might make an
inquiry into the matter and examine the parties
implicated. These discovered many individuals, servants of the queen, who had in some way or other
been accessory to her crimes—workmen who had been
engaged in making and adorning the statues, others
who had aided in introducing the young men into the
palace, and others, again, who had put them to death
and concealed their bodies. The case having been
sufficiently investigated, the king despatched ambassa-
dors to the rulers of Mexico and Tlacopan, giving them
information of the event, and signifying the day on
which the punishment of the queen and her accomplices
was to take place ; and he likewise sent through the
empire to summon all the lords to bring their wives
and their daughters, however young they might be, to
be witnesses of a punishment which he designed for a
great example. He also made a truce with all the
enemies of the empire, in order that they might come
freely to see it. The time having arrived, the number
of people gathered together was so great that, large
as was the city of Tezcuco, they could scarcely all find
room in it. The execution took place publicly, in
sight of the whole city. The queen was put to the
garrotte (a method of strangling by means of a rope
twisted round a stick), as well as her three gallants ;

and, from their being persons of high birth, their bodies were burned, together with the effigies before mentioned. The other parties who had been accessory to the crimes, who numbered more than two thousand persons, were also put to the garrotte, and burned in a pit made for the purpose in a ravine near a temple of the Idol of Adulterers. All applauded so severe and exemplary a punishment, except the Mexican lords, the relatives of the queen, who were much incensed at so public an example, and, although for the time they concealed their resentment, meditated future revenge. It was not without reason, says the chronicler, that the king experienced this disgrace in his household, since he was thus punished for an unworthy subterfuge made use of by his father to obtain his mother as a wife !

This Nezahualpilli, the successor of Nezahualcoyotl, was a monarch of scientific tastes, and, as Torquemada states, had a primitive observatory erected in his palace.

The Golden Age of Tezcuco

The period embraced by the life of this monarch and his predecessor may be regarded as the Golden Age of Tezcuco, and as semi-mythical. The palace of Nezahualcoyotl, according to the account of Ixtlilxochitl, extended east and west for 1234 yards, and for 978 yards from north to south. Enclosed by a high wall, it contained two large courts, one used as the municipal market-place, whilst the other was surrounded by administrative offices. A great hall was set apart for the special use of poets and men of talent, who held symposiums under its classic roof, or engaged in controversy in the surrounding corridors. The chronicles of the kingdom were also kept in this portion of the palace. The private apartments of the monarch adjoined this College of Bards. They were gorgeous in the extreme, and their description rivals that of the fabled Toltec city of Tollan. Rare stones and beautifully coloured plaster mouldings alternated with wonderful tapestries of splendid feather-work to make an enchanting display of florid decoration, and the gardens which surrounded this marvellous edifice were delightful retreats, where the lofty cedar and cypress over-hung sparkling fountains and luxurious baths. Fish darted hither and thither in the ponds, and the aviaries echoed to the songs of birds of wonderful plumage.

A Fairy Villa

According to Ixtlilxochitl, the king's villa of Tez-cotzinco was a residence which for sheer beauty had no equal in Persian romance, or in those dream-tales of Araby which in childhood we feel to be true, and in later life regretfully admit can only be known again by sailing the sea of Poesy or penetrating the mist-locked continent of Dream. The account of it which we have from the garrulous half-blood reminds us of the stately pleasure-dome decreed by Kubla Khan on the turbulent banks of the sacred Alph. A conical eminence was laid out in hanging gardens reached by an airy flight of five hundred and twenty marble steps. Gigantic walls contained an immense reservoir of water, in the midst of which was islanded a great rock carved with hieroglyphs describing the principal events in the reign of Nezahual-coyotl. In each of three other reservoirs stood a marble statue of a woman, symbolical of one of the three pro-vinces of Tezcuco. These great basins supplied the gardens beneath with a perennial flow of water, so directed as to leap in cascades over artificial rockeries or meander among mossy retreats with refreshing whisper, watering the roots of odoriferous shrubs and flowers and winding in and out of the shadow of the cypress woods. Here and there pavilions of marble arose over porphyry baths, the highly polished stone of which reflected the bodies of the bathers. The villa itself stood amidst a wilderness of stately cedars, which shielded it from the torrid heat of the Mexican sun. The architectural design of this delightful edifice was light and airy in the extreme, and the perfume of the surrounding gardens filled the spacious apartments with the delicious incense of nature. In this paradise the Tezcucan monarch sought in the company of his wives repose from the oppression of rule, and passed the lazy hours in gamesome sport and dance. The surrounding woods afforded him the pleasures of the chase, and art and nature combined to render his rural retreat a centre of pleasant recreation as well as of repose and refreshment.

Disillusionment

That some such palace existed on the spot in question it would be absurd to deny, as its stupendous pillars and remains still litter the terraces of Tezcotzinco. But, alas! we must not listen to the vapourings of the untrustworthy Ixtlilxochitl, who claims to have seen the place. It will be better to turn to a more modern authority, who visited the site about seventy-five years ago, and who has given perhaps the best account of it. He says :

"Fragments of pottery, broken pieces of obsidian knives and arrows, pieces of stucco, shattered terraces, and old walls were thickly dispersed over its whole surface. We soon found further advance on horseback impracticable, and, attaching our patient steeds to the nopal bushes, we followed our Indian guide on foot, scrambling upwards over rock and through tangled brushwood. On gaining the narrow ridge which connects the conical hill with one at the rear, we found the remains of a wall and causeway ; and, a little higher, reached a recess, where, at the foot of a small precipice, overhung with Indian fig and grass, the rock had been wrought by hand into a flat surface of large dimensions. In this perpendicular wall of rock a carved Toltec calendar existed formerly ; but the Indians, finding the place visited occasionally by foreigners from the capital, took it into their heads that there must be a silver vein there, and straightway set to work to find it, obliterating the sculpture, and driving a level beyond it into the hard rock for several yards. From this recess a few minutes' climb brought us to the summit of the hill. The sun was on the point of setting over the mountains on the other side of the valley, and the view spread beneath our feet was most glorious. The whole of the lake of Tezcuco, and the country and mountains on both sides, lay stretched before us.

" But, however disposed, we dare not stop long to gaze and admire, but, descending a little obliquely, soon came to the so-called bath, two singular basins, of perhaps two feet and a half diameter, cut into a bastion-like solid rock, projecting from the general outline of the hill, and surrounded by smooth carved seats and grooves, as we supposed—for I own the whole appearance of the locality was perfectly inexplicable to me. I have a suspicion that many of these horizontal planes and grooves were contrivances to aid their astronomical observations, one like that I have mentioned having been discovered by de Gama at Chapultepec.

" As to Montezuma's Bath, it might be his foot-bath if you will, but it would be a moral impossibility for any monarch of larger dimensions than Oberon to take a duck in it.

"The mountain bears the marks of human industry to its very apex, many of the blocks of porphyry of which it is composed being quarried into smooth horizontal planes. It is impossible to say at present what portion of the surface is artificial or not, such is the state of confusion observable in every part.

" By what means nations unacquainted with the use of iron constructed works of such a smooth polish, in rocks of such hardness, it is extremely difficult to say. Many think tools of mixed tin and copper were employed ; others, that patient friction was one of the main means resorted to. Whatever may have been the real appropriation of these inexplicable ruins, or the epoch of their construction, there can be no doubt but the whole of this hill, which I should suppose rises five or six hundred feet above the level of the plain, was covered with artificial works of one kind or another. They are doubtless rather of Toltec than of Aztec origin, and perhaps with still more probability attributable to a people of an age yet more remote."

The Noble Tlascalan

As may be imagined regarding a community where human sacrifice was rife, tales concerning those who were consigned to this dreadful fate were abundant. Perhaps the most striking of these is that relating to the noble Tlascalan warrior Tlalhuicole, who was captured in combat by the troops of Montezuma. Less than a year before the Spaniards arrived in Mexico war broke out between the Huexotzincans and the Tlascalans, to the former of whom the Aztecs acted as allies. On the battlefield there was captured by guile a very valiant Tlascalan leader called Tlalhuicole, so renowned for his prowess that the mere mention of his name was generally sufficient to deter any Mexican hero from attempting his capture. He was brought to Mexico in a cage, and presented to the Emperor Montezuma, who, on learning of his name and renown, gave him his liberty and overwhelmed him with honours. He further granted him permission to return to his own country, a boon he had never before extended to any captive. But Tlalhuicole refused his freedom, and replied that he would prefer to be sacrificed to the gods, according to the usual custom. Montezuma, who had the highest regard for him, and prized his life more than any sacrifice, would not consent to his immolation. At this juncture war broke out between Mexico and the Tarascans, and Montezuma announced the appointment of Tlalhuicole as chief of the expeditionary force. He accepted the command, marched against the Tarascans, and, having totally defeated them, returned to Mexico laden with an enormous booty and crowds of slaves. The city rang with his triumph. The emperor begged him to become a Mexican citizen, but he replied that on no account would he prove a traitor to his country. Montezuma then once more offered him his liberty, but he strenuously refused to return to Tlascala, having undergone the disgrace of defeat and capture. He begged Montezuma to terminate his unhappy existence by sacrificing him to the gods, thus ending the dishonour he felt in living on after having undergone defeat, and at the same time fulfilling the highest aspiration of his life—to die the death of a warrior on the stone of combat. Montezuma, himself the noblest pattern of Aztec chivalry, touched at his request, could not but agree with him that he had chosen the most fitting fate for a hero, and ordered him to be chained to the stone of combat, the blood-stained *temalacatl*. The most renowned of the Aztec warriors were pitted against him, and the emperor himself graced the sanguinary tournament with his presence. Tlalhuicole bore himself in the combat like a lion, slew eight warriors of renown, and wounded more than twenty. But at last he fell, covered with wounds, and was haled by the exulting priests to the altar of the terrible war-god Huitzilopochtli, to whom his heart was offered up.

The Haunting Mothers

It is only occasionally that we encounter either the gods or supernatural beings of any description in Mexican myth. But occasionally we catch sight of such beings as the Ciuapipiltin (Honoured Women), the spirits of those women who had died in childbed, a death highly venerated by the Mexicans, who regarded the woman who perished thus as the equal of a warrior who met his fate in battle. Strangely enough, these spirits were actively malevolent, probably because the moon-goddess (who was also the deity of evil exhalations) was evil in her tendencies, and they were regarded as possessing an affinity to her. It was supposed that they afflicted infants with various diseases, and Mexican parents took every precaution not to permit their offspring out of doors on the days when their influence was believed to be strong. They were said to haunt the cross-roads, and even to enter the bodies of weakly people, the better to work their evil will. The insane were supposed to be under their especial visitation. Temples were raised at the cross-roads in order to placate them, and loaves of bread, shaped like butterflies, were dedicated to them. They were represented as having faces of a dead white, and as blanching their arms and hands with a white powder known as *tisatl*. Their eyebrows were of a golden hue, and their raiment was that of Mexican ladies of the ruling class.

The Return of Papantzin[1]

One of the weirdest legends in Mexican tradition recounts how Papantzin, the sister of Montezuma II, returned from her tomb to prophesy to her royal brother concerning his doom and the fall of his empire at the hands of the Spaniards. On taking up the reins of government Montezuma had married this lady to one of his most illustrious servants, the governor of Tlatelulco, and after his death it would appear that she continued to exercise his almost vice-regal functions and to reside in his palace. In course of time she died, and her obsequies were attended by the emperor in person, accompanied by the greatest personages of his court and kingdom. The body was interred in a subterranean vault of his own palace, in close proximity to the royal baths, which stood in a sequestered part of the extensive grounds surrounding the royal residence. The entrance to the vault was secured by a stone slab of moderate weight, and when the numerous ceremonies prescribed for the interment of a royal personage had been completed the emperor and his suite retired. At daylight next morning one of the royal children, a little girl of some six years of age, having gone into the garden to seek her governess, espied the Princess Papan standing near the baths. The princess, who was her aunt, called to her, and requested her to bring her governess to her. The child did as she was bid, but her governess, thinking that imagination had played her a trick, paid little attention to what she said. As the child persisted in her statement, the governess at last followed her into the garden, where she saw Papan sitting on one of the steps of the baths.

[1] The suffix *tzin* after a Mexican name denotes either "lord" or "lady," according to the sex of the person alluded to.

The sight of the supposed dead princess filled the woman with such terror that she fell down in a swoon. The child then went to her mother's apartment, and detailed to her what had happened. She at once proceeded to the baths with two of her attendants, and at sight of Papan was also seized with affright. But the princess reassured her, and asked to be allowed to accompany her to her apartments, and that the entire affair should for the present be kept absolutely secret. Later in the day she sent for Tiçotzicatzin, her major-domo, and requested him to inform the emperor that she desired to speak with him immediately on matters of the greatest importance. The man, terrified, begged to be excused from the mission, and Papan then gave orders that her uncle Nezahualpilli, King of Tez-cuco, should be communicated with. That monarch, on receiving her request that he should come to her, hastened to the palace. The princess begged him to see the emperor without loss of time and to entreat him to come to her at once. Montezuma heard his story with surprise mingled with doubt. Hastening to his sister, he cried as he approached her : " Is it indeed you, my sister, or some evil demon who has taken your likeness ? " " It is I indeed, your Majesty," she replied. Montezuma and the exalted personages who accompanied him then seated them-selves, and a hush of expectation fell upon all as they were addressed by the princess in the following words :

" Listen attentively to what I am about to relate to you. You have seen me dead, buried, and now behold me alive again. By the authority of our ancestors, my brother, I am returned from the dwellings of the dead to prophesy to you certain things of prime importance.

The King's Sister is shown the Valley of Dry Bones
Gilbert James
(See page 141)

The Princess is given a Vision
William Sewell
(See page 141)

Papantzin's Story

" At the moment after death I found myself in a
spacious valley, which appeared to have neither commencement nor end, and was surrounded by lofty
mountains. Near the middle I came upon a road with
many branching paths. By the side of the valley there
flowed a river of considerable size, the waters of which
ran with a loud noise. By the borders of this I saw a
young man clothed in a long robe, fastened with a
diamond, and shining like the sun, his visage bright as
a star. On his forehead was a sign in the figure of a
cross. He had wings, the feathers of which gave forth
the most wonderful and glowing reflections and colours.
His eyes were as emeralds, and his glance was modest.
He was fair, of beautiful aspect and imposing presence.
He took me by the hand and said : 'Come hither.
It is not yet time for you to cross the river. You
possess the love of God, which is greater than you know
or can comprehend.' He then conducted me through
the valley, where I espied many heads and bones of
dead men. I then beheld a number of black folk,
horned, and with the feet of deer. They were engaged
in building a house, which was nearly completed.
Turning toward the east for a space, I beheld on the
waters of the river a vast number of ships manned by a
great host of men dressed differently from ourselves.
Their eyes were of a clear grey, their complexions
ruddy, they carried banners and ensigns in their hands
and wore helmets on their heads. They called themselves ' Sons of the Sun.' The youth who conducted
me and caused me to see all these things said that it
was not yet the will of the gods that I should cross
the river, but that I was to be reserved to behold the
future with my own eyes, and to enjoy the benefits of

the faith which these strangers brought with them ; that the bones I beheld on the plain were those of my countrymen who had died in ignorance of that faith, and had consequently suffered great torments ; that the house being builded by the black folk was an edifice prepared for those who would fall in battle with the seafaring strangers whom I had seen ; and that I was destined to return to my compatriots to tell them of the true faith, and to announce to them what I had seen that they might profit thereby."

Montezuma hearkened to these matters in silence, and felt greatly troubled. He left his sister's presence without a word, and, regaining his own apartments, plunged into melancholy thoughts.

Papantzin's resurrection is one of the best authenticated incidents in Mexican history, and it is a curious fact that on the arrival of the Spanish Conquistadores one of the first persons to embrace Christianity and receive baptism at their hands was the Princess Papan.

MEXICAN DEITY
From the Vienna Codex

CHAPTER IV : THE MAYA RACE
AND MYTHOLOGY

The Maya

IT was to the Maya—the people who occupied the territory between the isthmus of Tehuantepec and Nicaragua—that the civilisation of Central America owed most. The language they spoke was quite distinct from the Nahuatl spoken by the Nahua of Mexico, and in many respects their customs and habits were widely different from those of the people of Anahuac. It will be remembered that the latter were the heirs of an older civilisation, that, indeed, they had entered the valley of Mexico as savages, and that practically all they knew of the arts of culture was taught them by the remnants of the people whom they dispossessed. It was not thus with the Maya. Their arts and industries were of their own invention, and bore the stamp of an origin of considerable antiquity. They were, indeed, the supreme intellectual race of America, and on their coming into contact with the Nahua that people assimilated sufficient of their culture to raise them several grades in the scale of civilisation.

Were the Maya Toltecs?

It has already been stated that many antiquarians see in the Maya those Toltecs who because of the inroads of barbarous tribes quitted their native land of Anahuac and journeyed southward to seek a new home in Chiapas and Yucatan. It would be idle to attempt to uphold or refute such a theory in the absolute dearth of positive evidence for or against it. The architectural remains of the older race of Anahuac do not bear any striking likeness to Maya forms, and if the mythologies of the two peoples are in some particulars alike, that may well

143

be accounted for by their mutual adoption of deities and religious customs. On the other hand, it is distinctly noteworthy that the cult of the god Quetzalcoatl, which was regarded in Mexico as of alien origin, had a considerable vogue among the Maya and their allied races.

The Maya Kingdom

On the arrival of the Spaniards (after the celebrated march of Cortés from Mexico to Central America) the Maya were divided into a number of subsidiary states which remind us somewhat of the numerous little kingdoms of Palestine. That these had hived off from an original and considerably greater state there is good evidence to show, but internal dissension had played havoc with the polity of the central government of this empire, the disintegration of which had occurred at a remote period. In the semi-historical legends of this people we catch glimpses of a great kingdom, occasionally alluded to as the "Kingdom of the Great Snake," or the empire of Xibalba, realms which have been identified with the ruined city-centres of Palenque and Mitla. These identifications must be regarded with caution, but the work of excavation will doubtless sooner or later assist theorists in coming to conclusions which will admit of no doubt. The sphere of Maya civilisation and influence is pretty well marked, and embraces the peninsula of Yucatan, Chiapas, to the isthmus of Tehuantepec on the north, and the whole of Guatemala to the boundaries of the present republic of San Salvador. The true nucleus of Maya civilisation, however, must be looked for in that part of Chiapas which skirts the banks of the Usumacinta river and in the valleys of its tributaries. Here Maya art and architecture reached a height of splendour unknown elsewhere, and in this district, too, the strange Maya system of writing had its most skilful exponents. Although the arts and industries of the several districts inhabited by people of Maya race exhibited many superficial differences, these are so small as to make us certain of the fact that the various areas inhabited by Maya stock had all drawn their inspiration toward civilisation from one common nucleus, and had equally passed through a uniform civilisation and drawn sap from an original culture-centre.

The Maya Dialects

Perhaps the most effectual method of distinguishing the various branches of the Maya people from one another consists in dividing them into linguistic groups. The various dialects spoken by the folk of Maya origin, although they exhibit some considerable difference, yet display strongly that affinity of construction and resemblance in root which go to prove that they all emanate from one common mother-tongue. In Chiapas the Maya tongue itself is the current dialect, whilst in Guatemala no less than twenty-four dialects are in use, the principal of which are the Quiche, or Kiche, the Kakchiquel, the Zutugil, Coxoh Chol, and Pipil. These dialects and the folk who speak them are sufficient to engage our attention, as in them are enshrined the most remarkable myths and legends of the race, and by the men who used them were the greatest acts in Maya history achieved.

Whence Came the Maya?

Whence came these folk, then, who raised a civilisation by no means inferior to that of ancient Egypt, which, if it had had scope, would have rivalled in its achievements the glory of old Assyria ? We cannot tell. The mystery of its entrance into the land is as deep as the mystery of the ancient forests which now bury the remnants of its mighty monuments and enclose its temples in impenetrable gloom. Generations of antiquarians have attempted to trace the origin of this race to Egypt, Phœnicia, China, Burma. But the manifest traces of indigenous American origin are present in all its works, and the writers who have beheld in these likenesses to the art of Asiatic or African peoples have been grievously misled by superficial resemblances which could not have betrayed any one who had studied Maya affinities deeply.

Civilisation of the Maya

At the risk of repetition it is essential to point out that civilisation, which was a newly acquired thing with the Nahua peoples, was not so with the Maya. They were indisputably an older race, possessing institutions which bore the marks of generations of use, whereas the Nahua had only too obviously just entered into their heritage of law and order. When we first catch sight of the Maya kingdoms they are in the process of disintegration. Such strong young blood as the virile folk of Anahuac possessed did not flow in the veins of the people of Yucatan and Guatemala. They were to the Nahua much as the ancient Assyrians were to the hosts of Israel at the entrance of the latter into national existence. That there was a substratum of ethnical and cultural relationship, however, it would be impossible to deny. The institutions, architecture, habits, even the racial cast of thought of the two peoples, bore such a general resemblance as to show that many affinities of blood and cultural relationship existed between them. But it will not do to insist too strongly upon these. It may be argued with great probability that these relationships and likenesses exist because of the influence of Maya civilisation upon Mexican alone, or from the

inheritance by both Mexican and Maya people of a
still older culture of which we are ignorant, and the
proofs of which lie buried below the forests of Guatemala or the sands of Yucatan.

The Zapotecs

The influence of the Maya upon the Nahua was
a process of exceeding slowness. The peoples who
divided them one from another were themselves benefited by carrying Maya culture into Anahuac, or rather
it might be said that they constituted a sort of filter
through which the southern civilisation reached the
northern. These peoples were the Zapotecs, the Mixtecs,
and the Kuikatecs, by far the most important of whom
were the first-mentioned. They partook of the nature
and civilisation of both races, and were in effect a border
people who took from and gave to both Maya and Nahua,
much as the Jews absorbed and disseminated the cultures
of Egypt and Assyria. They were, however, of Nahua
race, but their speech bears the strongest marks of
having borrowed extensively from the Maya vocabulary.
For many generations these people wandered in a
nomadic condition from Maya to Nahua territory,
thus absorbing the customs, speech, and mythology
of each.

The Huasteca

But we should be wrong if we thought that the
Maya had never attempted to expand, and had never
sought new homes for their surplus population. That
they had is proved by an outlying tribe of Maya, the
Huasteca, having settled at the mouth of the Panuco
river, on the north coast of Mexico. The presence of
this curious ethnological island has of course given
rise to all sorts of queer theories concerning Toltec

relationship, whereas it simply intimates that before the era of Nahua expansion the Maya had attempted to colonise the country to the north of their territories, but that their efforts in this direction had been cut short by the influx of savage Nahua, against whom they found themselves unable to contend.

The Type of Maya Civilisation

Did the civilisation of the Maya differ, then, in type from that of the Nahua, or was it merely a larger expression of that in vogue in Anahuac? We may take it that the Nahua civilisation characterised the culture of Central America in its youth, whilst that of the Maya displayed it in its bloom, and perhaps in its senility. The difference was neither essential nor radical, but may be said to have arisen for the most part from climatic and kindred causes. The climate of Anahuac is dry and temperate, that of Yucatan and Guatemala is tropical, and we shall find even such religious conceptions of the two peoples as were drawn from a common source varying from this very cause, and coloured by differences in temperature and rainfall.

Maya History

Before entering upon a consideration of the art, architecture, or mythology of this strange and highly interesting people it will be necessary to provide the reader with a brief sketch of their history. Such notices of this as exist in English are few, and their value doubtful. For the earlier history of the people of Maya stock we depend almost wholly upon tradition and architectural remains. The net result of the evidence wrung from these is that the Maya civilisation was one and homogeneous, and that all the separate states must have at one period passed through a uniform condition of culture, to which they were all equally debtors, and that this is sufficient ground for the belief that all were at one time beneath the sway of one central power. For the later history we possess the writings of the Spanish fathers, but not in such profusion as in the case of Mexico. In fact the trustworthy original authors who deal with Maya history can almost be counted on the fingers of one hand. We are further confused in perusing these, and, indeed, throughout the study of Maya history, by discovering that many of the sites of Maya cities are designated by Nahua names. This is due to the fact that the Spanish conquerors were guided in their conquest of the Maya territories by Nahua, who naturally applied Nahuatlac designations to those sites of which the Spaniards asked the names. These appellations clung to the places in question ; hence the confusion, and the blundering theories which would read in these place-names relics of Aztec conquest.

The Nucleus of Maya Power

As has been said, the nucleus of Maya power and culture is probably to be found in that part of Chiapas which slopes down from the steep Cordilleras. Here the ruined sites of Palenque, Piedras Negras, and Ocosingo are eloquent of that opulence of imagination and loftiness of conception which go hand in hand with an advanced culture. The temples and palaces of this region bear the stamp of a dignity and consciousness of metropolitan power which are scarcely to be mistaken, so broad, so free is their architectural conception, so full to overflowing the display of the desire to surpass. But upon the necessities of religion and central organisation alone was this architectural artistry lavished. Its dignities were not profaned by its application to mere domestic uses, for, unless what were obviously palaces are excepted, not a single example of Maya domestic building has survived. This is of course accounted for by the circumstance that the people were sharply divided into the aristocratic and labouring classes, the first of which was closely identified with religion or kingship, and was housed in the ecclesiastical or royal buildings, whilst those of less exalted rank were perforce content with the shelter afforded by a hut built of perishable materials, the traces of which have long since passed away. The temples were, in fact, the nuclei of the towns, the centres round which the Maya communities were grouped, much in the same manner as the cities of Europe in the Middle Ages clustered and grew around the shadow of some vast cathedral or sheltering stronghold.

Early Race Movements

We shall leave the consideration of Maya tradition until we come to speak of Maya myth proper, and attempt to glean from the chaos of legend some veritable facts connected with Maya history. According to a manuscript of Kuikatec origin recently discovered, it is probable that a Nahua invasion of the Maya states of Chiapas and Tabasco took place about the ninth century of our era, and we must for the present regard that as the starting-point of Maya history. The south-western portions of the Maya territory were agitated about the same time by race movements, which turned northward toward Tehuantepec, and, flowing through Guatemala, came to rest in Acalan, on the borders of Yucatan, retarded, probably, by the inhospitable and waterless condition of that country. This Nahua invasion probably had the effect of driving the more peaceful Maya from their northerly settlements and forcing them farther south. Indeed, evidence is not wanting to show that the warlike Nahua pursued the pacific Maya into their new retreats, and for a space left them but little peace. This struggle it was which finally resulted in the breaking up of the Maya civilisation, which even at that relatively remote period had reached its apogee, its several races separating into numerous city-states, which bore a close political resemblance to those of Italy on the downfall of Rome. At this period, probably, began the cleavage between the Maya of Yucatan and those of Guatemala, which finally resolved itself into such differences of speech, faith, and architecture as almost to constitute them different peoples.

The Settlement of Yucatan

As the Celts of Wales and Scotland were driven into the less hospitable regions of their respective countries by the inroads of the Saxons, so was one branch of the Maya forced to seek shelter in the almost desert wastes of Yucatan. There can be no doubt that the Maya did not take to this barren and waterless land of their own accord. Thrifty and possessed of high agricultural attainments, this people would view with concern a removal to a sphere so forbidding after the rich and easily developed country they had inhabited for generations. But the inexorable Nahua were behind, and they were a peaceful folk, unused to the horrors of savage warfare. So, taking their courage in both hands, they wandered into the desert. Everything points to a late occupation of Yucatan by the Maya, and architectural effort exhibits deterioration, evidenced in a high conventionality of design and excess of ornamentation. Evidences of Nahua influence also are not wanting, a fact which is eloquent of the later period of contact which is known to have occurred between the peoples, and which alone is almost sufficient to fix the date of the settlement of the Maya in Yucatan. It must not be thought that the Maya in Yucatan formed one homogeneous state recognising a central authority. On the contrary, as is often the case with colonists, the several Maya bands of immigrants formed themselves into different states or kingdoms, each having its own separate traditions. It is thus a matter of the highest difficulty to so collate and criticise these traditions as to construct a history of the Maya race in Yucatan. As may be supposed, we find the various city-sites founded by divine beings who play a more or less important part in the Maya pantheon. Kukulcan, for example, is the first king of Mayapan, whilst Itzamna figures as the founder of the state of Itzamal. The gods were the spiritual leaders of these bands of Maya, just as Jehovah was the spiritual leader and guide of the Israelites in the desert. One is therefore not surprised to find in the *Popol Vuh*, the saga of the Kiche-Maya of Guatemala, that the god Tohil (The Rumbler) guided them to the site of the first Kiche city. Some writers on the subject appear to think that the incidents in such migration myths, especially the tutelage and guidance of the tribes by gods and the descriptions of desert scenery which they contain, suffice to stamp them as mere native versions of the Book of Exodus, or at the best myths sophisticated by missionary influence. The truth is that the conditions of migration undergone by the Maya were similar to those described in the Scriptures, and by no means merely reflect the Bible story, as short-sighted collators of both aver.

152

FLIGHT OF THE TUTUL XIUS

The Septs of Yucatan

The priest-kings of Mayapan, who claimed descent from Kukulcan or Quetzalcoatl, soon raised their state into a position of prominence among the surrounding cities. Those who had founded Chichen-Itza, and who were known as Itzaes, were, on the other hand, a caste of warriors who do not appear to have cherished the priestly function with such assiduity. The rulers of the Itzaes, who were known as the Tutul Xius, seem to have come, according to their traditions, from the western Maya states, perhaps from Nonohualco in Tabasco. Arriving from thence at the southern extremity of Yucatan, they founded the city of Ziyan Caan, on Lake Bacalar, which had a period of prosperity for at least a couple of generations. At the expiry of that period for some unaccountable reason they migrated northward, perhaps because at that particular time the incidence of power was shifting toward Northern Yucatan, and took up their abode in Chichen-Itza, eventually the sacred city of the Maya, which they founded.

The Cocomes

But they were not destined to remain undisturbed in their new sphere. The Cocomes of Mayapan, when at the height of their power, viewed with disfavour the settlement of the Tutul Xius. After it had flourished for a period of about 120 years it was overthrown by the Cocomes, who resolved it into a dependency, permitting the governors and a certain number of the people to depart elsewhere.

Flight of the Tutul Xius

Thus expelled, the Tutul Xius fled southward, whence they had originally come, and settled in Potonchan or Champoton, where they reigned for nearly 300 years. From this new centre, with the aid of Nahua mercenaries, they commenced an extension of territory northward, and entered into diplomatic relations with the heads of the other Maya states. It was at this time that they built Uxmal, and their power became so extensive that they reconquered the territory they had lost to the Cocomes. This on the whole appears to have been a period when the arts flourished under an enlightened policy, which knew how to make and keep friendly relations with surrounding states, and the splendid network of roads with which the country was covered and the many evidences of architectural excellence go to prove that the race had had leisure to achieve much in art and works of utility. Thus the city of Chichen-Itza was linked up with the island of Cozumel by a highway whereon thousands of pilgrims plodded to the temples of the gods of wind and moisture. From Itzamal, too, roads branched in every direction, in order that the people should have every facility for reaching the chief shrine of the country situated there. But the hand of the Cocomes was heavy upon the other Maya states which were tributary to them. As in the Yucatan of to-day, where the wretched henequen-picker leads the life of a veritable slave, a crushing system of helotage obtained. The Cocomes made heavy demands upon the Tutul Xius, who in their turn sweated the hapless folk under their sway past the bounds of human endurance. As in all tottering civilisations, the feeling of responsibility among the upper classes became dormant, and they abandoned themselves to the pleasures of life without thought of the morrow. Morality ceased to be regarded as a virtue, and rottenness was at the core of Maya life. Discontent quickly spread on every hand.

HUNAC EEL

The Revolution in Mayapan

The sequel was, naturally, revolution. Ground down by the tyranny of a dissolute oligarchy, the subject states rose in revolt. The Cocomes surrounded themselves by Nahua mercenaries, who succeeded in beating off the first wave of revolt, led by the king or regulus of Uxmal, who was defeated, and whose people in their turn rose against him, a circumstance which ended in the abandonment of the city of Uxmal. Once more were the Tutul Xius forced to go on pilgrimage, and this time they founded the city of Mani, a mere shadow of the splendour of Uxmal and Chichen.

Hunac Eel

If the aristocracy of the Cocomes was composed of weaklings, its ruler was made of sterner stuff. Hunac Eel, who exercised royal sway over this people, and held in subjection the lesser principalities of Yucatan, was not only a tyrant of harsh and vindictive temperament, but a statesman of judgment and experience, who courted the assistance of the neighbouring Nahua, whom he employed in his campaign against the new assailant of his absolutism, the ruler of Chichen-Itza. Mustering a mighty host of his vassals, Hunac Eel marched against the devoted city whose prince had dared to challenge his supremacy, and succeeded in inflicting a crushing defeat upon its inhabitants. But apparently the state was permitted to remain under the sovereignty of its native princes. The revolt, however, merely smouldered, and in the kingdom of Mayapan itself, the territory of the Cocomes, the fires of revolution began to blaze. This state of things continued for nearly a century. Then the crash came. The enemies of the Cocomes effected a junction. The people of Chichen-

155

Itza joined hands with the Tutul Xius, who had sought
refuge in the central highlands of Yucatan and those
city-states which clustered around the mother-city of
Mayapan. A fierce concerted attack was made, beneath
which the power of the Cocomes crumpled up completely. Not one stone was left standing upon another
by the exasperated allies, who thus avenged the helotage
of nearly 300 years. To this event the date 1436 is
assigned, but, like most dates in Maya history, considerable uncertainty must be attached to it.

The Last of the Cocomes

Only a remnant of the Cocomes survived. They
had been absent in Nahua territory, attempting to raise
fresh troops for the defence of Mayapan. These the
victors spared, and they finally settled in Zotuta, in the
centre of Yucatan, a region of almost impenetrable
forest.

It would not appear that the city of Chichen-Itza, the
prince of which was ever the head and front of the
rebellion against the Cocomes, profited in any way from
the fall of the suzerain power. On the contrary, tradition has it that the town was abandoned by its inhabitants, and left to crumble into the ruinous state in
which the Spaniards found it on their entrance into
the country. The probability is that its people quitted
it because of the repeated attacks made upon it by the
Cocomes, who saw in it the chief obstacle to their
universal sway ; and this is supported by tradition,
which tells that a prince of Chichen-Itza, worn out
with conflict and internecine strife, left it to seek the
cradle of the Maya race in the land of the setting
sun. Indeed, it is further stated that this prince
founded the city of Peten-Itza, on the lake of Peten, in
Guatemala.

The Prince who went to Found a City
Gilbert James
(See page 156)

THE MAYA TULAN

The Maya Peoples of Guatemala

When the Maya peoples of Guatemala, the Kiches and the Kakchiquels, first made their way into that territory, they probably found there a race of Maya origin of a type more advanced and possessed of more ancient traditions than themselves. By their connection with this folk they greatly benefited in the direction o. artistic achievement as well as in the industrial arts. Concerning these people we have a large body of tradition in the *Popol Vuh*, a native chronicle, the contents of which will be fully dealt with in the chapter relating to the Maya myths and legendary matter. We cannot deal with it as a veritable historical document, but there is little doubt that a basis of fact exists behind the tradition it contains. The difference between the language of these people and that of their brethren in Yucatan was, as has been said, one of dialect only, and a like slight distinction is found in their mythology, caused, doubtless, by the incidence of local conditions, and resulting in part from the difference between a level and comparatively waterless land and one of a semi-mountainous character covered with thick forests. We shall note further differences when we come to examine the art and architecture of the Maya race, and to compare those of its two most distinctive branches.

The Maya Tulan

It was to the city of Tulan, probably in Tabasco, that the Maya of Guatemala referred as being the starting-point of all their migrations. We must not confound this place with the Tollan of the Mexican traditions. It is possible that the name may in both cases be derived from a root meaning a place from which a tribe set forth, a starting-place, but geographical connection there is none. From here Nima-Kiche, the great Kiche, started on his migration to the mountains, accompanied by his three brothers. Tulan, says the *Popol Vuh*, had been a place of misfortune to man, for he had suffered much from cold and hunger, and, as at the building of Babel, his speech was so confounded that the first four Kiches and their wives were unable to comprehend one another. Of course this is a native myth created to account for the difference in dialect between the various branches of the Maya folk, and can scarcely have any foundation in fact, as the change in dialect would be a very gradual process. The brothers, we are told, divided the land so that one received the districts of Mames and Pocomams, another Verapaz, and the third Chiapas, while Nima-Kiche obtained the country of the Kiches, Kakchiquels, and Tzutuhils. It would be extremely difficult to say whether or not this tradition rests on any veritable historical basis. If so, it refers to a period anterior to the Nahua irruption, for the districts alluded to as occupied by these tribes were not so divided among them at the coming of the Spaniards.

Doubtful Dynasties

As with the earlier dynasties of Egypt, considerable doubt surrounds the history of the early Kiche monarchs. Indeed, a period of such uncertainty occurs that even the number of kings who reigned is lost in the hopeless confusion of varying estimates. From this chaos emerge the facts that the Kiche monarchs held the supreme power among the peoples of Guatemala, that they were the contemporaries of the rulers of Mexico city, and that they were often elected from among the princes of the subject states. Acxopil, the successor of Nima-Kiche, invested his second son with the government of the Kakchiquels, and placed his

youngest son over the Tzutuhils, whilst to his eldest
son he left the throne of the Kiches. Icutemal, his
eldest son, on succeeding his father, gifted the kingdom of
Kakchiquel to his eldest son, displacing his own brother
and thus mortally affronting him. The struggle which
ensued lasted for generations, embittered the relations
between these two branches of the Maya in Guatemala,
and undermined their joint strength. Nahua mercenaries were employed in the struggle on both sides,
and these introduced many of the uglinesses of Nahua
life into Maya existence.

The Coming of the Spaniards

This condition of things lasted up to the time of the
coming of the Spaniards. The Kakchiquels dated the
commencement of a new chronology from the episode of
the defeat of Cay Hun-Apu by them in 1492. They
may have saved themselves the trouble ; for the time
was at hand when the calendars of their race were to be
closed, and its records written in another script by
another people. One by one, and chiefly by reason of
their insane policy of allying themselves with the invader
against their own kin, the old kingdoms of Guatemala fell
as spoil to the daring Conquistadores, and their people
passed beneath the yoke of Spain—bondsmen who were
to beget countless generations of slaves.

The Riddle of Ancient Maya Writing

What may possibly be the most valuable sources of
Maya history are, alas ! sealed to us at present. We
allude to the native Maya manuscripts and inscriptions,
the writing of which cannot be deciphered by present-day
scholars. Some of the old Spanish friars who lived in
the times which directly succeeded the settlement of
the country by the white man were able to read and

even to write this script, but unfortunately they regarded it either as an invention of the Father of Evil or, as it was a native system, as a thing of no value. In a few generations all knowledge of how to decipher it was totally lost, and it remains to the modern world almost as a sealed book, although science has lavished all its wonderful machinery of logic and deduction upon it, and men of unquestioned ability have dedicated their lives to the problem of unravelling what must be regarded as one of the greatest and most mysterious riddles of which mankind ever attempted the solution.

The romance of the discovery of the key to the Egyptian hieroglyphic system of writing is well known. For centuries the symbols displayed upon the temples and monuments of the Nile country were so many meaningless pictures and signs to the learned folk of Europe, until the discovery of the Rosetta stone a hundred years ago made their elucidation possible. This stone bore the same inscription in Greek, demotic, and hieroglyphics, and so the discovery of the " alphabet " of the hidden script became a comparatively easy task. But Central America has no Rosetta stone, nor is it possible that such an aid to research can ever be found. Indeed, such " keys " as have been discovered or brought forward by scientists have proved for the most part unavailing.

The Maya Manuscripts

The principal Maya manuscripts which have escaped the ravages of time are the codices in the libraries of Dresden, Paris, and Madrid. These are known as the Codex Perezianus, preserved in the Bibliothèque Nationale at Paris, the Dresden Codex, long regarded as an Aztec manuscript, and the Troano Codex, so called from one of its owners, Señor Tro y Ortolano, found at

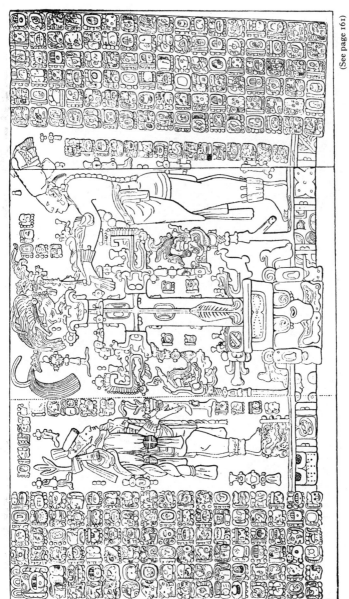

(See page 161)

" The Tablet of the Cross "

(See page 166)

Design on a Vase from Chamá representing Maya Deities

By permission of the Bureau of American Ethnology

Madrid in 1865. These manuscripts deal principally with Maya mythology, but as they cannot be deciphered with any degree of accuracy they do not greatly assist our knowledge of the subject.

The System of the Writing

The "Tablet of the Cross" gives a good idea of the general appearance of the writing system of the ancient peoples of Central America. The style varies somewhat in most of the manuscripts and inscriptions, but it is generally admitted that all of the systems employed sprang originally from one common source. The square figures which appear as a tangle of faces and objects are said to be "calculiform," or pebble-shaped, a not inappropriate description, and it is known from ancient Spanish manuscripts that they were read from top to bottom, and two columns at a time. The Maya tongue, like all native American languages, was one which, in order to express an idea, gathered a whole phrase into a single word, and it has been thought that the several symbols or parts in each square or sketch go to make up such a compound expression.

The first key (so called) to the hieroglyphs of Central America was that of Bishop Landa, who about 1575 attempted to set down the Maya alphabet from native sources. He was highly unpopular with the natives, whose literary treasures he had almost completely destroyed, and who in revenge deliberately misled him as to the true significance of the various symbols.

The first real step toward reading the Maya writing was made in 1876 by Léon de Rosny, a French student of American antiquities, who succeeded in interpreting the signs which denote the four cardinal points. As has been the case in so many discoveries of importance, the significance of these signs was simultaneously discovered by Professor Cyrus Thomas in America. In two of these four signs was found the symbol which meant "sun," almost, as de Rosny acknowledged, as a matter of course. However, the Maya word for "sun" (*kin*) also denotes "day," and it was later proved that this sign was also used with the latter meaning. The discovery of the sign stimulated further research to a great degree, and from the material now at their disposal Drs. Förstemann and Schellhas of Berlin were successful in discovering the sign for the moon and that for the Maya month of twenty days.

Clever Elucidations

In 1887 Dr. Seler discovered the sign for night (*akbal*), and in 1894 Förstemann unriddled the symbols for "beginning" and "end." These are two heads, the first of which has the sign *akbal*, just mentioned, for an eye. Now *akbal* means, as well as "night," "the beginning of the month," and below the face which contains it can be seen footsteps, or spots which resemble their outline, signifying a forward movement. The sign in the second head means "seventh," which in Maya also signifies "the end." From the frequent contrast of these terms there can be little doubt that their meaning is as stated.

"Union" is denoted by the sting of a rattlesnake, the coils of that reptile signifying to the Maya the idea of tying together. In contrast to this sign is the figure next to it, which represents a knife, and means "division" or "cutting." An important "letter" is the hand, which often occurs in both manuscripts and inscriptions. It is drawn sometimes in the act of grasping, with the thumb bent forward, and sometimes as pointing in a certain direction. The first seems to denote a tying together or joining, like the rattlesnake symbol, and the second Förstemann believes to represent a lapse of time. That it may represent futurity occurs as a more likely conjecture to the present writer.

The figure denoting the spring equinox was traced because of its obvious representation of a cloud from which three streams of water are falling upon the earth. The square at the top represents heaven. The obsidian knife underneath denotes a division or period of time cut off, as it were, from other periods of the year. That the sign means " spring " is verified by its position among the other signs of the seasons.

The sign for "week" was discovered by reason of its almost constant accompaniment of the sign for the number thirteen, the number of days in the Maya sacred week. The symbol of the bird's feather indicates the plural, and when affixed to certain signs signifies that the object indicated is multiplied. A bird's feather, when one thinks of it, is one of the most fitting symbols provided by nature to designate the plural, if the number of shoots on both sides of the stem are taken as meaning " many " or " two."

Water is depicted by the figure of a serpent, which reptile typifies the undulating nature of the element. The sign entitled " the sacrificial victim " is of deep human interest. The first portion of the symbol is the death-bird, and the second shows a crouching and beaten captive, ready to be immolated to one of the terrible Maya deities whose sanguinary religion demanded human sacrifice. The drawing which means " the day of the new year," in the month Ceh, was unriddled by the following means : The sign in the upper left-hand corner denotes the word "sun " or " day," that in the upper right-hand corner is the sign for "year." In the lower right-hand corner is the sign for "division," and in the lower left-hand the sign for the Maya month Ceh, already known from the native calendars.

From its accompaniment of a figure known to be a deity of the four cardinal points, whence all American tribes believed the wind to come, the symbol entitled "wind" has been determined.

Methods of Study

The method employed by those engaged in the elucidation of these hieroglyphs is typical of modern science. The various signs and symbols are literally "worn out" by a process of indefatigable examination. For hours the student sits staring at a symbol, drinking in every detail, however infinitesimal, until the drawing and all its parts are wholly and separately photographed upon the tablets of his memory. He then compares the several portions of the symbol with similar portions in other signs the value of which is known. From these he may obtain a clue to the meaning of the whole. Thus proceeding from the known to the unknown, he advances logically toward a complete elucidation of all the hieroglyphs depicted in the various manuscripts and inscriptions.

The method by which Dr. Seler discovered the hieroglyphs or symbols relating to the various gods of the Maya was both simple and ingenious. He says : "The way in which this was accomplished is strikingly simple. It amounts essentially to that which in ordinary life we call 'memory of persons,' and follows almost naturally from a careful study of the manuscripts. For, by frequently looking tentatively at the representations, one learns by degrees to recognise promptly similar and familiar figures of gods by the characteristic impression they make as a whole or by certain details, and the same is true of the accompanying hieroglyphs."

The Maya Numeral System

If Bishop Landa was badly hoaxed regarding the alphabet of the Maya, he was successful in discovering and handing down their numeral system, which was on a very much higher basis than that of many civilised peoples, being, for example, more practical and more fully evolved than that of ancient Rome. This system employed four signs altogether, the point for unity, a horizontal stroke for the number 5, and two signs for 20 and 0. Yet from these simple elements the Maya produced a method of computation which is perhaps as ingenious as anything which has ever been accomplished in the history of mathematics. In the Maya arithmetical system, as in ours, it is the position of the sign that gives it its value. The figures were placed in a vertical line, and one of them was employed as a decimal multiplier. The lowest figure of the column had the arithmetical value which it represented. The figures which appeared in the second, fourth, and each following place had twenty times the value of the preceding figures, while figures in the third place had eighteen times the value of those in the second place. This system admits of computation up to millions, and is one of the surest signs of Maya culture.

Much controversy has raged round the exact nature of the Maya hieroglyphs. Were they understood by the Indians themselves as representing ideas or merely pictures, or did they convey a given sound to the reader, as does our alphabet? To some extent controversy upon the point is futile, as those of the Spanish clergy who were able to learn the writing from the native Maya have confirmed its phonetic character, so that in reality each symbol must have conveyed a sound or sounds to the reader, not merely an idea or a picture. Recent research has amply proved this, so that the full elucidation of the long and painful puzzle on which so much learning and patience have been lavished may perhaps be at hand.

Mythology of the Maya

The Maya pantheon, although it bears a strong resemblance to that of the Nahua, differs from it in so many respects that it is easy to observe that at one period it must have been absolutely free from all Nahua influence. We may, then, provisionally accept the theory that at some relatively distant period the mythologies of the Nahua and Maya were influenced from one common centre, if they were not originally identical, but that later the inclusion in the cognate but divided systems of local deities and the superimposition of the deities and rites of immigrant peoples had caused such differentiation as to render somewhat vague the original likeness between them. In the Mexican mythology we have as a key-note the custom of human sacrifice. It has often been stated as exhibiting the superior status in civilisation of the Maya that their religion was free from the revolting practices which characterised the Nahua faith. This, however, is totally erroneous. Although the Maya were not nearly so prone to the practice of human sacrifice as were the Nahua, they frequently engaged in it, and the pictures which have been drawn of their bloodless offerings must not lead us to believe that they never indulged in this rite. It is known, for example, that they sacrificed maidens to the water-god at the period of the spring florescence, by casting them into a deep pool, where they were drowned.

QUETZALCOATL AMONG THE MAYA

Quetzalcoatl among the Maya

One of the most obvious of the mythological relationships between the Maya and Nahua is exhibited in the Maya cult of the god Quetzalcoatl. It seems to have been a general belief in Mexico that Quetzalcoatl was a god foreign to the soil ; or at least relatively aboriginal to his rival Tezcatlipoca, if not to the Nahua themselves. It is amusing to see it stated by authorities of the highest standing that his worship was free from bloodshed. But it does not appear whether the sanguinary rites connected with the name of Quetzalcoatl in Mexico were undertaken by his priests of their own accord or at the instigation and pressure of the pontiff of Huitzilopochtli, under whose jurisdiction they were. The designation by which Quetzalcoatl was known to the Maya was Kukulcan, which signifies "Feathered Serpent," and is exactly translated by his Mexican name. In Guatemala he was called Gucumatz, which word is also identical in Kiche with his other native appellations. But the Kukulcan of the Maya appears to be dissimilar from Quetzalcoatl in several of his attributes. The difference in climate would probably account for most of these. In Mexico Quetzalcoatl, as we have seen, was not only the Man of the Sun, but the original wind-god of the country. The Kukulcan of the Maya has more the attributes of a thunder-god. In the tropical climate of Yucatan and Guatemala the sun at midday appears to draw the clouds around it in serpentine shapes. From these emanate thunder and lightning and the fertilising rain, so that Kukulcan would appear to have appealed to the Maya more as a god of the sky who wielded the thunderbolts than a god of the atmosphere proper like Quetzalcoatl, though several of the stelæ in Yucatan represent

167

Kukulcan as he is portrayed in Mexico, with wind issuing from his mouth.

An Alphabet of Gods

The principal sources of our knowledge of the Maya deities are the Dresden, Madrid, and Paris codices alluded to previously, all of which contain many pictorial representations of the various members of the Maya pantheon. Of the very names of some of these gods we are so ignorant, and so difficult is the process of affixing to them the traditional names which are left to us as those of the Maya gods, that Dr. Paul Schellhas, a German student of Maya antiquities, has proposed that the figures of deities appearing in the Maya codices or manuscripts should be provisionally indicated by the letters of the alphabet. The figures of gods which thus occur are fifteen in number, and therefore take the letters of the alphabet from A to P, the letter J being omitted.

Difficulties of Comparison

Unluckily the accounts of Spanish authors concerning Maya mythology do not agree with the representations of the gods delineated in the codices. That the three codices have a mythology in common is certain. Again, great difficulty is found in comparing the deities of the codices with those represented by the carved and stucco bas-reliefs of the Maya region. It will thus be seen that very considerable difficulties beset the student in this mythological sphere. So few data have yet been collected regarding the Maya mythology that to dogmatise upon any subject connected with it would indeed be rash. But much has been accomplished in the past few decades, and evidence is slowly but surely accumulating from which sound conclusions can be drawn.

THE CALENDAR

The Conflict between Light and Darkness

We witness in the Maya mythology a dualism almost as complete as that of ancient Persia—the conflict between light and darkness. Opposing each other we behold on the one hand the deities of the sun, the gods of warmth and light, of civilisation and the joy of life, and on the other the deities of darksome death, of night, gloom, and fear. From these primal conceptions of light and darkness all the mythologic forms of the Maya are evolved. When we catch the first recorded glimpses of Maya belief we recognise that at the period when it came under the purview of Europeans the gods of darkness were in the ascendant and a deep pessimism had spread over Maya thought and theology. Its joyful side was subordinated to the worship of gloomy beings, the deities of death and hell, and if the cult of light was attended with such touching fidelity it was because the benign agencies who were worshipped in connection with it had promised not to desert mankind altogether, but to return at some future indefinite period and resume their sway of radiance and peace.

The Calendar

Like that of the Nahua, the Maya mythology was based almost entirely upon the calendar, which in its astronomic significance and duration was identical with that of the Mexicans. The ritual year of twenty "weeks" of thirteen days each was divided into four quarters, each of these being under the auspices of a different quarter of the heavens. Each "week" was under the supervision of a particular deity, as will be seen when we come to deal separately with the various gods.

Traditional Knowledge of the Gods

The heavenly bodies had important representation in the Maya pantheon. In Yucatan the sun-god was known as Kinich-ahau (Lord of the Face of the Sun). He was identified with the Fire-bird, or Arara, and was thus called Kinich-Kakmo (Fire-bird ; lit. Sun-bird). He was also the presiding genius of the north.

Itzamna, one of the most important of the Maya deities, was a moon-god, the father of gods and men. In him was typified the decay and recurrence of life in nature. His name was derived from the words he was supposed to have given to men regarding himself : " Itz en caan, itz en muyal " (" I am the dew of the heaven, I am the dew of the clouds "). He was tutelar deity of the west.

Chac, the rain-god, is the possessor of an elongated nose, not unlike the proboscis of a tapir, which of course is the spout whence comes the rain which he blows over the earth. He is one of the best represented gods on both manuscripts and monuments, and presides over the east. The black god Ekchuah was the god of merchants and cacao-planters. He is represented in the manuscripts several times.

Ix ch'el was the goddess of medicine, and Ix chebel yax was identified by the priest Hernandez with the Virgin Mary. There were also several deities, or rather genii, called Bacabs, who were the upholders of the heavens in the four quarters of the sky. The names of these were Kan, Muluc, Ix, and Cauac, representing the east, north, west, and south. Their symbolic colours were yellow, white, black, and red respectively. They corresponded in some degree to the four variants of the Mexican rain-god Tlaloc, foi many of the American races believed that rain, the fertiliser of the soil, emanated from the four points of the compass. We shall find still other deities when we come to discuss the *Popol Vuh*, the saga-book of the Kiche, but it is difficult to say how far these were connected with the deities of the Maya of Yucatan, concerning whom we have little traditional knowledge, and it is better to deal with them separately, pointing out resemblances where these appear to exist.

Maya Polytheism

On the whole the Maya do not seem to have been burdened with an extensive pantheon, as were the Nahua, and their polytheism appears to have been of a limited character. Although they possessed a number of divinities, these were in a great measure only different forms of one and the same divine power— probably localised forms of it. The various Maya tribes worshipped similar gods under different names. They recognised divine unity in the god Hunabku, who was invisible and supreme, but he does not bulk largely in their mythology, any more than does the universal All-Father in other early faiths. The sun is the great deity in Maya religion, and the myths which tell of the origin of the Maya people are purely solar. As the sun comes from the east, so the hero-gods who bring with them culture and enlightenment have an oriental origin. As Votan, as Kabil, the " Red Hand " who initiates the people into the arts of writing and architecture, these gods are civilising men of the sun as surely as is Quetzalcoatl.

The Bat-God

A sinister figure, the prince of the Maya legions of darkness, is the bat-god, Zotzilaha Chimalman, who dwelt in the " House of Bats," a gruesome cavern on the way to the abodes of darkness and death. He is undoubtedly a relic of cave-worship pure and simple. "The Maya," says an old chronicler, "have an immoderate fear of death, and they seem to have given it a figure peculiarly repulsive." We shall find this deity alluded to in the *Popol Vuh*, under the name Camazotz, in close proximity to the Lords of Death and Hell, attempting to bar the journey of the hero-gods across these dreary realms. He is frequently met with on the Copan reliefs, and a Maya clan, the Ah-zotzils, were called by his name. They were of Kakchiquel origin, and he was probably their totem.

Modern Research

We must now turn to the question of what modern research has done to elucidate the character of the various Maya deities. We have already seen that they have been provisionally named by the letters of the alphabet until such proof is forthcoming as will identify them with the traditional gods of the Maya, and we will now briefly examine what is known concerning them under their temporary designations.

God A

In the Dresden and other codices god A is represented as a figure with exposed vertebræ and skull-like countenance, with the marks of corruption on his body, and displaying every sign of mortality. On his head he wears a snail-symbol, the Aztec sign of birth, perhaps to typify the connection between birth and death. He also wears a pair of cross-bones. The hieroglyph which accompanies his figure represents a corpse's head with closed eyes, a skull, and a sacrificial knife. His symbol is that for the calendar day Cimi, which means death. He presides over the west, the home of the dead, the

The House of Bats
Gilbert James
(See page 171)

region toward which they invariably depart with the setting sun. That he is a death-god there can be no doubt, but of his name we are ignorant. He is probably identical with the Aztec god of death and hell, Mictlan, and is perhaps one of those Lords of Death and Hell who invite the heroes to the celebrated game of ball in the Kiche *Popol Vuh,* and hold them prisoners in their gloomy realm.

God B is the deity who appears most frequently in the manuscripts. He has a long, truncated nose, like that of a tapir, and we find in him every sign of a god of the elements. He walks the waters, wields fiery torches, and seats himself on the cruciform tree of the four winds which appears so frequently in American myth. He is evidently a culture-god or hero, as he is seen planting maize, carrying tools, and going on a journey, a fact which establishes his solar connection. He is, in fact, Kukulcan or Quetzalcoatl, and on examining him we feel that at least there can be no doubt concerning his identity.

Concerning god C matter is lacking, but he is evidently a god of the pole-star, as in one of the codices he is surrounded by planetary signs and wears a nimbus of rays.

God D is almost certainly a moon-god. He is represented as an aged man, with sunken cheeks and wrinkled forehead on which hangs the sign for night. His hieroglyph is surrounded by dots, to represent a starry sky, and is followed by the number 20, to show the duration of the moon. Like most moon deities he is connected with birth, for occasionally he wears the snail, symbol of parturition, on his head. It is probable that he is Itzamna, one of the greatest of Maya gods, who was regarded as the universal life-giver, and was probably of very ancient origin.

The Maize-God

God E is another deity whom we have no difficulty in identifying. He wears the leafed ear of maize as his head-dress. In fact, his head has been evolved out of the conventional drawings of the ear of maize, so we may say at once without any difficulty that he is a maize-god pure and simple, and a parallel with the Aztec maize-god Centeotl. Brinton calls this god Ghanan, and Schellhas thinks he may be identical with a deity Yum Kaax, whose name means "Lord of the Harvest Fields."

A close resemblance can be noticed between gods F and A, and it is thought that the latter resembles the Aztec Xipe, the god of human sacrifice. He is adorned with the same black lines running over the face and body, typifying gaping death-wounds.

The Sun-God

In G we may be sure that we have found a sun-god *par excellence*. His hieroglyph is the sun-sign, *kin*. But we must be careful not to confound him with deities like Quetzalcoatl or Kukulcan. He is, like the Mexican Totec, the sun itself, and not the Man of the Sun, the civilising agent, who leaves his bright abode to dwell with man and introduce him to the arts of cultured existence. He is the luminary himself, whose only acceptable food is human blood, and who must be fed full with this terrible fare or perish, dragging the world of men with him into a fathomless abyss of gloom. We need not be surprised, therefore, to see god G occasionally wearing the symbols of death.

God H would seem to have some relationship to the serpent, but what it may be is obscure, and no certain identification can be made.

THE GOD WITH THE ORNAMENTED NOSE

I is a water-goddess, an old woman with wrinkled brown body and claw-like feet, wearing on her head a grisly snake twisted into a knot, to typify the serpent-like nature of water. She holds in her hands an earthenware pot from which water flows. We cannot say that she resembles the Mexican water-goddess, Chalchihuit-licue, wife of Tlaloc, who was in most respects a deity of a beneficent character. I seems a personification of water in its more dreadful aspect of floods and water-spouts, as it must inevitably have appeared to the people of the more torrid regions of Central America, and that she was regarded as an agent of death is shown from her occasionally wearing the cross-bones of the death-god.

"The God with the Ornamented Nose"

God K is scientifically known as "the god with the ornamented nose," and is probably closely related to god B. Concerning him no two authorities are at one, some regarding him as a storm-god, whose proboscis, like that of Kukulcan, is intended to represent the blast of the tempest. But we observe certain stellar signs in con-nection with K which would go to prove that he is, in-deed, one of the Quetzalcoatl group. His features are constantly to be met with on the gateways and corners of the ruined shrines of Central America, and have led many "antiquarians" to believe in the existence of an elephant-headed god, whereas his trunk-like snout is merely a funnel through which he emitted the gales over which he had dominion, as a careful study of the *pinturas* shows, the wind being depicted issuing from the snout in question. At the same time, the snout may have been modelled on that of the tapir. "If the rain-god Chac is distinguished in the Maya manuscript by a peculiarly long nose curving over the mouth, and if in the other forms of the rain-god, to which, as it seems, the name of Balon Zacab belongs, the nose widens out and sends out shoots, I believe that the tapir which was employed identically with Chac, the Maya rain-god, furnished the model," says Dr. Seler. Is K, then, the same as Chac ? Chac bears every sign of affinity with the Mexican rain-god Tlaloc, whose face was evolved from the coils of two snakes, and also some resemblance to the snouted features of B and K. But, again, the Mexican pictures of Quetzalcoatl are not at all like those of Tlaloc, so that there can be no affinity between Tlaloc and K. Therefore if the Mexican Tlaloc and the Maya Chac be identical, and Tlaloc differs from Quetzalcoatl, who in turn is identical with B and K, it is clear that Chac has nothing to do with K.

The Old Black God

God L Dr. Schellhas has designated "the Old Black God," from the circumstance that he is depicted as an old man with sunken face and toothless gums, the upper, or sometimes the lower, part of his features being covered with black paint. He is represented in the Dresden MS. only. Professor Cyrus Thomas, of New York, thinks that he is the god Ekchuah, who is traditionally described as black, but Schellhas fits this designation to god M. The more probable theory is that of Förstemann, who sees in L the god Votan, who is identical with the Aztec earth-god, Tepeyollotl. Both deities have similar face markings, and their dark hue is perhaps symbolical of the subterranean places where they were supposed to dwell.

The Travellers' God

God M is a veritable black god, with reddish lips. On his head he bears a roped package resembling the loads carried by the Maya porter class, and he is found in violent opposition with F, the enemy of all who wander into the unknown wastes. A god of this description has been handed down by tradition under the name of Ekchuah, and his blackness is probably symbolical of the black or deeply bronzed skin of the porter class among the natives of Central America, who are constantly exposed to the sun. He would appear to be a parallel to the Aztec Yacatecutli, god of travelling merchants or chapmen.

The God of Unlucky Days

God N is identified by Schellhas with the demon Uayayab, who presided over the five unlucky days which it will be recollected came at the end of the Mexican and Maya year. He was known to the Maya as " He by whom the year is poisoned." After modelling his image in clay they carried it out of their villages, so that his baneful influence might not dwell therein.

Goddess O is represented as an old woman engaged in the avocation of spinning, and is probably a goddess of the domestic virtues, the tutelar of married females.

The Frog-God

God P is shown with the body and fins of a frog on a blue background, evidently intended to represent water. Like all other frog-gods he is, of course, a deity of water, probably in its agricultural significance. We find him sowing seed and making furrows, and when we remember the important part played by frog deities in the agriculture of Anahuac we should have no difficulty in classing him with these. Seler asserts his identity with Kukulcan, but no reason except the circumstance of his being a rain-god can be advanced to establish the identity. He wears the year-sign on his head, probably with a seasonal reference.

Maya Architecture

It was in the wonderful architectural system which it developed without outside aid that the Maya people most individually expressed itself. As has been said, those buildings which still remain, and which have excited the admiration of generations of archæologists, are principally confined to examples of ecclesiastical and governmental architecture, the dwellings of the common people consisting merely of the flimsiest of wattle-and-daub structures, which would fall to pieces shortly after they were abandoned.

Buried in dense forests or mouldering on the sun-exposed plains of Yucatan, Honduras, and Guatemala, the cities which boasted these edifices are for the most part situated away from modern trade routes, and are not a little difficult to come at. It is in Yucatan, the old home of the Cocomes and Tutul Xius, that the most perfect specimens of Maya architecture are to be found, especially as regards its later development, and here, too, it may be witnessed in its decadent phase.

Methods of Building

The Maya buildings were almost always erected upon a mound or *ku*, either natural or artificial, generally the latter. In this we discover affinities with the Mexican *teocalli* type. Often these *kus* stood alone, without any superincumbent building save a small altar to prove their relation to the temple type of Anahuac. The typical Maya temple was built on a series of earth terraces arranged in exact parallel order, the buildings themselves forming the sides of a square. The mounds are generally concealed by plaster or faced with stone, the variety employed being usually a hard sandstone, of which the Maya had a good supply in the quarries of Chiapas and Honduras. Moderate in weight, the difficulty of transport was easily overcome, whilst large blocks could be readily quarried. It will thus be seen that the Maya had no substantial difficulties to surmount in connection with building the large edifices and temples they raised, except, perhaps, the lack of metal tools to shape and carve and quarry the stone which they used. And although they exhibit considerable ingenuity in such architectural methods as they employed, they were still surprisingly ignorant of some of the first essentials and principles of the art.

No Knowledge of the Arch

For example, they were totally ignorant of the principles upon which the arch is constructed. This difficulty they overcame by making each course of masonry overhang the one beneath it, after the method employed by a boy with a box of bricks, who finds that he can only make "doorways" by this means, or by the simple expedient—also employed by the Maya—of placing a slab horizontally upon two upright pillars. In consequence it will readily be seen that the superimposition of a second story upon such an insecure foundation was scarcely to be thought of, and that such support for the roof as towered above the doorway would necessarily require to be of the most substantial description. Indeed, this portion of the building often appears to be more than half the size of the rest of the edifice. This space gave the Maya builders a splendid chance for mural decoration, and it must be said they readily seized it and made the most of it, ornamental façades being perhaps the most typical features in the relics of Maya architecture.

Pyramidal Structures

But the Maya possessed another type of building which permitted of their raising more than one story. This was the pyramidal type, of which many examples remain. The first story was built in the usual manner, and the second was raised by increasing the height of the mound at the back of the building until it was upon a level with the roof—another device well known to the boy with the box of bricks. In the centre of the space thus made another story could be erected, which was entered by a staircase outside the building. Hampered by their inability to build to any appreciable height, the Maya architects made up for the deficiency by constructing edifices of considerable length and breadth, the squat appearance of which is counter-balanced by the beautiful mural decoration of the sides and façade.

Definiteness of Design

He would be a merely superficial observer who would form the conclusion that these specimens of an architecture spontaneously evolved were put together without survey, design, or previous calculation. That as much thought entered into their construction as is lavished upon his work by a modern architect is proved by the manner in which the carved stones fit into one another. It would be absurd to suppose that these tremendous façades bristling with scores of intricate designs could have been first placed in position and subsequently laden with the bas-reliefs they exhibit. It is plain that they were previously worked apart and separately from one entire design. Thus we see that the highest capabilities of the architect were essential in a measure to the erection of these imposing structures.

FASCINATION OF THE SUBJECT

Architectural Districts

Although the mason-craft of the Maya peoples was essentially similar in all the regions populated by its various tribes and offshoots, there existed in the several localities occupied by them certain differences in construction and ornamentation which would almost justify us in dividing them into separate architectural spheres. In Chiapas, for example, we find the bas-relief predominant, whether in stone or stucco. In Honduras we find a stiffness of design which implies an older type of architecture, along with caryatides and memorial pillars of human shape. In Guatemala, again, we find traces of the employment of wood. As the civilisation of the Maya cannot be well comprehended without some knowledge of their architecture, and as that art was unquestionably their national *forte* and the thing which most sharply distinguished them from the semi-savage peoples that surrounded them, it will be well to consider it for a space as regards its better-known individual examples.

Fascination of the Subject

He would indeed be dull of imagination and of spirit who could enter into the consideration of such a subject as this without experiencing some thrill from the mystery which surrounds it. Although familiarised with the study of the Maya antiquities by reason of many years of close acquaintance with it, the author cannot approach the theme without a feeling of the most intense awe. We are considering the memorials of a race isolated for countless thousands of years from the rest of humanity—a race which by itself evolved a civilisation in every respect capable of comparison with those of ancient Egypt or Assyria. In these

impenetrable forests and sun-baked plains mighty works
were raised which tell of a culture of a lofty type. We
are aware that the people who reared them entered into
religious and perhaps philosophical considerations their
interpretations of which place them upon a level with the
most enlightened races of antiquity; but we have only
stepped upon the margin of Maya history. What dread
secrets, what scenes of orgic splendour have those carven
walls witnessed? What solemn priestly conclave, what
magnificence of rite, what marvels of initiation, have
these forest temples known? These things we shall
never learn. They are hidden from us in a gloom as
palpable as that of the tree-encircled depths in which we
find these shattered works of a once powerful hierarchy.

Mysterious Palenque

One of the most famous of these ancient centres of
priestly domination is Palenque, situated in the modern
state of Chiapas. This city was first brought into
notice by Don José Calderon in 1774, when he discovered no less than eighteen palaces, twenty great
buildings, and a hundred and sixty houses, which
proves that in his day the primeval forest had not made
such inroads upon the remaining buildings as it has
during the past few generations. There is good
evidence besides this that Palenque was standing at
the time of Cortés' conquest of Yucatan. And here it
will be well at once to dispel any conception the reader
may have formed concerning the vast antiquity of
these cities and the structures they contain. The very
oldest of them cannot be of a date anterior to the
thirteenth century, and few Americanists of repute
would admit such an antiquity for them. There may
be remains of a fragmentary nature here and there in
Central America which are relatively more ancient.

(See page 182)

Part of the Palace and Tower, Palenque

Photo C. B. Waite, Mexico

But no temple or edifice which remains standing can claim a greater antiquity.

Palenque is built in the form of an amphitheatre, and nestles on the lowest slopes of the Cordilleras. Standing on the central pyramid, the eye is met by a ring of ruined palaces and temples raised upon artificial terraces. Of these the principal and most imposing is the Palace, a pile reared upon a single platform, forming an irregular quadrilateral, with a double gallery on the east, north, and west sides, surrounding an inner structure with a similar gallery and two court-yards. It is evident that there was little system or plan observed in the construction of this edifice, an unusual circumstance in Maya architecture. The dwelling apartments were situated on the southern side of the structure, and here there is absolute confusion, for buildings of all sorts and sizes jostle each other, and are reared on different levels.

Our interest is perhaps at first excited by three sub-terraneous apartments down a flight of gloomy steps. Here are to be found three great stone tables, the edges of which are fretted with sculptured symbols. That these were altars admits of little doubt, although some visitors have not hesitated to call them dining-tables! These constitute only one of the many puzzles in this building of 228 feet frontage, with a depth of 180 feet, which at the same time is only about 25 feet high!

On the north side of the Palace pyramid the façade of the Palace has crumbled into complete ruin, but some evidences of an entrance are still noticeable. There were probably fourteen doorways in all in the frontage, with a width of about 9 feet each, the piers of which were covered with figures in bas-relief. The inside of the galleries is also covered at intervals with similar designs, or medallions, many of which are probably representations of priests or priestesses who once dwelt within the classic shades and practised strange rites in the worship of gods long since forgotten. One of these is of a woman with delicate features and high-bred countenance, and the frame or rim surrounding it is decorated in a manner recalling the Louis XV style.

The east gallery is 114 feet long, the north 185 feet, and the west 102 feet, so that, as remarked above, a lack of symmetry is apparent. The great court is reached by a Mayan arch which leads on to a staircase, on each side of which grotesque human figures of the Maya type are sculptured. Whom they are intended to portray or what rite they are engaged in it would indeed be difficult to say. That they are priests may be hazarded, for they appear to be dressed in the ecclesiastical *maxtli* (girdle), and one seems to be decorated with the beads seen in the pictures of the death-god. Moreover, they are mitred.

The courtyard is exceedingly irregular in shape. To the south side is a small building which has assisted our knowledge of Maya mural decoration; especially valuable is the handsome frieze with which it is adorned, on which we observe the rather familiar feathered serpent (Kukulcan or Quetzalcoatl). Everywhere we notice the flat Maya head—a racial type, perhaps brought about by deformation of the cranium in youth. One of the most important parts of the Palace from an architectural point of view is the east front of the inner wing, which is perhaps the best preserved, and exhibits the most luxurious ornamentation. Two roofed galleries supported by six pillars covered with bas-reliefs are reached by a staircase on which hieroglyphic signs still remain. The reliefs in cement are still faintly to be discerned on the pillars, and must have been of great beauty. They represent mythological characters in various attitudes. Above, seven enormous heads frown on the explorer in grim menace. The effect of the entire façade is rich in the extreme, even in ruin, and from it we can obtain a faint idea of the splendours of this wonderful civilisation.

An Architectural Curiosity

One of the few towers to be seen among the ruins of Maya architecture stands at Palenque. It is square in shape and three stories in height, with sloping roof, and is not unlike the belfry of some little English village church.

The building we have been describing, although traditionally known as a " palace," was undoubtedly a great monastery or ecclesiastical habitation. Indeed, the entire city of Palenque was solely a priestly centre, a place of pilgrimage. The bas-reliefs with their representations of priests and acolytes prove this, as does the absence of warlike or monarchical subjects.

The Temple of Inscriptions

The Temple of Inscriptions, perched on an eminence some 40 feet high, is the largest edifice in Palenque. It has a façade 74 feet long by 25 feet deep, composed of a great gallery which runs along the entire front of the fane. The building has been named from the inscriptions with which certain flagstones in the central apartment are covered. Three other temples occupy a piece of rising ground close by. These are the Temple of the Sun, closely akin in type to many Japanese temple buildings ; the Temple of the Cross, in which a wonderful altar-piece was discovered ; and the Temple of the Cross No. II. In the Temple of the

Cross the inscribed altar gave its name to the building. In the central slab is a cross of the American pattern, its roots springing from the hideous head of the goddess Chicomecohuatl, the Earth-mother, or her Maya equivalent. Its branches stretch to where on the right and left stand two figures, evidently those of a priest and acolyte, performing some mysterious rite. On the apex of the tree is placed the sacred turkey, or " Emerald Fowl," to which offerings of maize paste are made. The whole is surrounded by inscriptions. (See illustration facing p. 160.)

Aké and Itzamal

Thirty miles east of Merida lies Aké, the colossal and primeval ruins of which speak of early Maya occupation. Here are pyramids, tennis-courts, and gigantic pillars which once supported immense galleries, all in a state of advanced ruin. Chief among these is the great pyramid and gallery, a mighty staircase rising toward lofty pillars, and somewhat reminiscent of Stonehenge. For what purpose it was constructed is quite unknown.

The House of Darkness

One ruin, tradition calls " The House of Darkness." Here no light enters save that which filters in by the open doorway. The vaulted roof is lost in a lofty gloom. So truly have the huge blocks of which the building is composed been laid that not even a needle could be inserted between them. The whole is coated with a hard plaster or cement.

The Palace of Owls

The Knuc (Palace of Owls), where a beautiful frieze of diamond-shaped stones intermingling with spheres may be observed, is noteworthy. All here is undoubtedly of the first Yucatec era, the time when the Maya first overran the country.

At Itzamal the chief object of interest is the great pyramid of Kinich-Kakmo (The Sun's Face with Fiery Rays), the base of which covers an area of nearly 650 square feet. To this shrine thousands were wont to come in times of panic or famine, and from the summit, where was housed the glittering idol, the smoke of sacrifice ascended to the cloudless sky, whilst a multitude of white-robed priests and augurs chanted and prophesied. To the south of this mighty pile stand the ruins of the Ppapp-Hol-Chac (The House of Heads and Lightnings), the abode of the chief priest.

Itzamna's Fane

At Itzamal, too, stood one of the chief temples of the great god Itzamna, the legendary founder of the Maya Empire. Standing on a lofty pyramid, four roads radiated from it, leading to Tabasco, Guatemala, and Chiapas ; and here they brought the halt, the maimed, and the blind, aye, even the dead, for succour and resurrection, such faith had they in the mighty power of Kab-ul (The Miraculous Hand), as they designated the deity. The fourth road ran to the sacred isle of Cozumel, where first the men of Spain found the Maya cross, and supposed it to prove that St. Thomas had discovered the American continent in early times, and had converted the natives to a Christianity which had become debased.

Bearded Gods

To the west arose another pyramid, on the summit of which was built the palace of Hunpictok (The

Commander-in-chief of Eight Thousand Flints), in allusion, probably, to the god of lightning, Hurakan, whose gigantic face, once dominating the basement wall, has now disappeared. This face possessed huge mustachios, appendages unknown to the Maya race ; and, indeed, we are struck with the frequency with which Mexican and Mayan gods and heroes are adorned with beards and other hirsute ornaments both on the monuments and in the manuscripts. Was the original governing class a bearded race ? It is scarcely probable. Whence, then, the ever-recurring beard and moustache ? These may have been developed in the priestly class by constant ceremonial shaving, which often produces a thin beard in the Mongolians—as witness the modern Japanese, who in imitating a custom of the West often succeed in producing quite respectable beards.

A Colossal Head

Not far away is to be found a gigantic head, probably that of the god Itzamna. It is 13 feet in height, and the features were formed by first roughly tracing them in rubble, and afterwards coating the whole with plaster. The figure is surrounded by spirals, symbols of wind or speech. On the opposite side of the pyramid alluded to above is found a wonderful bas-relief representing a tiger couchant, with a human head of the Maya type, probably depicting one of the early ancestors of the Maya, Balam-Quitze (Tiger with the Sweet Smile), of whom we read in the *Popol Vuh*.

Chichen-Itza

At Chichen-Itza, in Yucatan, the chief wonder is the gigantic pyramid-temple known as El Castillo. It is reached by a steep flight of steps, and from it the vast

Teocalli or Pyramid of Papantla
Photo C. B. Waite, Mexico

The Nunnery, Chichen-Itza
Photo C. B. Waite, Mexico
(See page 188)

The King who loved a Princess

Gilbert James

(See page 189)

ruins of Chichen radiate in a circular manner. To the east is the market-place, to the north a mighty temple, and a tennis-court, perhaps the best example of its kind in Yucatan, whilst to the west stand the Nunnery and the Chichan-Chob, or prison. Concerning Chichen-Itza Cogolludo tells the following story : " A king of Chichen called Canek fell desperately in love with a young princess, who, whether she did not return his affection or whether she was compelled to obey a parental mandate, married a more powerful Yucatec *cacique*. The discarded lover, unable to bear his loss, and moved by love and despair, armed his dependents and suddenly fell upon his successful rival. Then the gaiety of the feast was exchanged for the din of war, and amidst the confusion the Chichen prince disappeared, carrying off the beautiful bride. But conscious that his power was less than his rival's, and fearing his vengeance, he fled the country with most of his vassals." It is a historical fact that the inhabitants of Chichen abandoned their city, but whether for the reason given in this story or not cannot be discovered.

The Nunnery

The Nunnery at Chichen is a building of great beauty of outline and decoration, the frieze above the doorway and the fretted ornamentation of the upper story exciting the admiration of most writers on the subject. Here dwelt the sacred women, the chief of whom, like their male prototypes, were dedicated to Kukulcan and regarded with much reverence. The base of the building is occupied by eight large figures, and over the door is the representation of a priest with a *panache*, whilst a row of gigantic heads crowns the north façade. Here, too, are figures of the wind-god,

with projecting lips, which many generations of antiquarians took for heads of elephants with waving
trunks ! The entire building is one of the gems of
Central American architecture, and delights the eye of
archæologist and artist alike. In El Castillo are
found wonderful bas-reliefs depicting bearded men,
evidently the priests of Quetzalcoatl, himself bearded,
and to the practised eye one of these would appear to
be wearing a false hirsute appendage, as kings were wont
to do in ancient Egypt. Were these beards artificial
and symbolical?

The "Writing in the Dark"

The Akab-sib (Writing in the Dark) is a bas-
relief found on the lintel of an inner door at the
extremity of the building. It represents a figure seated
before a vase, with outstretched forefinger, and whence
it got its traditional appellation it would be hard to say,
unless the person represented is supposed to be in the
act of writing. The figure is surrounded by inscriptions. At Chichen were found a statue of Tlaloc, the
god of rain or moisture, and immense torsos representing Kukulcan. There also was a terrible well
into which men were cast in time of drought as a
propitiation to the rain-god.

Kabah

At Kabah there is a marvellous frontage which strikingly recalls that of a North American Indian totem-
house in its fantastic wealth of detail. The ruins are
scattered over a large area, and must all have been at
one time painted in brilliant colours. Here two horses'
heads in stone were unearthed, showing that the natives
had copied faithfully the steeds of the conquering
Spaniards. Nothing is known of the history of Kabah,

Details of the Nunnery at Chichen-Itza

Photo C. B. Waite, Mexico

(See page 189)

The Old Woman who took an Egg home
Gilbert James

(See page 192)

but its neighbour, Uxmal, fifteen miles distant, is much more famous.

Uxmal

The imposing pile of the Casa del Gobernador (Governor's Palace, so called) at Uxmal is perhaps the best known and described of all the aboriginal buildings of Central America. It occupies three successive colossal terraces, and its frieze runs in a line of 325 feet, and is divided into panels, each of which frames a gigantic head of priest or deity. The striking thing concerning this edifice is that although it has been abandoned for over three hundred years it is still almost as fresh architecturally as when it left the builder's hands. Here and there a lintel has fallen, or stones have been removed in a spirit of vandalism to assist in the erection of a neighbouring *hacienda*, but on the whole we possess in it the most unspoiled piece of Yucatec building in existence. On the side of the palace where stands the main entrance, directly over the gateway, is the most wonderful fretwork and ornamentation, carried out in high relief, above which soar three eagles in hewn stone, surmounted by a plumed human head. In the plinth are three heads, which in type recall the Roman, surrounded by inscriptions. A clear proof of the comparative lateness of the period in which Uxmal was built is found in the circumstance that all the lintels over the doorways are of wood, of which much still exists in a good state of preservation. Many of the joists of the roofs were also of timber, and were fitted into the stonework by means of specially carved ends.

The Dwarf's House

There is also a nunnery which forcibly recalls that at Chichen, and is quite as elaborate and flamboyant in its architectural design. But the real mystery at Uxmal is the Casa del Adivino (The Prophet's House), also locally known as "The Dwarf's House." It consists of two portions, one of which is on the summit of an artificial pyramid, whilst the other, a small but beautifully finished chapel, is situated lower down facing the town. The loftier building is reached by an exceedingly steep staircase, and bears every evidence of having been used as a sanctuary, for here were discovered cacao and copal, recently burnt, by Cogolludo as late as 1656, which is good evidence that the Yucatecs did not all at once abandon their ancient faith at the promptings of the Spanish fathers.

The Legend of the Dwarf

In his *Travels in Yucatan* Stephens has a legend relating to this house which may well be given in his own words : "An old woman," he says, "lived alone in her hut, rarely leaving her chimney-corner. She was much distressed at having no children, and in her grief one day took an egg, wrapped it up carefully in cotton cloth, and put it in a corner of her hut. She looked every day in great anxiety, but no change in the egg was observable. One morning, however, she found the shell broken, and a lovely tiny creature was stretching out its arms to her. The old woman was in raptures. She took it to her heart, gave it a nurse, and was so careful of it that at the end of a year the baby walked and talked as well as a grown-up man. But he stopped growing. The good old woman in her joy and delight exclaimed that the baby should be a great chief. One day she told him to go to the king's palace and engage him in a trial of strength. The dwarf begged hard not to be sent on such an enterprise. But the old woman insisted on his going, and he was obliged to obey. When ushered into the presence of the sovereign he threw down his gauntlet. The latter smiled, and asked him to lift a stone of three arobes (75 lb.). The child returned crying to his mother, who sent him back, saying, 'If the king can lift the stone, you can lift it too.' The king did take it up, but so did the dwarf. His strength was tried in many other ways, but all the king did was as easily done by the dwarf. Wroth at being outdone by so puny a creature, the prince told the dwarf that unless he built a palace loftier than any in the city he should die. The affrighted dwarf returned to the old woman, who bade him not to despair, and the next morning they both awoke in the palace which is still standing. The king saw the palace with amazement. He instantly sent for the dwarf, and desired him to collect two bundles of *cogoiol* (a kind of hard wood), with one of which he would strike the dwarf on the head, and consent to be struck in return by his tiny adversary. The latter again returned to his mother moaning and lamenting. But the old woman cheered him up, and, placing a *tortilla* on his head, sent him back to the king. The trial took place in the presence of all the state grandees. The king broke the whole of his bundle on the dwarf's head without hurting him in the least, seeing which he wished to save his own head from the impending ordeal ; but his word had been passed before his assembled court, and he could not well refuse. The dwarf struck, and at the second blow the king's skull was broken to pieces. The spectators immediately proclaimed the victorious dwarf their sovereign. After this the old woman disappeared. But in the village of Mani, fifty miles distant, is a deep well leading to a subterraneous passage which extends as far as Merida. In this passage is an old woman sitting on the bank of a river shaded by a great tree, having a serpent by her side. She sells water in small quantities, accepting no money, for she must have human beings, innocent babies, which are devoured by the serpent. This old woman is the dwarf's mother."

The interpretation of this myth is by no means difficult. The old woman is undoubtedly the rain-goddess, the dwarf the Man of the Sun who emerges from the cosmic egg. In Yucatan dwarfs were sacred to the sun-god, and were occasionally sacrificed to him, for reasons which appear obscure.

The Mound of Sacrifice

Another building at Uxmal the associations of which render it of more than passing interest is the Pyramid of Sacrifice, an edifice built on the plan of the Mexican *teocalli*. Indeed, it is probably of Aztec origin, and may even have been erected by the mercenaries who during the fifteenth century swarmed from Mexico into Yucatan and Guatemala to take service with the rival chieftains who carried on civil war in those states. Beside this is another mound which was crowned by a very beautiful temple, now in an advanced state of ruin. The "Pigeon House" is an ornate pile with pinnacles pierced by large openings which probably served as dovecotes. The entire architecture of Uxmal displays a type more primitive than that met elsewhere in Yucatan. There is documentary evidence to prove that so late as 1673 the Indians still worshipped in the ruins of Uxmal, where they burnt copal, and performed "other detestable sacrifices." So that even a hundred and fifty years of Spanish rule had not sufficed to wean the natives from the worship of the older gods to whom their fathers had for generations bowed down. This would also seem conclusive evidence that the ruins of Uxmal at least were the work of the existing race.

THE HORSE-GOD

The Phantom City

In his *Travels in Central America* Stephens recounts a fascinating story told him by a priest of Santa Cruz del Quiche, to the effect that four days' journey from that place a great Indian city was to be seen, densely populated, and preserving the ancient civilisation of the natives. He had, indeed, beheld it from the summit of a cliff, shining in glorious whiteness many leagues away. This was perhaps Lorillard City, discovered by Suarez, and afterwards by Charnay. In general type Lorillard closely resembles Palenque. Here was found a wonderfully executed stone idol, which Charnay thought represented a different racial type from that seen in the other Central American cities. The chief finds of interest in this ancient city were the intricate bas-reliefs, one over the central door of a temple, probably a symbolic representation of Quetzalcoatl, who holds the rain-cross, in both hands, and is seen *vis-à-vis* with an acolyte, also holding the symbol, though it is possible that the individual represented may have been the high-priest of Quetzalcoatl or Kukulcan. Another bas-relief represents a priest sacrificing to Kukulcan by passing a rope of maguey fibre over his tongue for the purpose of drawing blood —an instance of the substitution in sacrifice of the part for the whole.

The Horse-God

At Peten-Itza, Cortés left his horse, which had fallen sick, to the care of the Indians. The animal died under their mismanagement and because of the food offered it, and the terrified natives, fancying it a divine being, raised an image of it, and called it Izimin Chac (Thunder and Lightning), because they had seen its rider discharge a firearm, and they imagined that the flash and the report had proceeded from the creature. The sight of the idol aroused such wrath in the zealous bosom of a certain Spanish monk that he broke it with a huge stone—and, but for the interference of the *cacique*, would have suffered death for his temerity. Peten was a city " filled with idols," as was Tayasal, close at hand, where in the seventeenth century no less than nine new temples were built, which goes to prove that the native religion was by no means extinct. One of these new temples, according to Villagutierre, had a Spanish balcony of hewn stone ! In the Temple of the Sun at Tikal, an adjoining city, is a wonderful altar panel, representing an unknown deity, and here also are many of those marvellously carved idols of which Stephens gives such capital illustrations in his fascinating book.

Copan

Copan, one of the most interesting of these wondrous city-centres, the name of which has, indeed, become almost a household word, is in the same district as the towns just described, and abounds chiefly in monolithic images. It yielded after a desperate struggle to Hernandez de Chaves, one of Alvarado's lieutenants, in 1530. The monolithic images so abundantly re-presented here are evolved from the stelæ and the bas-relief, and are not statues in the proper sense of the term, as they are not completely cut away from the stone background out of which they were carved. An altar found at Copan exhibits real skill in sculpture, the head-dresses, ornaments, and expressions of the eight figures carved on its sides being elaborate in the extreme and exceedingly lifelike. Here again we notice a fresh racial type, which goes to prove that one race alone cannot have been responsible for these marvellous ruined cities and all that they contain and signify. We have to imagine a shifting of races and a fluctuation of peoples in Central America such as we know took place in Europe and Asia before we can rightly understand the ethnological problems of the civilised sphere of the New World, and any theory which does not take due account of such conditions is doomed to failure.

Mitla

We now come to the last of these stupendous remnants of a vanished civilisation—Mitla, by no means the least of the works of civilised man in Central America. At the period of the conquest the city occupied a wide area, but at the present time only six palaces and three ruined pyramids are left standing. The great palace is a vast edifice in the shape of the letter T, and measures 130 feet in its greater dimension, with an apartment of a like size. Six monolithic columns which supported the roof still stand in gigantic isolation, but the roof itself has long fallen in. A dark passage leads to the inner court, and the walls of this are covered with mosaic work in panels which recalls somewhat the pattern known as the " Greek fret." The lintels over the doorways are of huge blocks of stone nearly eighteen feet long. Of this building Viollet-le-Duc says : " The monuments of Greece and Rome in their best time can alone compare with the splendour of this great edifice."

A Place of Sepulture

The ruins at Mitla bear no resemblance to those of Mexico or Yucatan, either as regards architecture or ornamentation, for whereas the Yucatec buildings possess overlapping walls, the palaces of Mitla consist of perpendicular walls intended to support flat roofs. Of these structures the second and fourth palaces alone are in such a state of preservation as to permit of general description. The second palace shows by its sculptured lintel and two inner columns that the same arrangement was observed in its construction as in the great palace just described. The fourth palace has on its southern façade oblong panels and interesting caryatides or pillars in the shape of human figures. These palaces consisted of four upper apartments, finely sculptured, and a like number of rooms on the lower story, which was occupied by the high-priest, and to which the king came to mourn on the demise of a relative. Here, too, the priests were entombed, and in an adjoining room the idols were kept. Into a huge underground chamber the bodies of eminent warriors and sacrificial victims were cast. Attempts have been made to identify Mitla with Mictlan, the Mexican Hades, and there is every reason to suppose that the identification is correct. It must be borne in mind that Mictlan was as much a place of the dead as a place of punishment, as was the Greek Hades, and therefore might reasonably signify a place of sepulture, such as Mitla undoubtedly was. The following passages from the old historians of Mitla, Torquemada and Burgoa, throw much light on this aspect of the city, and besides are full of the most intense interest and curious information, so that they may be given *in extenso*. But before passing on to them we should for a moment glance at Seler's suggestion that the American race imagined that their ancestors had originally issued from the underworld through certain caverns into the light of day, and that this was the reason why Mitla was not only a burial-place but a sanctuary.

Great Palace of Mitla

Interior of an Apartment in the Palace of Mitla

(See page 197)

(See page 199)

Hall of the Columns, Palace of Mitla

By permission of the Bureau of American Ethnology

An Old Description of Mitla

Of Mitla Father Torquemada writes :

"When some monks of my order, the Franciscan, passed, preaching and shriving, through the province of Zapoteca, whose capital city is Tehuantepec, they came to a village which was called Mictlan, that is, Underworld [Hell]. Besides mentioning the large number of people in the village they told of buildings which were prouder and more magnificent than any which they had hitherto seen in New Spain. Among them was a temple of the evil spirit and living-rooms for his demoniacal servants, and among other fine things there was a hall with ornamented panels, which were constructed of stone in a variety of arabesques and other very remarkable designs. There were doorways there, each one of which was built of but three stones, two upright at the sides and one across them, in such a manner that, although these doorways were very high and broad, the stones sufficed for their entire construction. They were so thick and broad that we were assured there were few like them. There was another hall in these buildings, or rectangular temples, which was erected entirely on round stone pillars, very high and very thick, so thick that two grown men could scarcely encircle them with their arms, nor could one of them reach the finger-tips of the other. These pillars were all in one piece, and, it was said, the whole shaft of a pillar measured 5 ells from top to bottom, and they were very much like those of the Church of Santa Maria Maggiore in Rome, very skilfully made and polished."

Father Burgoa gives a more exact description. He says :

"The Palace of the Living and of the Dead was built

for the use of this person [the high-priest of the Zapotecs]. . . . They built this magnificent house or pantheon in the shape of a rectangle, with portions rising above the earth and portions built down into the earth, the latter in the hole or cavity which was found below the surface of the earth, and ingeniously made the chambers of equal size by the manner of joining them, leaving a spacious court in the middle ; and in order to secure four equal chambers they accomplished what barbarian heathen (as they were) could only achieve by the powers and skill of an architect. It is not known in what stone-pit they quarried the pillars, which are so thick that two men can scarcely encircle them with their arms. These are, to be sure, mere shafts without capital or pedestal, but they are wonderfully regular and smooth, and they are about 5 ells high and in one piece. These served to support the roof, which consists of stone slabs instead of beams. The slabs are about 2 ells long, 1 ell broad, and half an ell thick, extending from pillar to pillar. The pillars stand in a row, one behind the other, in order to receive the weight. The stone slabs are so regular and so exactly fitted that, without any mortar or cement, at the joints they resemble mortised beams. The four rooms, which are very spacious, are arranged in exactly the same way and covered with the same kind of roofing. But in the construction of the walls the greatest architects of the earth have been surpassed, as I have not found this kind of architecture described either among the Egyptians or among the Greeks, for they begin at the base with a narrow outline and, as the structure rises in height, spread out in wide copings at the top, so that the upper part exceeds the base in breadth and looks as if it would fall over. The inner side of the walls consists of a mortar or stucco of such hardness that no one knows with what kind of liquid it could have been mixed. The outside is of such extraordinary workmanship that on a masonry wall about an ell in height there are placed stone slabs with a projecting edge, which form the support for an endless number of small white stones, the smallest of which are a sixth of an ell long, half as broad, and a quarter as thick, and which are as smooth and regular as if they had all come from one mould. They had so many of these stones that, setting them in, one beside the other, they formed with them a large number of different beautiful geometric designs, each an ell broad and running the whole length of the wall, each varying in pattern up to the crowning piece, which was the finest of all. And what has always seemed inexplicable to the greatest architects is the adjustment of these little stones without a single handful of mortar, and the fact that without tools, with nothing but hard stones and sand, they could achieve such solid work that, though the whole structure is very old and no one knows who made it, it has been preserved until the present day.

Human Sacrifice at Mitla

"I carefully examined these monuments some thirty years ago in the chambers above ground, which are constructed of the same size and in the same way as those below ground, and, though single pieces were in ruins because some stones had become loosened, there was still much to admire. The doorways were very large, the sides of each being of single stones of the same thickness as the wall, and the lintel was made out of another stone which held the two lower ones together at the top. There were four chambers above ground and four below. The latter were arranged according to their purpose in such a way that one front chamber served as chapel and sanctuary for the idols, which were placed on a great stone which served as an altar. And for the more important feasts which they celebrated with sacrifices, or at the burial of a king or great lord, the high-priest instructed the lesser priests or the subordinate temple officials who served him to prepare the chapel and his vestments and a large quantity of the incense used by them. And then he descended with a great retinue, while none of the common people saw him or dared to look in his face, convinced that if they did so they would fall dead to the earth as a punishment for their boldness. And when he entered the chapel they put on him a long white cotton garment made like an alb, and over that a garment shaped like a dalmatic, which was embroidered with pictures of wild beasts and birds ; and they put a cap on his head, and on his feet a kind of shoe woven of many coloured feathers. And when he had put on these garments he walked with solemn mien and measured step to the altar, bowed low before the idols, renewed the incense, and then in quite unintelligible murmurs he began to converse with these images, these depositories of infernal spirits, and continued in this sort of prayer with hideous grimaces and writhings, uttering inarticulate sounds, which filled all present with fear and terror, till he came out of that diabolical trance and told those standing around the lies and fabrications which the spirit had imparted to him or which he had invented himself. When human beings were sacrificed the ceremonies were multiplied, and the assistants of the high-priest stretched the victim out upon a large stone, baring his breast, which they tore open with a great stone knife, while the body writhed in fearful convulsions, and they laid the heart bare, ripping it out, and with it the soul, which the devil took, while they carried the heart to the high-priest that he might offer it to the idols by holding it to their mouths, among other ceremonies; and the body was thrown into the burial-place of their 'blessed,' as they called them. And if after the sacrifice he felt inclined to detain those who begged any favour he sent them word by the subordinate priests not to leave their houses till their gods were appeased, and he commanded them to do penance meanwhile, to fast and to speak with no woman, so that, until this father of sin had interceded for the absolution of the penitents and had declared the gods appeased, they did not dare to cross their thresholds.

" The second (underground) chamber was the burial-place of these high-priests, the third that of the kings of Theozapotlan, whom they brought hither richly dressed in their best attire, feathers, jewels, golden necklaces, and precious stones, placing a shield in the left hand and a javelin in the right, just as they used them in war. And at their burial rites great mourning prevailed; the instruments which were played made mournful sounds; and with loud wailing and continuous sobbing they chanted the life and exploits of their lord until they laid him on the structure which they had prepared for this purpose.

Living Sacrifices

" The last (underground) chamber had a second door at the rear, which led to a dark and gruesome room. This was closed with a stone slab, which occupied the whole entrance. Through this door they threw the bodies of the victims and of the great lords and chieftains who had fallen in battle, and they brought them from the spot where they fell, even

when it was very far off, to this burial-place; and so
great was the barbarous infatuation of those Indians
that, in the belief of the happy life which awaited them,
many who were oppressed by diseases or hardships
begged this infamous priest to accept them as living
sacrifices and allow them to enter through that portal
and roam about in the dark interior of the mountain,
to seek the feasting-places of their forefathers. And
when any one obtained this favour the servants of the
high-priest led him thither with special ceremonies,
and after they allowed him to enter through the small
door they rolled the stone before it again and took
leave of him, and the unhappy man, wandering in that
abyss of darkness, died of hunger and thirst, beginning
already in life the pain of his damnation, and on
account of this horrible abyss they called this village
Liyobaa.

The Cavern of Death

" When later there fell upon these people the light
of the Gospel, its servants took much trouble to instruct
them, and to find out whether this error, common to all
these nations, still prevailed; and they learned from the
stories which had been handed down that all were convinced that this damp cavern extended more than thirty
leagues underground, and that its roof was supported
by pillars. And there were people, zealous prelates
anxious for knowledge, who, in order to convince these
ignorant people of their error, went into this cave accompanied by a large number of people bearing lighted
torches and firebrands, and descended several large steps.
And they soon came upon many great buttresses which
formed a kind of street. They had prudently brought
a quantity of rope with them to use as guiding-lines,
that they might not lose themselves in this confusing
204

labyrinth. And the putrefaction and the bad odour and the dampness of the earth were very great, and there was also a cold wind which blew out their torches. And after they had gone a short distance, fearing to be over-powered by the stench, or to step on poisonous reptiles, of which some had been seen, they resolved to go out again, and to completely wall up this back door oɪ hell. The four buildings above ground were the only ones which still remained open, and they had a court and chambers like those underground; and the ruins of these have lasted even to the present day.

Palace of the High-Priest

"One of the rooms above ground was the palace of the high-priest, where he sat and slept, for the apart-ment offered room and opportunity for everything. The throne was like a high cushion, with a high back to lean against, all of tiger-skin, stuffed entirely with delicate feathers, or with fine grass which was used for this purpose. The other seats were smaller, even when the king came to visit him. The authority of this devilish priest was so great that there was no one who dared to cross the court, and to avoid this the other three chambers had doors in the rear, through which even the kings entered. For this purpose they had alleys and passage-ways on the outside above and below, by which people could enter and go out when they came to see the high-priest. . . .

"The second chamber above ground was that of the priests and the assistants of the high-priest. The third was that of the king when he came. The fourth was that of the other chieftains and captains, and though the space was small for so great a number, and for so many different families, yet they accommodated themselves to each other out of respect for the place, and avoided dissensions and factions. Furthermore, there was no other administration of justice in this place than that of the high-priest, to whose unlimited power all bowed.

Furniture of the Temples

"All the rooms were clean, and well furnished with mats. It was not the custom to sleep on bedsteads, however great a lord might be. They used very tastefully braided mats, which were spread on the floor, and soft skins of animals and delicate fabrics for coverings. Their food consisted usually of animals killed in the hunt—deer, rabbits, armadillos, &c., and also birds, which they killed with snares or arrows. The bread, made of their maize, was white and well kneaded. Their drinks were always cold, made of ground chocolate, which was mixed with water and pounded maize. Other drinks were made of pulpy and of crushed fruits, which were then mixed with the intoxicating drink prepared from the agave ; for since the common people were forbidden the use of intoxicating drinks, there was always an abundance of these on hand."

CHAPTER V : MYTHS OF THE MAYA

Mythology of the Maya

OUR knowledge of the mythology of the Maya is by no means so full and comprehensive as in the case of Mexican mythology. Traditions are few and obscure, and the hieroglyphic matter is closed to us. But one great mine of Maya-Kiche mythology exists which furnishes us with much information regarding Kiche cosmogony and pseudo-history, with here and there an interesting allusion to the various deities of the Kiche pantheon. This is the *Popol Vuh*, a volume in which a little real history is mingled with much mythology. It was composed in the form in which we now possess it by a Christianised native of Guatemala in the seventeenth century, and copied in Kiche, in which it was originally written, by one Francisco Ximenes, a monk, who also added to it a Spanish translation.

The Lost "Popol Vuh"

For generations antiquarians interested in this wonderful compilation were aware that it existed somewhere in Guatemala, and many were the regrets expressed regarding their inability to unearth it. A certain Don Felix Cabrera had made use of it early in the nineteenth century, but the whereabouts of the copy he had seen could not be discovered. A Dr. C. Scherzer, of Austria, resolved, if possible, to discover it, and paid a visit to Guatemala in 1854 for that purpose. After a diligent search he succeeded in finding the lost manuscript in the University of San Carlos in the city of Guatemala. Ximenes, the copyist, had placed it in the library of the convent of Chichicastenango, whence it passed to the San Carlos library in 1830.

MYTHS OF MEXICO AND PERU

Genuine Character of the Work

Much doubt has been cast upon the genuine character of the *Popol Vuh*, principally by persons who were almost if not entirely ignorant of the problems of pre-Columbian history in America. Its genuine character, however, is by no means difficult to prove. It has been stated that it is a mere *réchauffé* of the known facts of Maya history coloured by Biblical knowledge, a native version of the Christian Bible. But such a theory will not stand when it is shown that the matter it contains squares with the accepted facts of Mexican mythology, upon which the *Popol Vuh* throws considerable light. Moreover, the entire work bears the stamp of being a purely native compilation, and has a flavour of great antiquity. Our knowledge of the general principles of mythology, too, prepares us for the unqualified acceptance of the material of the *Popol Vuh*, for we find there the stories and tales, the conceptions and ideas connected with early religion which are the property of no one people, but of all peoples and races in an early social state.

Likeness to other Pseudo-Histories

We find in this interesting book a likeness to many other works of early times. The *Popol Vuh* is, indeed, of the same *genre* and class as the *Heimskringla* of Snorre, the history of Saxo Grammaticus, the Chinese history in the *Five Books*, the Japanese *Nihongi*, and many other similar compilations. But it surpasses all these in pure interest because it is the only native American work that has come down to us from pre-Columbian times.

The name "Popol Vuh" means "The Collection of Written Leaves," which proves that the book must

208

THE CREATION-STORY

have contained traditional matter reduced to writing at
a very early period. It is, indeed, a compilation of
mythological character, interspersed with pseudo-history,
which, as the account reaches modern times, shades
off into pure history and tells the deeds of authentic
personages. The language in which it was written, the
Kiche, was a dialect of the Maya-Kiche tongue spoken
at the time of the conquest in Guatemala, Honduras,
and San Salvador, and still the tongue of the native
populations in these districts.

The Creation-Story

The beginning of this interesting book is taken up
with the Kiche story of the creation, and what occurred
directly subsequent to that event. We are told that
the god Hurakan, the mighty wind, a deity in whom
we can discern a Kiche equivalent to Tezcatlipoca,
passed over the universe, still wrapped in gloom. He
called out "Earth," and the solid land appeared. Then
the chief gods took counsel among themselves as to
what should next be made. These were Hurakan,
Gucumatz or Quetzalcoatl, and Xpiyacoc and Xmucane, the mother and father gods. They agreed that
animals should be created. This was accomplished,
and they next turned their attention to the framing of
man. They made a number of mannikins carved out
of wood. But these were irreverent and angered the
gods, who resolved to bring about their downfall.
Then Hurakan (The Heart of Heaven) caused the
waters to be swollen, and a mighty flood came upon
the mannikins. Also a thick resinous rain descended
upon them. The bird Xecotcovach tore out their eyes,
the bird Camulatz cut off their heads, the bird Cotz-
balam devoured their flesh, the bird Tecumbalam
broke their bones and sinews and ground them into

powder. Then all sorts of beings, great and small, abused the mannikins. The household utensils and domestic animals jeered at them, and made game of them in their plight. The dogs and hens said : " Very badly have you treated us and you have bitten us. Now we bite you in turn." The millstones said : " Very much were we tormented by you, and daily, daily, night and day, it was squeak, screech, screech, holi, holi, huqi, huqi,[1] for your sake. Now you shall feel our strength, and we shall grind your flesh and make meal of your bodies." And the dogs growled at the unhappy images because they had not been fed, and tore them with their teeth. The cups and platters said : " Pain and misery you gave us, smoking our tops and sides, cooking us over the fire, burning and hurting us as if we had no feeling. Now it is your turn, and you shall burn." The unfortunate mannikins ran hither and thither in their despair. They mounted upon the roofs of the houses, but the houses crumbled beneath their feet ; they tried to climb to the tops of the trees, but the trees hurled them down ; they were even repulsed by the caves, which closed before them. Thus this ill-starred race was finally destroyed and overthrown, and the only vestiges of them which remain are certain of their progeny, the little monkeys which dwell in the woods.

Vukub-Cakix, the Great Macaw

Ere the earth was quite recovered from the wrathful flood which had descended upon it there lived a being orgulous and full of pride, called Vukub-Cakix (Seven-times-the-colour-of-fire—the Kiche name for the great macaw bird). His teeth were of emerald, and other

[1] These words are obviously onomatopoetic, and are evidently intended to imitate the sound made by a millstone.

parts of him shone with the brilliance of gold and silver. In short, it is evident that he was a sun-and-moon god of prehistoric times. He boasted dreadfully, and his conduct so irritated the other gods that they resolved upon his destruction. His two sons, Zipacna and Cabrakan (Cockspur or Earth-heaper, and Earthquake), were earthquake-gods of the type of the Jötuns of Scandinavian myth or the Titans of Greek legend. These also were prideful and arrogant, and to cause their downfall the gods despatched the heavenly twins Hun-Apu and Xbalanque to earth, with instructions to chastise the trio.

Vukub-Cakix prided himself upon his possession of the wonderful nanze-tree, the tapal, bearing a fruit round, yellow, and aromatic, upon which he breakfasted every morning. One morning he mounted to its summit, whence he could best espy the choicest fruits, when he was surprised and infuriated to observe that two strangers had arrived there before him, and had almost denuded the tree of its produce. On seeing Vukub, Hun-Apu raised a blow-pipe to his mouth and blew a dart at the giant. It struck him on the mouth, and he fell from the top of the tree to the ground. Hun-Apu leapt down upon Vukub and grappled with him, but the giant in terrible anger seized the god by the arm and wrenched it from the body. He then returned to his house, where he was met by his wife, Chimalmat, who inquired for what reason he roared with pain. In reply he pointed to his mouth, and so full of anger was he against Hun-Apu that he took the arm he had wrenched from him and hung it over a blazing fire. He then threw himself down to bemoan his injuries, consoling himself, however, with the idea that he had avenged himself upon the disturbers of his peace.

Whilst Vukub-Cakix moaned and howled with the dreadful pain which he felt in his jaw and teeth (for the dart which had pierced him was probably poisoned) the arm of Hun-Apu hung over the fire, and was turned round and round and basted by Vukub's spouse, Chimalmat. The sun-god rained bitter imprecations upon the interlopers who had penetrated to his paradise and had caused him such woe, and he gave vent to dire threats of what would happen if he succeeded in getting them into his power.

But Hun-Apu and Xbalanque were not minded that Vukub-Cakix should escape so easily, and the recovery of Hun-Apu's arm must be made at all hazards. So they went to consult two great and wise magicians, Xpiyacoc and Xmucane, in whom we see two of the original Kiche creative deities, who advised them to proceed with them in disguise to the dwelling of Vukub, if they wished to recover the lost arm. The old magicians resolved to disguise themselves as doctors, and dressed Hun-Apu and Xbalanque in other garments to represent their sons.

Shortly they arrived at the mansion of Vukub, and while still some way off they could hear his groans and cries. Presenting themselves at the door, they accosted him. They told him that they had heard some one crying out in pain, and that as famous doctors they considered it their duty to ask who was suffering.

Vukub appeared quite satisfied, but closely questioned the old wizards concerning the two young men who accompanied them.

" They are our sons," they replied.

" Good," said Vukub. "Do you think you will be able to cure me ? "

" We have no doubt whatever upon that head,"

answered Xpiyacoc. "You have sustained very bad injuries to your mouth and eyes."

"The demons who shot me with an arrow from their blow-pipe are the cause of my sufferings," said Vukub. "If you are able to cure me I shall reward you richly."

"Your Highness has many bad teeth, which must be removed," said the wily old magician. "Also the balls of your eyes appear to me to be diseased."

Vukub appeared highly alarmed, but the magicians speedily reassured him.

"It is necessary," said Xpiyacoc, "that we remove your teeth, but we will take care to replace them with grains of maize, which you will find much more agreeable in every way."

The unsuspicious giant agreed to the operation, and very quickly Xpiyacoc, with the help of Xmucane, removed his teeth of emerald, and replaced them by grains of white maize. A change quickly came over the Titan. His brilliancy speedily vanished, and when they removed the balls of his eyes he sank into insensibility and died.

All this time the wife of Vukub was turning Hun-Apu's arm over the fire, but Hun-Apu snatched the limb from above the brazier, and with the help of the magicians replaced it upon his shoulder. The discomfiture of Vukub was then complete. The party left his dwelling feeling that their mission had been accomplished.

The Earth-Giants

But in reality it was only partially accomplished, because Vukub's two sons, Zipacna and Cabrakan, still remained to be dealt with. Zipacna was daily employed in heaping up mountains, while Cabrakan, his brother, shook them in earthquake. The vengeance of Hun-Apu and Xbalanque was first directed against Zipacna, and they conspired with a band of young men to bring about his death.

The young men, four hundred in number, pretended to be engaged in building a house. They cut down a large tree, which they made believe was to be the roof-tree of their dwelling, and waited in a part of the forest through which they knew Zipacna must pass. After a while they could hear the giant crashing through the trees. He came into sight, and when he saw them standing round the giant tree-trunk, which they could not lift, he seemed very much amused.

"What have you there, O little ones?" he said laughing.

"Only a tree, your Highness, which we have felled for the roof-tree of a new house we are building."

"Cannot you carry it?" asked the giant disdainfully.

"No, your Highness," they made answer; "it is much too heavy to be lifted even by our united efforts."

With a good-natured laugh the Titan stooped and lifted the great trunk upon his shoulder. Then, bidding them lead the way, he trudged through the forest, evidently not disconcerted in the least by his great burden. Now the young men, incited by Hun-Apu and Xbalanque, had dug a great ditch, which they pretended was to serve for the foundation of their new house. Into this they requested Zipacna to descend, and, scenting no mischief, the giant readily complied. On his reaching the bottom his treacherous acquaintances cast huge trunks of trees upon him, but on hearing them coming down he quickly took refuge in a small side tunnel which the youths had constructed to serve as a cellar beneath their house.

Imagining the giant to be killed, they began at once to express their delight by singing and dancing, and to lend colour to his stratagem Zipacna despatched several

The Twins make an Imitation Crab
Gilbert James
(See page 215)

friendly ants to the surface with strands of hair, which the young men concluded had been taken from his dead body. Assured by the seeming proof of his death, the youths proceeded to build their house upon the tree-trunks which they imagined covered Zipacna's body, and, producing a quantity of *pulque*, they began to make merry over the end of their enemy. For some hours their new dwelling rang with revelry.

All this time Zipacna, quietly hidden below, was listening to the hubbub and waiting his chance to revenge himself upon those who had entrapped him.

Suddenly arising in his giant might, he cast the house and all its inmates high in the air. The dwelling was utterly demolished, and the band of youths were hurled with such force into the sky that they remained there, and in the stars we call the Pleiades we can still discern them wearily waiting an opportunity to return to earth.

The Undoing of Zipacna

But Hun-Apu and Xbalanque, grieved that their comrades had so perished, resolved that Zipacna must not be permitted to escape so easily. He, carrying the mountains by night, sought his food by day on the shore of the river, where he wandered catching fish and crabs. The brothers made a large artificial crab, which they placed in a cavern at the bottom of a ravine. They then cunningly undermined a huge mountain, and awaited events. Very soon they saw Zipacna wandering along the side of the river, and asked him where he was going.

"Oh, I am only seeking my daily food," replied the giant.

"And what may that consist of?" asked the brothers.

215

" Only of fish and crabs," replied Zipacna.

" Oh, there is a crab down yonder," said the crafty brothers, pointing to the bottom of the ravine. " We espied it as we came along. Truly, it is a great crab, and will furnish you with a capital breakfast."

" Splendid ! " cried Zipacna, with glistening eyes. "I must have it at once," and with one bound he leapt down to where the cunningly contrived crab lay in the cavern.

No sooner had he reached it than Hun-Apu and Xbalanque cast the mountain upon him ; but so desperate were his efforts to get free that the brothers feared he might rid himself of the immense weight of earth under which he was buried, and to make sure of his fate they turned him into stone. Thus at the foot of Mount Meahŭan, near Vera Paz, perished the proud Mountain-Maker.

The Discomfiture of Cabrakan

Now only the third of this family of boasters re-mained, and he was the most proud of any.

" I am the Overturner of Mountains ! " said he.

But Hun-Apu and Xbalanque had made up their minds that not one of the race of Vukub should be left alive.

At the moment when they were plotting the over-throw of Cabrakan he was occupied in moving mountains. He seized the mountains by their bases and, exerting his mighty strength, cast them into the air ; and of the smaller mountains he took no account at all. While he was so employed he met the brothers, who greeted him cordially.

" Good day, Cabrakan," said they. " What may you be doing ? "

" Bah ! nothing at all," replied the giant. " Cannot you see that I am throwing the mountains about, which is my usual occupation ? And who may you be that ask such stupid questions ? What are your names ?"

"We have no names," replied they. "We are only hunters, and here we have our blow-pipes, with which we shoot the birds that live in these mountains. So you see that we do not require names, as we meet no one."

Cabrakan looked at the brothers disdainfully, and was about to depart when they said to him : "Stay ; we should like to behold these mountain-throwing feats of yours."

This aroused the pride of Cabrakan.

"Well, since you wish it," said he, "I will show you how I can move a really great mountain. Now, choose the one you would like to see me destroy, and before you are aware of it I shall have reduced it to dust."

Hun-Apu looked around him, and espying a great peak pointed toward it. "Do you think you could overthrow that mountain ?" he asked.

"Without the least difficulty," replied Cabrakan, with a great laugh. "Let us go toward it."

"But first you must eat," said Hun-Apu. "You have had no food since morning, and so great a feat can hardly be accomplished fasting."

The giant smacked his lips. "You are right," he said, with a hungry look. Cabrakan was one of those people who are always hungry. "But what have you to give me ?"

"We have nothing with us," said Hun-Apu.

"Umph !" growled Cabrakan, "you are a pretty fellow. You ask me what I will have to eat, and then tell me you have nothing," and in his anger he seized one of the smaller mountains and threw it into the sea, so that the waves splashed up to the sky.

"Come," said Hun-Apu, "don't get angry. We

have our blow-pipes with us, and will shoot a bird for your dinner."

On hearing this Cabrakan grew somewhat quieter.

"Why did you not say so at first?" he growled. "But be quick, because I am hungry."

Just at that moment a large bird passed overhead, and Hun-Apu and Xbalanque raised their blow-pipes to their mouths. The darts sped swiftly upward, and both of them struck the bird, which came tumbling down through the air, falling at the feet of Cabrakan.

"Wonderful, wonderful!" cried the giant. "You are clever fellows indeed," and, seizing the dead bird, he was going to eat it raw when Hun-Apu stopped him.

"Wait a moment," said he. "It will be much nicer when cooked," and, rubbing two sticks together, he ordered Xbalanque to gather some dry wood, so that a fire was soon blazing.

The bird was then suspended over the fire, and in a short time a savoury odour mounted to the nostrils of the giant, who stood watching the cooking with hungry eyes and watering lips.

Before placing the bird over the fire to cook, however, Hun-Apu had smeared its feathers with a thick coating of mud. The Indians in some parts of Central America still do this, so that when the mud dries with the heat of the fire the feathers will come off with it, leaving the flesh of the bird quite ready to eat. But Hun-Apu had done this with a purpose. The mud that he spread on the feathers was that of a poisoned earth, called *tizate*, the elements of which sank deeply into the flesh of the bird.

When the savoury mess was cooked, he handed it to Cabrakan, who speedily devoured it.

"Now," said Hun-Apu, "let us go toward that

great mountain and see if you can lift it as you boast."

But already Cabrakan began to feel strange pangs.

"What is this?" said he, passing his hand across his brow. "I do not seem to see the mountain you mean."

"Nonsense," said Hun-Apu. "Yonder it is, see, to the east there."

"My eyes seem dim this morning," replied the giant.

"No, it is not that," said Hun-Apu. "You have boasted that you could lift this mountain, and now you are afraid to try."

"I tell you," said Cabrakan, "that I have difficulty in seeing. Will you lead me to the mountain?"

"Certainly," said Hun-Apu, giving him his hand, and with several strides they were at the foot of the eminence.

"Now," said Hun-Apu, "see what you can do, boaster."

Cabrakan gazed stupidly at the great mass in front of him. His knees shook together so that the sound was like the beating of a war-drum, and the sweat poured from his forehead and ran in a little stream down the side of the mountain.

"Come," cried Hun-Apu derisively, "are you going to lift the mountain or not?"

"He cannot," sneered Xbalanque. "I knew he could not."

Cabrakan shook himself into a final effort to regain his senses, but all to no purpose. The poison rushed through his blood, and with a groan he fell dead before the brothers.

Thus perished the last of the earth-giants of Guatemala, whom Hun-Apu and Xbalanque had been sent to destroy.

The Second Book

The second book of the *Popol Vuh* outlines the history of the hero-gods Hun-Apu and Xbalanque. We are told that Xpiyacoc and Xmucane, the father and mother gods, had two sons, Hunhun-Apu and Vukub-Hunapu, the first of whom had by his wife Xbakiyalo two sons, Hunbatz and Hunchouen. The weakness of the whole family was the native game of ball, possibly the Mexican-Mayan game of *tlachtli*, a sort of hockey. To this pastime the natives of Central America were greatly addicted, and numerous remains of *tlachtli* courts are to be found in the ruined cities of Yucatan and Guatemala. The object of the game was to " putt " the ball through a small hole in a circular stone or goal, and the player who succeeded in doing this might demand from the audience all their clothes and jewels. The game, as we have said, was exceedingly popular in ancient Central America, and there is good reason to believe that inter-city matches took place between the various city-states, and were accompanied by a partisanship and rivalry as keen as that which finds expression among the crowd at our principal football matches to-day.

A Challenge from Hades

On one occasion Hunhun-Apu and Vukub-Hunapu played a game of ball which in its progress took them into the vicinity of the realm of Xibalba (the Kiche Hades). The rulers of that drear abode, imagining that they had a chance of capturing the brothers, extended a challenge to them to play them at ball, and this challenge Hun-Came and Vukub-Came, the sovereigns of the Kiche Hell, despatched by four messengers in the shape of owls. The brothers accepted the challenge, and, bidding farewell to their mother Xmucane and their respective sons and nephews, followed the feathered messengers down the long hill which led to the Underworld.

The Fooling of the Brethren

The American Indian is grave and taciturn. If there is one thing he fears and dislikes more than another it is ridicule. To his austere and haughty spirit it appears as something derogatory to his dignity, a slur upon his manhood. The hero-brothers had not been long in Xibalba when they discovered that it was the intention of the Lords of Hades to fool them and subject them to every species of indignity. After crossing a river of blood, they came to the palace of the Lords of Xibalba, where they espied two seated figures in front of them. Thinking that they recognised in them Hun-Came and Vukub-Came, they saluted them in a becoming manner, only to discover to their mortification that they were addressing figures of wood. This incident excited the ribald jeers of the Xibalbans, who scoffed at the brothers. Next they were invited to sit on the seat of honour, which they found to their dismay to be a red-hot stone, a circumstance which caused unbounded amusement to the inhabitants of the Underworld. Then they were imprisoned in the House of Gloom, where they were sacrificed and buried. The head of Hunhun-Apu was, however, suspended from a tree, upon the branches of which grew a crop of gourds so like the dreadful trophy as to be indistinguishable from it. The fiat went forth that no one in Xibalba must eat of the fruit of that tree. But the Lords of Xibalba had reckoned without feminine curiosity and its unconquerable love of the forbidden.

The Princess Xquiq

One day—if day ever penetrated to that gloomy and unwholesome place—a princess of Xibalba called Xquiq (Blood), daughter of Cuchumaquiq, a notability of Xibalba, passed under the tree, and, observing the desirable fruit with which it was covered, stretched out her hand to pluck one of the gourds. Into the outstretched palm the head of Hunhun-Apu spat, and told Xquiq that she would become a mother. Before she returned home, however, the hero-god assured her that no harm would come to her, and that she must not be afraid. In a few months' time the princess's father heard of her adventure, and she was doomed to be slain, the royal messengers of Xibalba, the owls, receiving commands to despatch her and to bring back her heart in a vase. But on the way she overcame the scruples of the owls by splendid promises, and they substituted for her heart the coagulated sap of the bloodwort plant.

The Birth of Hun-Apu and Xbalanque

Xmucane, left at home, looked after the welfare of the young Hunbatz and Hunchouen, and thither, at the instigation of the head of Hunhun-Apu, went Xquiq for protection. At first Xmucane would not credit her story, but upon Xquiq appealing to the gods a miracle was performed on her behalf, and she was permitted to gather a basket of maize where no maize grew to prove the authenticity of her claim. As a princess of the Underworld, it is not surprising that she should be connected with such a phenomenon, as it is from deities of that region that we usually expect the phenomena of growth to proceed. Shortly afterwards, when she had won the good graces of the aged

The Princess and the Gourds

Gilbert James

(See page 222)

The Princess who made Friends of the Owls

Gilbert James

(See page 222)

Xmucane, her twin sons were born, the Hun-Apu and Xbalanque whom we have already met as the central figures of the first book.

The Divine Children

But the divine children were both noisy and mischievous. They tormented their venerable grandmother with their shrill uproar and tricky behaviour. At last Xmucane, unable to put up with their habits, turned them out of doors. They took to an outdoor life with surprising ease, and soon became expert hunters and skilful in the use of the *serbatana* (blow-pipe), with which they shot birds and small animals. They were badly treated by their half-brothers Hunbatz and Hunchouen, who, jealous of their fame as hunters, annoyed them in every possible manner. But the divine children retaliated by turning their tormentors into hideous apes. The sudden change in the appearance of her grandsons caused Xmucane the most profound grief and dismay, and she begged that they who had brightened her home with their singing and flute-playing might not be condemned to such a dreadful fate. She was informed by the divine brothers that if she could behold their antics unmoved by mirth her wish would be granted. But the capers they cut and their grimaces caused her such merriment that on three separate occasions she was unable to restrain her laughter, and the men-monkeys took their leave.

The Magic Tools

The childhood of Hun-Apu and Xbalanque was full of such episodes as might be expected from these beings. We find, for example, that on attempting to clear a *milpa* (maize plantation) they employed magic tools which could be trusted to undertake a good day's work whilst they were absent at the chase. Returning at night, they smeared soil over their hands and faces, for the purpose of deluding Xmucane into the belief that they had been toiling all day in the fields. But the wild beasts met in conclave during the night, and replaced all the roots and shrubs which the magic tools had cleared away. The twins recognised the work of the various animals, and placed a large net on the ground, so that if the creatures came to the spot on the following night they might be caught in its folds. They did come, but all made good their escape save the rat. The rabbit and deer lost their tails, however, and that is why these animals possess no caudal appendages! The rat, in gratitude for their sparing its life, told the brothers the history of their father and uncle, of their heroic efforts against the powers of Xibalba, and of the existence of a set of clubs and balls with which they might play *tlachtli* on the ball-ground at Ninxor-Carchah, where Hunhun-Apu and Vukub-Hunapu had played before them.

The Second Challenge

But the watchful Hun-Came and Vukub-Came soon heard that the sons and nephews of their first victims had adopted the game which had led these last into the clutches of the cunning Xibalbans, and they resolved to send a similar challenge to Hun-Apu and Xbalanque, thinking that the twins were unaware of the fate of Hunhun-Apu and Vukub-Hunapu. They therefore despatched messengers to the home of Xmucane with a challenge to play them at the ball-game, and Xmucane, alarmed by the nature of the message, sent a louse to warn her grandsons. The louse, unable to proceed as quickly as he wished, permitted himself to be swallowed by a toad, the toad by a serpent, and the serpent by the bird Voc, the messenger of Hurakan. At the end of the journey the other animals duly liberated each other, but the toad could not rid himself of the louse, who had in reality hidden himself in the toad's gums, and had not been swallowed at all. At last the message was delivered, and the twins returned to the abode of Xmucane, to bid farewell to their grandmother and mother. Before leaving they each planted a cane in the midst of the hut, saying that it would wither if any fatal accident befell them.

The Tricksters Tricked

They then proceeded to Xibalba, on the road trodden by Hunhun-Apu and Vukub-Hunapu, and passed the river of blood as the others had done. But they adopted the precaution of despatching ahead an animal called Xan as a sort of spy or scout. They commanded this animal to prick all the Xibalbans with a hair from Hun-Apu's leg, in order that they might discover which of them were made of wood, and incidentally learn the names of the others as they addressed one another when pricked by the hair. They were thus enabled to ignore the wooden images on their arrival at Xibalba, and they carefully avoided the red-hot stone. Nor did the ordeal of the House of Gloom affright them, and they passed through it scatheless. The inhabitants of the Underworld were both amazed and furious with disappointment. To add to their annoyance, they were badly beaten in the game of ball which followed. The Lords of Hell then requested the twins to bring them four bouquets of flowers from the royal garden of Xibalba, at the same time commanding the gardeners to keep good watch over the flowers so that none of them might be removed. But the brothers called to their aid a swarm of ants, who succeeded in returning with the flowers. The anger of the Xibalbans increased to a white fury, and they incarcerated Hun-Apu and Xbalanque in the House of Lances, a dread abode where demons armed with sharp spears thrust at them fiercely. But they bribed the lancers and escaped. The Xibalbans slit the beaks of the owls who guarded the royal gardens, and howled in fury.

The Houses of the Ordeals

They were next thrust into the House or Cold. Here they escaped a dreadful death from freezing by warming themselves with burning pine-cones. Into the House of Tigers and the House of Fire they were thrown for a night each, but escaped from both. But they were not so lucky in the House of Bats. As they threaded this place of terror, Camazotz, Ruler of the Bats, descended upon them with a whirring of leathern wings, and with one sweep of his sword-like claws cut off Hun-Apu's head. (See Mictlan, pp. 95, 96.) But a tortoise which chanced to pass the severed neck of the hero's prostrate body and came into contact with it was immediately turned into a head, and Hun-Apu arose from his terrible experience not a whit the worse.

These various houses in which the brothers were forced to pass a certain time forcibly recall to our minds the several circles of Dante's Hell. Xibalba was to the Kiche not a place of punishment, but a dark place of horror and myriad dangers. No wonder the Maya had what Landa calls " an immoderate fear of death " if they believed that after it they would be transported to such a dread abode !

With the object of proving their immortal nature to their adversaries, Hun-Apu and Xbalanque, first

In the House of Bats
William Sewell
(See page 226)

arranging for their resurrection with two sorcerers, Xulu and Pacaw, stretched themselves upon a bier and died. Their bones were ground to powder and thrown into the river. They then went through a kind of evolutionary process, appearing on the fifth day after their deaths as men-fishes and on the sixth as old men, ragged and tatterdemalion in appearance, killing and restoring each other to life. At the request of the princes of Xibalba, they burned the royal palace and restored it to its pristine splendour, killed and resuscitated the king's dog, and cut a man in pieces, bringing him to life again. The Lords of Hell were curious about the sensation of death, and asked to be killed and resuscitated. The first portion of their request the hero-brothers speedily granted, but did not deem it necessary to pay any regard to the second.

Throwing off all disguise, the brothers assembled the now thoroughly cowed princes of Xibalba, and announced their intention of punishing them for their animosity against themselves, their father and uncle. They were forbidden to partake in the noble and classic game of ball—a great indignity in the eyes of Maya of the higher caste—they were condemned to menial tasks, and they were to have sway over the beasts of the forest alone. After this their power rapidly waned. These princes of the Underworld are described as being owl-like, with faces painted black and white, as symbolical of their duplicity and faithless disposition.

As some reward for the dreadful indignities they had undergone, the souls of Hunhun-Apu and Vukub-Hunapu, the first adventurers into the darksome region of Xibalba, were translated to the skies, and became the sun and moon, and with this apotheosis the second book ends.

We can have no difficulty, in the light of comparative

mythology, in seeing in the matter of this book a version of "the harrying of hell" common to many mythologies. In many primitive faiths a hero or heroes dares the countless dangers of Hades in order to prove to the savage mind that the terrors of death can be overcome. In Algonquian mythology Blue-Jay makes game of the Dead Folk whom his sister Ioi has married, and Balder passes through the Scandinavian Helheim. The god must first descend into the abyss and must emerge triumphant if humble folk are to possess assurance of immortality.

The Reality of Myth

It is from such matter as that found in the second book of the *Popol Vuh* that we are enabled to discern how real myth can be on occasion. It is obvious, as has been pointed out, that the dread of death in the savage mind may give rise to such a conception of its vanquishment as appears in the *Popol Vuh*. But there is reason to suspect that other elements have also entered into the composition of the myth. It is well known that an invading race, driving before them the remnants of a conquered people, are prone to regard these in the course of a few generations as almost supernatural and as denizens of a sphere more or less infernal. Their reasons for this are not difficult of comprehension. To begin with, a difference in ceremonial ritual gives rise to the belief that the inimical race practises magic. The enemy is seldom seen, and, if perceived, quickly takes cover or "vanishes." The majority of aboriginal races were often earth- or cave-dwellers, like the Picts of Scotland, and such the originals of the Xibalbans probably were.

The invading Maya-Kiche, encountering such a folk in the cavernous recesses of the hill-slopes of Guatemala, would naturally refer them to the Underworld. The cliff-dwellings of Mexico and Colorado exhibit manifest signs of the existence of such a cave-dwelling race. In the latter state is the Cliff Palace Cañon, a huge natural recess, within which a small city was actually built, which still remains in excellent preservation. In some such semi-subterranean recess, then, may the city of " Xibalba " have stood.

The Xibalbans

We can see, too, that the Xibalbans were not merely a plutonic race. Xibalba is not a Hell, a place of punishment for sin, but a place of the dead, and its inhabitants were scarcely " devils," nor evil gods. The transcriber of the *Popol Vuh* says of them : " In the old times they did not have much power. They were but annoyers and opposers of men, and, in truth, they were not regarded as gods." The word Xibalba is derived from a root meaning " to fear," from which comes the name for a ghost or phantom. Xibalba was thus the " Place of Phantoms."

The Third Book

The opening of the third book finds the gods once more deliberating as to the creation of man. Four men are evolved as the result of these deliberations. These beings were moulded from a paste of yellow and white maize, and were named Balam-Quitze (Tiger with the Sweet Smile), Balam-Agab (Tiger of the Night), Mahacutah (The Distinguished Name), and Iqi-Balam (Tiger of the Moon).

But the god Hurakan who had formed them was not overpleased with his handiwork, for these beings were too much like the gods themselves. The gods once more took counsel, and agreed that man must be less perfect and possess less knowledge than this new race. He must not become as a god. So Hurakan breathed a cloud over their eyes in order that they might only see a portion of the earth, whereas before they had been able to see the whole round sphere of the world. After this the four men were plunged into a deep sleep, and four women were created, who were given them as wives. These were Caha-Paluma (Falling Water), Choima (Beautiful Water), Tzununiha (House of the Water), and Cakixa (Water of Parrots, or Brilliant Water), who were espoused to the men in the respective order given above.

These eight persons were the ancestors of the Kiche only, after which were created the forerunners of the other peoples. At this time there was no sun, and comparative darkness lay over the face of the earth. Men knew not the art of worship, but blindly lifted their eyes to heaven and prayed the Creator to send them quiet lives and the light of day. But no sun came, and dispeace entered their hearts. So they journeyed to a place called Tulan-Zuiva (The Seven Caves)—practically the same as Chicomoztoc in the Aztec myth— and there gods were vouchsafed to them. The names of these were Tohil, whom Balam-Quitze received; Avilix, whom Balam-Agab received; and Hacavitz, granted to Mahacutah. Iqi-Balam received a god, but as he had no family his worship and knowledge died out.

The Granting of Fire

Grievously did the Kiche feel the want of fire in the sunless world they inhabited, but this the god Tohil (The Rumbler, the Fire-god) quickly provided them with. However, a mighty rain descended and extinguished all the fires in the land. These, however,

How the Sun appeared like the Moon

Gilbert James

(See page 230)

were always supplied again by Tohil, who had only to strike his feet together to produce fire. In this figure there is no difficulty in seeing a fully developed thunder-god.

The Kiche Babel

Tulan-Zuiva was a place of great misfortune to the Kiche, for here the race suffered alienation in its different branches by reason of a confounding of their speech, which recalls the story of Babel. Owing to this the first four men were no longer able to comprehend each other, and determined to leave the place of their mischance and to seek the leadership of the god Tohil into another and more fortunate sphere. In this journey they met with innumerable hardships. They had to cross many lofty mountains, and on one occasion had to make a long *détour* across the bed of the ocean, the waters of which were miraculously divided to permit of their passage. At last they arrived at a mountain which they called Hacavitz, after one of their deities, and here they remained, for it had been foretold that here they should see the sun. At last the luminary appeared. Men and beasts went wild with delight, although his beams were by no means strong, and he appeared more like a reflection in a mirror than the strong sun of later days whose fiery beams speedily sucked up the blood of victims on the altar. As he showed his face the three tribal gods of the Kiche were turned into stone, as were the gods or totems connected with the wild animals. Then arose the first Kiche town, or permanent dwelling-place.

The Last Days of the First Men

Time passed, and the first men of the Kiche race grew old. Visions came to them, in which they were exhorted by the gods to render human sacrifices, and in order to obey the divine injunctions they raided the neighbouring lands, the folk of which made a spirited resistance. But in a great battle the Kiche were miraculously assisted by a horde of wasps and hornets, which flew in the faces of their foes, stinging and blinding them, so that they could not wield weapon nor see to make any effective resistance. After this battle the surrounding races became tributary to them.

Death of the First Men

Now the first men felt that their death-day was nigh, and they called their kin and dependents around them to hear their dying words. In the grief of their souls they chanted the song " Kamucu," the song " We see," that they had sung so joyfully when they had first seen the light of day. Then they parted from their wives and sons one by one. And of a sudden they were not, and in their place was a great bundle, which was never opened. It was called the " Majesty Enveloped." So died the first men of the Kiche.

In this book it is clear that we have to deal with the problem which the origin and creation of man presented to the Maya-Kiche mind. The several myths connected with it bear a close resemblance to those of other American peoples. In the mythology of the American Indian it is rare to find an Adam, a single figure set solitary in a world without companionship of some sort. Man is almost invariably the child of Mother Earth, and emerges from some cavern or subterranean country fully grown and fully equipped for the upper earth-life. We find this type of myth in the mythologies of the Aztecs, Peruvians, Choctaws, Blackfeet Indians, and those of many other American tribes.

American Migrations

We also find in the story of the Kiche migration a striking similarity to the migration myths of other American races. But in the Kiche myth we can trace a definite racial movement from the cold north to the warm south. The sun is not at first born. There is darkness. When he does appear he is weak and his beams are dull and watery like those of the luminary in a northern clime. Again, there are allusions to the crossing of rivers by means of " shining sand " which covered them, which might reasonably be held to imply the presence upon them of ice. In this connection we may quote from an Aztec migration myth which appears almost a parallel to the Kiche story.

" This is the beginning of the record of the coming of the Mexicans from the place called Aztlan. It is by means of the water that they came this way, being four tribes, and in coming they rowed in boats. They built their huts on piles at the place called the grotto of Quineveyan. It is there from which the eight tribes issued. The first tribe is that of the Huexotzincos, the second the Chalcas, the third the Xochimilcos, the fourth the Cuitlavacas, the fifth the Mallinalcas, the sixth the Chichimecas, the seventh the Tepanecas, the eighth the Matlatzincas. It is there where they were founded in Colhuacan. They were the colonists of it since they landed there, coming from Aztlan. . . . It is there that they soon afterwards went away from, carrying with them their god Vitzillopochtli. . . . There the eight tribes opened up our road by water."

The " Wallum Olum," or painted calendar records, of the Leni-Lenape Indians contain a similar myth.

" After the flood," says the story, " the Lenape with the manly turtle beings dwelt close together at the cave house and dwelling of Talli. . . . They saw that the snake-land was bright and wealthy. Having all agreed, they went over the water of the frozen sea to possess the land. It was wonderful when they all went over the smooth deep water of the frozen sea at the gap of the snake sea in the great ocean."

Do these myths contain any essence of the truth? Do they refer to an actual migration when the ancestors of certain American tribes crossed the frozen ocean of the Kamchatka Strait and descended from the sunless north and the boreal night of these sub-Arctic regions to a more genial clime? Can such a tradition have been preserved throughout the countless ages which must have passed between the arrival of proto-Mongolian man in America and the writing or composition of the several legends cited? Surely not. But may there not have been later migrations from the north? May not hordes of folk distantly akin to the first Americans have swept across the frozen strait, and within a few generations have made their way into the warmer regions, as we know the Nahua did? The Scandinavian vikings who reached north-eastern America in the tenth century found there a race totally distinct from the Red Man, and more approaching the Esquimaux, whom they designated Skrellingr, or " Chips," so small and misshapen were they. Such a description could hardly have been applied to the North American Indian as we know him. From the legends of the Red race of North America we may infer that they remained for a number of generations in the Far West of the North American continent before they migrated eastward. And a guess might be hazarded to the effect that, arriving in

America somewhere about the dawn of the Christian era, they spread slowly in a south-easterly direction, arriving in the eastern parts of North America about the end of the eleventh century, or even a little later. This would mean that such a legend as that which we have just perused would only require to have survived a thousand years, provided the *Popol Vuh* was first composed about the eleventh century, as appears probable. But such speculations are somewhat dangerous in the face of an almost complete lack of evidence, and must be met with the utmost caution and treated as surmises only.

Cosmogony of the "Popol Vuh"

We have now completed our brief survey of the mythological portion of the *Popol Vuh*, and it will be well at this point to make some inquiries into the origin and nature of the various gods, heroes, and similar personages who fill its pages. Before doing so, however, let us glance at the creation-myth which we find detailed in the first book. We can see by internal evidence that this must be the result of the fusion of more than one creation-story. We find in the myth that mention is made of a number of beings each of whom appears to exercise in some manner the functions of a creator or "moulder." These beings also appear to have similar attributes. There is evidently here the reconciliation of early rival faiths. We know that this occurred in Peruvian cosmogony, which is notoriously composite, and many another mythology, European and Asiatic, exhibits a like phenomenon. Even in the creation-story as given in Genesis we can discover the fusion of two separate accounts from the allusion to the creative power as both " Jahveh " and " Elohim," the plural ending of the second name proving the presence of polytheistic as well as monotheistic conceptions.

Antiquity of the "Popol Vuh"

These considerations lead to the assumption that the *Popol Vuh* is a mythological collection of very considerable antiquity, as the fusion of religious beliefs is a comparatively slow process. It is, of course, in the absence of other data, impossible to fix the date of its origin, even approximately. We possess only the one version of this interesting work, so that we are compelled to confine ourselves to the consideration of that alone, and are without the assistance which philology would lend us by a comparison of two versions of different dates.

The Father-Mother Gods

We discover a pair of dual beings concerned in the Kiche creation. These are Xpiyacoc and Xmucane, the Father-Mother deities, and are obviously Kiche equivalents to the Mexican Ometecutli-Omeciuatl, whom we have already noticed (pp. 103-4). The former is the male fructifier, whilst the name of the latter signifies "Female Vigour." These deities were probably regarded as hermaphroditic, as numerous North American Indian gods appear to be, and may be analogous to the "Father Sky" and "Mother Earth" of so many mythologies.

Gucumatz

We also find Gucumatz concerned in the Kiche scheme of creation. He was a Maya-Kiche form of the Mexican Quetzalcoatl, or perhaps the converse was the case. The name signifies, like its Nahua equivalent, "Serpent with Green Feathers."

METRICAL ORIGIN OF THE POPOL VUH

Hurakan

Hurakan, the wind-god, "He who hurls below," whose name perhaps signifies "The One-legged," is probably the same as the Nahua Tezcatlipoca. It has been suggested that the word "hurricane" has been evolved from the name of this god, but the derivation seems rather too fortuitous to be real. Hurakan had the assistance of three sub-gods, Cakulha-Hurakan (Lightning), Chipi-Cakulha (Lightning-flash), and Raxa-Cakulha (Track of the Lightning).

Hun-Apu and Xbalanque

Hun-Apu and Xbalanque, the hero-gods, appear to have the attributes of demi-gods in general. The name Hun-Apu means "Master" or "Magician," and Xbalanque "Little Tiger." We find many such figures in American myth, which is rich in hero-gods.

Vukub-Cakix and his Sons

Vukub-Cakix and his progeny are, of course, earth-giants like the Titans of Greek mytnology or the Jötuns of Scandinavian story. The removal of the emerald teeth of Vukub-Cakix and their replacement by grains of maize would seem to be a mythical interpretation or allegory of the removal of the virgin turf of the earth and its replacement by maize-seed. Therefore it is possible that Vukub-Cakix is an earth-god, and not a prehistoric sun-and-moon god, as stated by Dr. Seler.[1]

Metrical Origin of the "Popol Vuh"

There is reason to believe that the *Popol Vuh* was originally a metrical composition. This would assist the

---

[1] See my remarks on this subject in *The Popol Vuh*, pp. 41, 52 (London, 1908).

hypothesis of its antiquity, on the ground that it was for generations recited before being reduced to writing. Passages here and there exhibit a decided metrical tendency, and one undoubtedly applies to a descriptive dance symbolical of sunrise. It is as follows :

> "'Ama x-u ch'ux ri Vuch ?'
> 'Ve,' x-cha ri mama.
> Ta chi xaquinic.
> Quate ta chi gecumarchic.
> Cahmul xaquin ri mama.
> 'Ca xaquin-Vuch,' ca cha vinak vacamic.ˣ

This may be rendered freely :

> "'Is the dawn about to be ?'
> 'Yes,' answered the old man.
> Then he spread apart his legs.
> Again the darkness appeared.
> Four times the old man spread his legs.
> 'Now the opossum spreads his legs,'
> Say the people."

It is obvious that many of these lines possess the well-known quality of savage dance-poetry, which displays itself in a rhythm of one long foot followed by two short ones. We know that the Kiche were very fond of ceremonial dances, and of repeating long chants which they called *nugum tzih*, or "garlands of words," and the *Popol Vuh*, along with other matter, probably contained many of these.

Pseudo-History of the Kiche

The fourth book of the *Popol Vuh* contains the pseudo-history of the Kiche kings. It is obviously greatly confused, and it would be difficult to say how much of it originally belonged to the *Popol Vuh* and how much had been added or invented by its latest compiler. One cannot discriminate between saga and history, or between monarchs and gods, the real and the fabulous. Interminable conflicts are the theme of most of the book, and many migrations are recounted.

Queen Móo

Whilst dealing with Maya pseudo-history it will be well to glance for a moment at the theories of the late Augustus Le Plongeon, who lived and carried on excavations in Yucatan for many years. Dr. Le Plongeon was obsessed with the idea that the ancient Maya spread their civilisation all over the habitable globe, and that they were the originators of the Egyptian, Palestinian, and Hindu civilisations, besides many others. He furthermore believed himself to be the true elucidator of the Maya system of hieroglyphs, which in his estimation were practically identical with the Egyptian. We will not attempt to refute his theories, as they are based on ignorance of the laws which govern philology, anthropology, and mythology. But he possessed a thorough knowledge of the Maya tongue, and his acquaintance with Maya customs was extensive and peculiar. One of his ideas was that a certain hall among the ruins of Chichen-Itza had been built by a Queen Móo, a Maya princess who after the tragic fate of her brother-husband and the catastrophe which ended in the sinking of the continent of Atlantis fled to Egypt, where she founded the ancient Egyptian civilisation. It would be easy to refute this theory. But the tale as told by Dr. Le Plongeon possesses a sufficiency of romantic interest to warrant its being rescued from the little-known volume in which he published it.[1]

We do not learn from Dr. Le Plongeon's book by what course of reasoning he came to discover that the

[1] *Queen Móo and the Egyptian Sphinx* (London, 1896).

name of his heroine was the rather uneuphonious one of Móo. Probably he arrived at it by the same process as that by which he discovered that certain Mayan architectural ornaments were in reality Egyptian letters. But it will be better to let him tell his story in his own words. It is as follows :

The Funeral Chamber

" As we are about to enter the funeral chamber hallowed by the love of the sister-wife, Queen Móo, the beauty of the carvings on the zapote beam that forms the lintel of the doorway calls our attention. Here is represented the antagonism of the brothers Aac and Coh, that led to the murder of the latter by the former. Carved on the lintel are the names of these personages, represented by their totems—a leopard head for Coh, and a boar head as well as a turtle for Aac, this word meaning both boar and turtle in Maya. Aac is pictured within the disk of the sun, his protective deity which he worshipped, according to mural inscriptions at Uxmal. Full of anger he faces his brother. In his right hand there is a badge ornamented with feathers and flowers. The threatening way in which this is held suggests a concealed weapon. . . . The face of Coh also expresses anger. With him is the feathered serpent, emblematic of royalty, thence of the country, more often represented as a winged serpent protecting Coh. In his left hand he holds his weapon down, whilst his right hand clasps his badge of authority, with which he covers his breasts as for protection, and demanding the respect due to his rank. . . .

" Passing between the figures of armed chieftains sculptured on the jambs of the doorway, and seeming like sentinels guarding the entrance of the funeral chamber, we notice one wearing a headdress similar to

Queen Móo has her Destiny foretold

Gilbert James

(See page 241)

The Rejected Suitor

From *Queen Móo and the Egyptian Sphinx*, by Augustus Le Plongeon. M.D.

(See page 243)

the crown of Lower Egypt, which formed part of the *pshent* of the Egyptian monarchs.

The Frescoes

" The frescoes in the funeral chamber of Prince Coh's Memorial Hall, painted in water-colours taken from the vegetable kingdom, are divided into a series of *tableaux* separated by blue lines. The plinths, the angles of the room, and the edges of the ceiling, being likewise painted blue, indicate that this was intended for a funeral chamber. . . . The first scene represents Queen Móo while yet a child. She is seated on the back of a peccary, or American wild boar, under the royal umbrella of feathers, emblem of royalty in Mayach, as it was in India, Chaldea, and other places. She is consulting a *h-men*, or wise man ; listening with profound attention to the decrees of fate as revealed by the cracking of the shell of an armadillo exposed to a slow fire on a brazier, the condensing on it of the vapour, and the various tints it assumes. This mode of divination is one of the customs of the Mayas. . . .

The Soothsayers

" In front of the young Queen Móo, and facing her, is seated the soothsayer, evidently a priest of high rank, judging from the colours, blue and yellow, of the feathers of his ceremonial mantle. He reads the decrees of fate on the shell of the armadillo, and the scroll issuing from his throat says what they are. By him stands the winged serpent, emblem and protective genius of the Maya Empire. His head is turned towards the royal banner, which he seems to caress. His satisfaction is reflected in the mild and pleased expression of his face. Behind the priest, the position of whose hand is the same as that of Catholic priests in blessing their congregation, and the significance of which is well known to occultists, are the ladies-in-waiting of the young Queen.

The Royal Bride

" In another *tableau* we again see Queen Móo, no longer a child, but a comely young woman. She is not seated under the royal umbrella or banner, but she is once more in the presence of the *h-men*, whose face is concealed by a mask representing an owl's head. She, pretty and coquettish, has many admirers, who vie with each other for the honour of her hand. In company with one of her wooers she comes to consult the priest, accompanied by an old lady, her grandmother probably, and her female attendants. According to custom the old lady is the spokeswoman. She states to the priest that the young man, he who sits on a low stool between two female attendants, desires to marry the Queen. The priest's attendant, seated also on a stool, back of all, acts as crier, and repeats in a loud voice the speech of the old lady.

Móo's Refusal

" The young Queen refuses the offer. The refusal is indicated by the direction of the scroll issuing from her mouth. It is turned backward, instead of forward towards the priest, as would be the case if she assented to the marriage. The *h-men* explains that Móo, being a daughter of the royal family, by law and custom must marry one of her brothers. The youth listens to the decision with due respect to the priest, as shown by his arm being placed across his breast, the left hand resting on the right shoulder. He does not accept the refusal in a meek spirit, however. His clenched fist, his foot raised as in the act of stamping, betoken anger and disappointment, while the attendant behind him expostulates, counselling patience and resignation, judging by the position and expression of her left-hand palm upward.

The Rejected Suitor

"In another *tableau* we see the same individual whose offer of marriage was rejected by the young Queen in consultation with a *nubchi*, or prophet, a priest whose exalted rank is indicated by his head-dress, and the triple breastplate he wears over his mantle of feathers. The consulter, evidently a person of importance, has come attended by his *hachetail*, or confidential friend, who sits behind him on a cushion. The expression on the face of the said consulter shows that he does not accept patiently the decrees of fate, although conveyed by the interpreter in as conciliatory a manner as possible. The adverse decision of the gods is manifested by the sharp projecting centre part of the scroll, but it is wrapped in words as persuasive and consoling, preceded by as smooth a preamble as the rich and beautiful Maya language permits and makes easy. His friend is addressing the prophet's assistant. Reflecting the thoughts of his lord, he declares that the *nubchi's* fine discourse and his pretended reading of the will of the gods are all nonsense, and exclaims 'Pshaw!' which contemptuous exclamation is pictured by the yellow scroll, pointed at both ends, escaping from his nose like a sneeze. The answer of the priest's assistant, evidenced by the gravity of his features, the assertive position of his hand, and the bluntness of his speech, is evidently 'It is so!'

Aac's Fierce Wooing

" Her brother Aac is madly in love with Móo. He is portrayed approaching the interpreter of the will of the gods, divested of his garments in token of humility in presence of their majesty and of submission to their decrees. He comes full of arrogance, arrayed in gorgeous attire, and with regal pomp. He comes not as a suppliant to ask and accept counsel, but haughty, he makes bold to dictate. He is angered at the refusal of the priest to accede to his demand for his sister Móo's hand, to whose totem, an armadillo on this occasion, he points imperiously. It was on an armadillo's shell that the fates wrote her destiny when consulted by the performance of the *Pou* ceremony. The yellow flames of wrath darting from all over his person, the sharp yellow scroll issuing from his mouth, symbolise Aac's feelings. The pontiff, however, is unmoved by them. In the name of the gods with serene mien he denies the request of the proud nobleman, as his speech indicates. The winged serpent, genius of the country, that stands erect and ireful by Aac, is also wroth at his pretensions, and shows in its features and by sending its dart through Aac's royal banner a decided opposition to them, expressed by the ends of his speech being turned backwards, some of them terminating abruptly, others in sharp points.

Prince Coh

" Prince Coh sits behind the priest as one of his attendants. He witnesses the scene, hears the calm negative answer, sees the anger of his brother and rival, smiles at his impotence, is happy at his discomfiture. Behind him, however, sits a spy who will repeat his words, report his actions to his enemy. He listens, he watches. The high-priest himself, Cay, their elder brother, sees the storm that is brewing behind the dissensions of Coh and Aac. He trembles at the thought of the misfortunes that will surely befall the dynasty of the Cans, of the ruin and misery of the country that will certainly follow. Divested of his priestly raiment, he comes nude and humble as it is proper for men in the presence of the gods, to ask their advice how best to avoid the impending calamities. The chief of the auspices is in the act of reading their decrees on the palpitating entrails of a fish. The sad expression on his face, that of humble resignation on that of the pontiff, of deferential astonishment on that of the assistant, speak of the inevitable misfortunes which are to come in the near future.

" We pass over interesting battle scenes . . . in which the defenders have been defeated by the Mayas. Coh will return to his queen loaded with spoils that he will lay at her feet with his glory, which is also hers.

The Murder of Coh

" We next see him in a terrible altercation with his brother Aac. The figures in that scene are nearly life-size, but so much disfigured and broken as to make it impossible to obtain good tracings. Coh is portrayed without weapons, his fists clenched, looking menacingly at his foe, who holds three spears, typical of the three wounds he inflicted in his brother's back when he killed him treacherously. Coh is now laid out, being prepared for cremation. His body has been opened at the ribs to extract the viscera and heart, which, after being charred, are to be preserved in a stone urn with cinnabar, where the writer found them in 1875. His sister-wife, Queen Móo, in sad contemplation of the remains of the beloved, . . . kneels at his feet. . . . The winged

245

serpent, protective genius of the country, is pictured
without a head. The ruler of the country has been
slain. He is dead. The people are without a chief."

The Widowhood of Moo

The widowhood of Móo is then said to be portrayed
in subsequent pictures. Other suitors, among them
Aac, make their proposals to her, but she refuses them
all. "Aac's pride being humiliated, his love turned to
hatred. His only wish henceforth was to usurp the
supreme power, to wage war against the friend of his
childhood. He made religious disagreement the pre-
text. He proclaimed that the worship of the sun was
to be superior to that of the winged serpent, the genius
of the country ; also to that of the worship of ancestors,
typified by the feathered serpent, with horns and a flame
or halo on the head. . . . Prompted by such evil passions, he put himself at the head of his own vassals,
and attacked those who had remained faithful to Queen
Móo and to Prince Coh's memory. At first Móo's
adherents successfully opposed her foes. The contend-
ing parties, forgetting in the strife that they were
children of the same soil, blinded by their prejudices,
let their passions have the better of their reason. At
last Queen Móo fell a prisoner in the hands of her
enemy."

The Manuscript Troano

Dr. Le Plongeon here assumes that the story is taken
up by the Manuscript Troano. As no one is able to
decipher this manuscript completely, he is pretty safe in
nis assertion. Here is what the *pintura* alluded to says
regarding Queen Móo, according to our author :

"The people of Mayach having been whipped into
submission and cowed, no longer opposing much resist-

ance, the lord seized her by the hair, and, in common with others, caused her to suffer from blows. This happened on the ninth day of the tenth month of the year Kan. Being completely routed, she passed to the opposite sea-coast in the southern parts of the country, which had already suffered much injury."

Here we shall leave the Queen, and those who have been sufficiently credulous to create and believe in her and her companions. We do not aver that the illustrations on the walls of the temple at Chichen do not allude to some such incident, or series of incidents, as Dr. Le Plongeon describes, but to bestow names upon the *dramatis personæ* in the face of almost complete inability to read the Maya script and a total dearth of accompanying historical manuscripts is merely futile, and we must regard Dr. Le Plongeon's narrative as a quite fanciful rendering of probability. At the same time, the light which he throws—if some obviously unscientific remarks be deducted—on the customs of the Maya renders his account of considerable interest, and that must be our excuse for presenting it here at some length.

PIECE OF POTTERY REPRESENTING
TAPIR (FROM GUATEMALA)

CHAPTER VI: THE CIVILISATION OF OLD PERU

Old Peru

IF the civilisation of ancient Peru did not achieve the standard of general culture reached by the Mexicans and Maya, it did not fall far short of the attainment of these peoples. But the degrading despotism under which the peasantry groaned in Inca times, and the brutal and sanguinary tyranny of the Apu-Ccapac Incas, make the rulers of Mexico at their worst appear as enlightened when compared with the Peruvian governing classes. The Quichua-Aymara race which inhabited Peru was inferior to the Mexican in general mental culture, if not in mental capacity, is is proved by its inability to invent any method of written communication or any adequate time-reckoning. In imitative art, too, the Peruvians were weak, save in pottery and rude modelling, and their religion savoured much more of the materialistic, and was altogether of a lower cultus.

The Country

The country in which the interesting civilisation of the Inca race was evolved presents physical features which profoundly affected the history of the race. In fact, it is probable that in no country in the world has the configuration of the land so modified the events in the life of the people dwelling within its borders. The chain of the Andes divides into two branches near the boundary between Bolivia and Chili, and, with the Cordillera de la Costa, encloses at a height of over 3000 feet the Desaguadero, a vast tableland with an area equal to France. To the north of this is Cuzco, the ancient capital of the Incas, to the south Potosi, the most elevated town in the world, whilst between them lies Lake Titicaca, the largest body of fresh water in South America. The whole country is dreary and desolate in the extreme. Cereals cannot ripen, and animals are rare. Yet it was in these desolate regions that the powerful and highly organised empire of Peru arose—an empire extending over an area 3000 miles long by 400 broad.

The Andeans

The prehistoric natives of the Andean region had evolved a civilisation long before the days of the Inca dynasties, and the cyclopean ruins of their edifices are to be found at intervals scattered over a wide field on the slopes of the range under the shadow of which they dwelt. Their most extraordinary achievement was probably the city of Tiahuanaco, on the southern shore of Lake Titicaca, built at a level 13,000 feet above the sea, occupying nearly half an acre in extent, and constructed of enormous megalithic blocks of trachytic rock. The great doorway, carved out of a single block of rock, is 7 feet in height by $13\frac{1}{2}$ feet wide, and $1\frac{1}{2}$ feet thick. The upper portion of this massive portal is carved with symbolic figures. In the centre is a figure in high relief, the head surrounded by solar rays, and in each hand a sceptre, the end of which terminates in the head of a condor. This figure is flanked on either side by three tiers of kneeling suppliants, each of whom is winged and bears a sceptre similar in design to the central ones. Elsewhere are mighty blocks of stone, some 36 feet long, remains of enormous walls, standing monoliths, and in earlier times colossal statues were seen on the site. When the Spanish conquerors arrived no tradition remained regarding the founders of these structures, and their

249

origin still remains a mystery ; but that they represent the remains of the capital of some mighty prehistoric kingdom is practically admitted.

A Strange Site

The greatest mystery of all regarding the ruins at Tiahuanaco is the selection of the site. For what reason did the prehistoric rulers of Peru build here ? The surroundings are totally unsuitable for the raising of such edifices, and the tableland upon which they are placed is at once desolate and difficult of access. The snow-line is contiguous, and breathing at such a height is no easy matter. There is no reason to suppose that climatic conditions in the day of these colossal builders were different from those which obtain at the present time. In face of these facts the position of Tiahuanaco remains an insoluble riddle.

Sacsahuaman and Ollantay

Other remains of these prehistoric people are found in various parts of Peru. At Sacsahuaman, perched on a hill above the city of Cuzco, is an immense fortified work six hundred yards long, built in three lines of wall consisting of enormous stones, some of which are twenty-seven feet in length. Pissac is also the site of wonderful ruined masonry and an ancient observatory. At Ollantay-tampu, forty-five miles to the north of Cuzco, is another of these gigantic fortresses, built to defend the valley of the Yucay. This stronghold is constructed for the most part of red porphyry, and its walls average twenty-five feet in height. The great cliff on which Ollantay is perched is covered from end to end with stupendous walls which zigzag from point to point of it like the salient angles of some modern fortalice. At intervals are placed round towers of stone provided

Doorway of Tiahuanaco
Carved out of a single block of stone

(See page 249)

Fortress at Ollantay-tampu

By permission of the late Sir Clements Markham

(See page 250)

with loopholes, from which doubtless arrows were discharged at the enemy. This outwork embraces a series of terraces, world-famous because of their gigantic outline and the problem of the use to which they were put. It is now practically agreed that these terraces were employed for the production of maize, in order that during a prolonged investment the beleaguered troops and country-folk might not want for a sufficiency of provender. The stone of which this fortress was built was quarried at a distance of seven miles, in a spot upwards of three thousand feet above the valley, and was dragged up the steep declivity of Ollantay by sheer human strength. The nicety with which the stones were fitted is marvellous.

The Drama-Legend of Ollantay

Among the dramatic works with which the ancient Incas were credited is that of *Apu-Ollanta*, which may recount the veritable story of a chieftain after whom the great stronghold was named. It was probably divided into scenes and supplied with stage directions at a later period, but the dialogue and songs are truly aboriginal. The period is that of the reign of the Inca Yupanqui Pachacutic, one of the most celebrated of the Peruvian monarchs. The central figure of the drama is a chieftain named Ollanta, who conceived a violent passion for a daughter of the Inca named Curi-Coyllur (Joyful Star). This passion was deemed unlawful, as no mere subject who was not of the blood-royal might aspire to the hand of a daughter of the Inca. As the play opens we overhear a dialogue between Ollanta and his man-servant Piqui-Chaqui (Flea-footed), who supplies what modern stage-managers would designate the " comic relief." They are talking of Ollanta's love for the princess, when they are confronted by the

high-priest of the Sun, who tries to dissuade the rash
chieftain from the dangerous course he is taking by
means of a miracle. In the next scene Curi-Coyllur is
seen in company with her mother, sorrowing over the
absence of her lover. A harvest song is here followed
by a love ditty of undoubtedly ancient origin. The
third scene represents Ollanta's interview with the Inca
in which he pleads his suit and is slighted by the
scornful monarch. Ollanta defies the king in a
resounding speech, with which the first act concludes.
In the first scene of the second act we are informed
that the disappointed chieftain has raised the standard
of rebellion, and the second scene is taken up with the
military preparations consequent upon the announcement of a general rising. In the third scene Rumi-
ñaui as general of the royal forces admits defeat by the
rebels.

The Love-Story of Curi-Coyllur

Curi-Coyllur gives birth to a daughter, and is
imprisoned in the darksome Convent of Virgins.
Her child, Yma Sumac (How Beautiful), is brought
up in the same building, but is ignorant of the near
presence of her mother. The little girl tells her
guardian of groans and lamentations which she has
heard in the convent garden, and of the tumultuous
emotions with which these sad sounds fill her heart.
The Inca Pachacutic's death is announced, and the
accession of his son, Yupanqui. Rebellion breaks out
once more, and the suppression of the malcontents is
again entrusted to Rumi-ñaui. That leader, having
tasted defeat already, resorts to cunning. He conceals
his men in a valley close by, and presents himself
covered with blood before Ollanta, who is at the
head of the rebels. He states that he has been

" Mother and child are united "

William Sewell

(See page 253)

(See page 250)

The Inca Fortress of Pissac

By permission of the late Sir Clements Markham

barbarously used by the royal troops, and that he desires to join the rebels. He takes part with Ollanta and his men in a drunken frolic, in which he incites them to drink heavily, and when they are overcome with liquor he brings up his troops and makes them prisoners.

Mother and Child

Yma Sumac, the beautiful little daughter of Curi-Coyllur, requests her guardian, Pitu Salla, so pitifully to be allowed to visit her mother in her dungeon that the woman consents, and mother and child are united. Ollanta is brought as a prisoner before the new Inca, who pardons him. At that juncture Yma Sumac enters hurriedly, and begs the monarch to free her mother, Curi-Coyllur. The Inca proceeds to the prison, restores the princess to her lover, and the drama concludes with the Inca bestowing his blessing upon the pair.

The play was first put into written form in the seventeenth century, has often been printed, and is now recognised as a genuine aboriginal production.

The Races of Peru

Many races went to make up the Peruvian people as they existed when first discovered by the conquering Spaniards. From the south came a civilising race which probably found a number of allied tribes, each existing separately in its own little valley, speaking a different dialect, or even language, from its neighbours, and in many instances employing different customs. Although tradition alleged that these invaders came from the north by sea within historical times, the more probable theory of their origin is one which states that they had followed the course of the affluents of the Amazon to the valleys where they dwelt when the more enlightened folk from the south came upon them. The remains of this aboriginal people—for, though they spoke diverse languages, the probability is that they were of one or not more than two stocks—are still found scattered over the coastal valleys in pyramidal mounds and adobe-built dwellings.

The Coming of the Incas

The arrival of the dominant race rudely broke in upon the peaceful existence of the aboriginal folk. This race, the Quichua-Aymara, probably had its place of origin in the Altaplanicie highlands of Bolivia, the eastern cordillera of the Andes. This they designated Tucuman (World's End), just as the Kiche of Guatemala were wont to describe the land of their origin as Ki Pixab (Corner of the Earth). The present republic of Argentina was at a remote period covered by a vast, partially land-locked sea, and beside the shores of this the ancestors of the Quichua-Aymara race may have settled as fishers and fowlers. They found a more permanent settlement on the shores of Lake Titicaca, where their traditions state that they made considerable advances in the arts of civilisation. It was, indeed, from Titicaca that the sun emerged from the sacred rock where he had erstwhile hidden himself. Here, too, the llama and paco were domesticated and agricultural life initiated, or perfected. The arts of irrigation and terrace-building—so marked as features of Peruvian civilisation—were also invented in this region, and the basis of a composite advancement laid.

The Quichua-Aymara

This people consisted of two groups, the Quichua and Aymara, so called from the two kindred tongues spoken by each respectively. These possess a common

254

grammatical structure, and a great number of words are common to both. They are in reality varying forms of one speech. From the valley of Titicaca the Aymara spread from the source of the Amazon river to the higher parts of the Andes range, so that in course of time they exhibited those qualities which stamp the mountaineer in every age and clime. The Quichua, on the other hand, occupied the warm valleys beyond the river Apurimac, to the north-west of the Aymara-speaking people—a tract equal to the central portion of the modern republic of Peru. The name "Quichua" implies a warm valley or sphere, in contradistinction to the "Yunca," or tropical districts of the coast and lowlands.

The Four Peoples

The metropolitan folk or Cuzco considered Peru to be divided into four sections—that of the Colla-suyu, with the valley of Titicaca as its centre, and stretching from the Bolivian highlands to Cuzco ; the Conti-suyu, between the Colla-suyu and the ocean ; the Quichua Chinchay-suyu, of the north-west ; and the Anti-suyu, of the *montaña* region. The Inca people, coming suddenly into these lands, annexed them with surprising rapidity, and, making the aboriginal tribes dependent upon their rule, spread themselves over the face of the country. Thus the ancient chroniclers. But it is obvious that such rapid conquest was a practical impossibility, and it is now understood that the Inca power was consolidated only some hundred years before the coming of Pizarro.

The Coming of Manco Ccapac

Peruvian myth has its Quetzalcoatl in Manco Ccapac, a veritable son of the sun. The Life-giver, observing the deplorable condition of mankind, who seemed to exist for war and feasting alone, despatched his son, Manco Ccapac, and his sister-wife, Mama Oullo Huaca, to earth for the purpose of instructing the degraded peoples in the arts of civilised life. The heavenly pair came to earth in the neighbourhood of Lake Titicaca, and were provided with a golden wedge which they were assured would sink into the earth at the precise spot on which they should commence their missionary labours. This phenomenon occurred at Cuzco, where the wedge disappeared. The derivation of the name Cuzco, which means "Navel," or, in more modern terms, "Hub of the Universe," proves that it was regarded as a great culture-centre. On this spot the civilising agents pitched their camp, gathering the uncultured folk of the country around them. Whilst Manco taught the men the arts of agriculture, Mama Oullo instructed the women in those of weaving and spinning. Great numbers gathered in the vicinity of Cuzco, and the foundations of a city were laid. Under the mild rule of the heavenly pair the land of Peru abounded in every desirable thing, like the Eden of Genesis. The legend of Manco Ccapac as we have it from an old Spanish source is worth giving. It is as follows : "There [in Tiahuanaco] the creator began to raise up the people and nations that are in that region, making one of each nation in clay, and painting the dresses that each one was to wear ; those that were to wear their hair, with hair, and those that were to be shorn, with hair cut. And to each nation was given the language that was to be spoken, and the songs to be sung, and the seeds and food that they were to sow. When the creator had finished painting and making the said nations and figures of clay, he gave life and soul to each one, as well man as woman, and ordered that they should pass under the earth. Thence each nation came up in the places to which he ordered them to go. Thus they say that some came out of caves, others issued from hills, others from fountains, others from the trunks of trees. From this cause and others, and owing to having come forth and multiplied from those places, and to having had the beginning of their lineage in them, they made *huacas*[1] and places of worship of them, in memory of the origin of their lineage. Thus each nation uses the dress with which they invest their *huaca;* and they say that the first that was born in that place was there turned into stone. Others say that they were turned into falcons, condors, and other animals and birds. Hence the *huacas* they use are in different shapes."

The Peruvian Creation-Story

The Incan Peruvians believed that all things emanated from Pachacamac, the all-pervading spirit, who provided the plants and animals (which they believed to be produced from the earth) with "souls." The earth itself they designated Pachacamama (Earth-Mother). Here we observe that Pachacamac was more the maker and moulder than the originator of matter, a view common to many American mythologies. Pachacamac it was who breathed the breath of life into man, but the Peruvian conception of him was only evolved in later Inca times, and by no means existed in the early days of Inca rule, although he was probably worshipped before this under another and less exalted shape. The mere exercise of will or thought was sufficient, according to the Peruvians, to accomplish the creative act. In the prayers to the creator, and in other portions of Inca rite, we read such expressions as "Let a man be," "Let a woman be," and "The creative word," which go to prove that the Peruvian consciousness had fully

[1] Sacred things.

grasped the idea of a creator capable of evolving matter out of nothingness. Occasionally we find the sun acting as a kind of demiurge or sub-creator. He it is who in later legend founds the city of Cuzco, and sends thither three eggs composed of gold, silver, and copper, from which spring the three classes of Peruvians, kings, priests, and slaves. The inevitable deluge occurs, after which we find the prehistoric town of Tiahuanaco regarded as the theatre of a new creation of man. Here the creator made man, and separated him into nations, making one of each nation out of the clay of the earth, painting the dresses that each was to wear, and endowing them with national songs, languages, seeds to sow suitable to the environment of each, and food such as they would require. Then he gave the peoples life and soul, and commanded them to enter the bowels of the earth, whence they came upward in the places where he ordered them to go. Perhaps this is one of the most complete ("wholesale" would be a better word) creation-myths in existence, and we can glean from its very completeness that it is by no means of simple origin, but of great complexity. It is obviously an attempt to harmonise several conflicting creation-stories, notably those in which the people are spoken of as emanating from caves, and the later one of the creation of men at Tiahuanaco, probably suggested to the Incas by the immense ruins at that place, for which they could not otherwise account.

Local Creation-Myths

In some of the more isolated valleys of Peru we discover local creation-myths. For example, in the coastal valley of Irma Pachacamac was not considered to be the creator of the sun, but to be himself a descendant of it. The first human beings created by

" Making one of each nation out of the clay of the earth "
William Sewell
(See page 258)

him were speedily separated, as the man died of hunger, but the woman supported herself by living on roots. The sun took compassion upon her and gave her a son whom Pachacamac slew and buried. But from his teeth there grew maize, from his ribs the long white roots of the manioc plant, and from his flesh various esculent plants.

The Character of Inca Civilisation

Apart from the treatment which they meted out to the subject races under their sway, the rule of the Inca monarchs was enlightened and contained the elements of high civilisation. It is scarcely clear whether the Inca race arrived in the country at such a date as would have permitted them to profit by adopting the arts and sciences of the Andean people who preceded them. But it may be affirmed that their arrival considerably post-dated the fall of the megalithic empire of the Andeans, so that in reality their civilisation was of their own manufacture. As architects they were by no means the inferiors of the prehistoric race, if the examples of their art did not bulk so massively, and the engineering skill with which they pushed long, straight tunnels through vast mountains and bridged seemingly impassable gorges still excites the wonder of modern experts. They also made long, straight roads after the most improved macadamised model. Their temples and palaces were adorned with gold and silver images and ornaments ; sumptuous baths supplied with hot and cold water by means of pipes laid in the earth were to be found in the mansions of the nobility, and much luxury and real comfort prevailed.

An Absolute Theocracy

The empire of Peru was the most absolute theocracy the world has ever seen. The Inca was the direct representative of the sun upon earth, the head of a socio-religious edifice intricate and highly organised. This colossal bureaucracy had ramifications into the very homes of the people. The Inca was represented in the provinces by governors of the blood-royal. Officials were placed above ten thousand families, a thousand families, and even ten families, upon the principle that the rays of the sun enter everywhere, and that therefore the light of the Inca must penetrate to every corner of the empire. There was no such thing as personal freedom. Every man, woman, and child was numbered, branded, and under surveillance as much as were the llamas in the royal herds. Individual effort or enterprise was unheard of. Some writers have stated that a system of state socialism obtained in Peru. If so, then state surveillance in Central Russia might also be branded as socialism. A man's life was planned for him by the authorities from the age of five years, and even the woman whom he was to marry was selected for him by the Government officials. The age at which the people should marry was fixed at not earlier than twenty-four years for a man and eighteen for a woman. Coloured ribbons worn round the head indicated the place of a person's birth or the province to which he belonged.

A Golden Temple

One of the most remarkable monuments of the Peruvian civilisation was the Coricancha (Town of Gold) at Cuzco, the principal fane of the sun-god. Its inner and outer walls were covered with plates of pure gold. Situated upon an eminence eighty feet high, the temple looked down upon gardens filled, according to the conquering Spaniards, with treasures of gold and silver. The animals, insects, the very trees, say the chroniclers, were of the precious metals, as were the spades, hoes, and other implements employed for keeping the ground in cultivation. Through the pleasances rippled the river Huatenay. Such was the glittering Intipampa (Field of the Sun). That the story is true, at least in part, is proved by the traveller Squier, who speaks of having seen in several houses in Cuzco sheets of gold preserved as relics which came from the Temple of the Sun. These, he says, were scarcely as thick as paper, and were stripped off the walls of the Coricancha by the exultant Spanish soldiery.

The Great Altar

But this house of gold had but a roof of thatch ! The Peruvians were ignorant of the principle of the arch, or else considered the feature unsuitable, for some reason best known to their architects. The doorways were formed of huge monoliths, and the entire aspect of the building was cyclopean. The interior displayed an ornate richness which impressed even the Spaniards, who had seen the wealth of many lands and Oriental kingdoms, and the gold-lust must have swelled within their hearts at sight of the great altar, behind which was a huge plate of the shining metal engraved with the features of the sun-god. The surface of this plate was enriched by a thousand gems, the scintillation of which was, according to eye-witnesses, almost insupportable. Around this dazzling sphere were seated the mummified corpses of the Inca kings, each on his throne, with sceptre in hand.

Planetary Temples

Surrounding the Coricancha several lesser temples clustered, all of them dedicated to one or other of the planetary bodies—to the moon, to Cuycha, the

rainbow, to Chasca, the planet Venus. In the temple
of the moon, the mythic mother of the Inca dynasty, a
great plate of silver, like the golden one which represented the face of the sun-god, depicted the features
of the moon-goddess, and around this the mummies
of the Inca queens sat in a semicircle, like their
spouses in the greater neighbouring fane. In the
rainbow temple of Cuycha the seven-hued arch of
heaven was depicted by a great arc of gold skilfully
tempered or painted in suitable colours. All the
utensils in these temples were of gold or silver. In
the principal building twelve large jars of silver held
the sacred grain, and even the pipes which conducted the
water-supply through the earth to the sanctuary were
of silver. Pedro Pizarro himself, besides other credible
eye-witnesses, vouched for these facts. The colossal
representation of the sun became the property of a certain Mancio Serra de Leguicano, a reckless cavalier and
noted gambler, who lost it on a single throw of the
dice ! Such was the spirit of the adventurers who conquered this golden realm for the crown of Spain. The
walls of the Coricancha are still standing, and this
marvellous shrine of the chief luminary of heaven, the
great god of the Peruvians, is now a Christian church.

The Mummies of Peru

The fact that the ancient Peruvians had a method
of mummification has tempted many " antiquarians "
to infer therefrom that they had some connection with
ancient Egypt. These theories are so numerous as to
give the unsophisticated reader the idea that a regular
system of immigration was carried on between Egypt
and America. As a matter of fact the method of
mummification in vogue in Peru was entirely different from that employed by the ancient Egyptians.

THE MUMMIES OF PERU

Peruvian mummies are met with at apparently all stages of the history of the native races. Megalithic tombs and monuments contain them in the doubled-up posture so common among early peoples all over the world. These megalithic tombs, or *chulpas*, as they are termed, are composed of a mass of rough stones and clay, faced with huge blocks of trachyte or basalt, so put together as to form a cist, in which the mummy was placed. The door invariably faces the east, so that it may catch the gleams of the rising sun—a proof of the prevalence of sun-worship. Squier alludes to one more than 24 feet high. An opening 18 inches square gave access to the sepulchral chamber, which was 11 feet square by 13 feet high. But the tomb had been entered before, and after getting in with much difficulty the explorer was forced to retreat empty-handed.

Many of these *chulpas* are circular, and painted in gay primary colours. They are very numerous in Bolivia, an old Peruvian province, and in the basin of Lake Titicaca they abound. The dead were wrapped in llama-skins, on which the outlines of the eyes and mouth were carefully marked. The corpse was then arrayed in other garments, and the door of the tomb walled up. In some parts of Peru the dead were mummified and placed in the dwelling-houses beside the living. In the rarefied air of the plateaus the bodies rapidly became innocuous, and the custom was not the insanitary one we might imagine it to be.

On the Pacific coast the method of mummification was somewhat different. The body was reduced to a complete state of desiccation, and was deposited in a tomb constructed of stone or adobe. Vases intended to hold maize or *chicha* liquor were placed beside the corpse, and copper hatchets, mirrors of polished stone, earrings, and bracelets have been discovered in these burial-places. Some of the remains are wrapped in rich cloth, and vases of gold and silver were placed beside them. Golden plaques are often discovered in the mouths, probably symbolic of the sun. The bodies exhibit no traces of embalming, and are usually in a sitting posture. Some of them have evidently been dried before inhumation, whilst others are covered with a resinous substance. They are generally accompanied by the various articles used during life ; the men have their weapons and ornaments, women their household implements, and children their toys. The dryness of the climate, as in Egypt, keeps these relics in a wonderful state of preservation. In the grave of a woman were found not only vases of every shape, but also some cloth she had commenced to weave, which her death had perhaps prevented her from completing. Her light brown hair was carefully combed and plaited, and the legs from the ankle to the knee were painted red, after the fashion in vogue among Peruvian beauties, while little bladders of toilet-powder and gums were thoughtfully placed beside her for her use in the life to come.

Laws and Customs

The legal code of the Incas was severe in the extreme. Murderers and adulterers were punished by death, and the unpardonable sin appears to have been blasphemy against the sun, or his earthly representative, the Inca. The Virgin of the Sun (or nun) who broke her vow was buried alive, and the village from whence she came was razed to the ground. Flogging was administered for minor offences. A peculiar and very trying punishment must have been that of carrying a heavy stone for a certain time.

On marriage a home was apportioned to each couple, and land assigned to them sufficient for their support. When a child was born a separate allowance was given it—one *fanega* for a boy, and half that amount for a girl, the *fanega* being equal to the area which could be sown with a hundred pounds of maize. There is something repulsive in the Inca code, with its grandmotherly legislation ; and if this tyranny was beneficent, it was devised merely to serve its own ends and hound on the unhappy people under its control like dumb, driven cattle. The outlook of the average native was limited in the extreme. The Inca class of priests and warriors retained every vestige of authority ; and that they employed their power unmercifully to grind down the millions beneath them was a sufficient excuse for the Spanish Conquistadores in dispossessing them of the empire they had so harshly administered.

The public ground was divided afresh every year according to the number of the members of each family, and agrarian laws were strictly fixed. Private property did not exist among the people of the lower classes, who merely farmed the lot which each year was placed at their disposal. Besides this, the people had perforce to cultivate the lands sacred to the Inca, and only the aged and the sick could evade this duty.

The Peruvian Calendar

The standard chronology known to the Peru of the Incas was a simple lunar reckoning. But the four principal points in the sun's course were denoted by means of the *intihuatana*, a device consisting of a large rock surmounted by a small cone, the shadow of which, falling on certain notches on the stone below, marked the date of the great sun-festivals. The Peruvians, however, had no definite calendar. At Cuzco, the

capital, the solstices were gauged by pillars called
pachacta unanchac, or indicators of time, which were
placed in four groups (two pillars to a group) on
promontories, two in the direction of sunrise and two
in that of sunset, to mark the extreme points of the
sun's rising and setting. By this means they were
enabled to distinguish the arrival and departure of the
solstices, during which the sun never went beyond
the middle pair of pillars. The Inca astronomer's
approximation to the year was 360 days, which were
divided into twelve moons of thirty days each. These
moons were not calendar months in the correct sense,
but simply a succession of lunations, which commenced
with the winter solstice. This method, which must
ultimately have proved confusing, does not seem to
have been altered to co-ordinate with the reckoning of
the succession of years. The names of the twelve
moons, which had some reference to the daily life of
the Peruvian, were as follows :

Huchuy Pucuy Quilla (Small Growing Moon), approximately
January.

Hatun Pucuy Quilla (Great Growing Moon), approximately
February.

Pancar Pucuy Quilla (Flower-growing Moon), approximately
March.

Ayrihua Quilla (Twin Ears Moon), approximately April.

Aymuray Quilla (Harvest Moon), approximately May.

Auray Cusqui Quilla (Breaking Soil), approximately June.

Chahua Huarqui Quilla (Irrigation Moon), approximately July.

Tarpuy Quilla (Sowing Moon), approximately August.

Ccoya Raymi Quilla (Moon of the Moon Feast), approximately
September.

Uma Raymi Quilla (Moon of the Feast of the Province of Uma),
approximately October.

Ayamarca Raymi Quilla (Moon of the Feast of the Province of
Ayamarca), approximately November.

Ccapac Raymi Quilla (Moon of the Great Feast of the Sun),
approximately December.

The Festivals

That the Peruvian standard of time, as with all American people, was taken from the natural course of the moon is known chiefly from the fact that the principal religious festivals began on the new moon following a solstice or equinox. The ceremonies connected with the greatest festival, the Ccapac Raymi, were made to date near the lunar phases, the two stages commencing with the ninth day of the December moon and twenty-first day, or last quarter. But while these lunar phases indicated certain festivals, it very often happened that the civil authorities followed a reckoning of their own, in preference to accepting ecclesiastical rule. Considerable significance was attached to each month by the Peruvians regarding the nature of their festivals. The solstices and equinoxes were the occasions of established ceremonies. The arrival of the winter solstice, which in Peru occurs in June, was celebrated by the Intip Raymi (Great Feast of the Sun). The principal Peruvian feast, which took place at the summer solstice, when the new year was supposed to begin, was the national feast of the great god Pachacamac, and was called Ccapac Raymi. Molina, Fernandez, and Garcilasso, however, date the new year from the winter solstice. The third festival of the Inca year, the Ccapac Sitŭa, or Ccoya Raymi (Moon Feast), which is signalled by the beginning of the rainy season, occurred in September. In general character these festivals appear to have been simple, and even childlike. The sacrifice of animals taken from sacred herds of llamas was doubtless a principal feature of the ceremony, accompanied by the offering up of *maguey*, or maize spirit, and followed by the performance of symbolic dances.

The Llama

The llama was the chief domestic animal of Peru. All llamas were the property of the Inca. Like the camel, its distant relative, this creature can subsist for long periods upon little nourishment, and it is suitable for the carriage of moderate loads. Each year a certain amount of llama wool was given to the Peruvian family, according to the number of women it contained, and these wove it into garments, whatever was over being stored away in the public cloth-magazines for the general use. The large flocks of llamas and alpacas also afforded a supply of meat for the people such as the Mexicans never possessed. Naturally much attention was given to the breeding of these animals, and the alpaca was as carefully regarded by the Peruvian as the sheep by the farmer of to-day. The guanacos and vicuñas, wild animals of the llama or auchenia family, were also sources of food- and wool-supply.

Architecture of the Incas

The art in which the Incan Peruvians displayed the greatest advance was that of architecture. The earlier style of Inca building shows that it was closely modelled, as has already been pointed out, on that of the megalithic masons of the Tiahuanaco district, but the later style shows stones laid in regular courses, varying in length. No cement or mortar of any kind was employed, the structure depending for stability upon the accuracy with which the stones were fitted to each other. An enormous amount of labour must have been expended upon this part of the work, for in the monuments of Peruvian architecture which still exist it is impossible to insert even a needle between the stones of which they are composed. The palaces and temples were built around a courtyard, and most of the principal buildings had a hall of considerable dimensions attached to them, which, like the baronial halls of the England of the Middle Ages, served for feasting or ceremony. In this style is built the front of the palace on the Colcampata, overlooking the city of Cuzco, under the fortress which is supposed to have been the dwelling of Manco Ccapac, the first Inca. Palaces at Yucay and Chinchero are also of this type.

Unsurpassed Workmanship

In an illuminating passage upon Inca architecture Sir Clements Markham, the greatest living authority upon matters Peruvian, says :

" In Cuzco the stone used is a dark trachyte, and the coarse grain secured greater adhesion between the blocks. The workmanship is unsurpassed, and the world has nothing to show in the way of stone-cutting and fitting to equal the skill and accuracy displayed in the Ynca structures of Cuzco. No cement is used, and the larger stones are in the lowest row, each ascending course being narrower, which presents a most pleasing effect. The edifices were built round a court, upon which the rooms opened, and some of the great halls were 200 paces long by 60 wide, the height being 35 to 40 feet, besides the spring of the roof. The roofs were thatch ; and we are able to form an idea of their construction from one which is still preserved, after a lapse of three centuries. This is on a circular building called the Sondor-huasi, at Azangaro, and it shows that even thatch in the hands of tasteful builders will make a sightly roof for imposing edifices, and that the interior ornament of such a roof may be exceedingly beautiful."

The Temple of Viracocha

The temple of Viracocha, at Cacha, in the valley of the Vilcamayu, is built on a plan different from that of any other sacred building in Peru. Its ruins consist of a wall of adobe or clay 40 feet high and 330 long, built on stone foundations 8 feet in height. The roof was supported on twenty-five columns, and the width of the structure was 87 feet. It was a place of pilgrimage, and the caravanserais where the Faithful were wont to be housed still stand around the ruined fane.

Titicaca

The most sacred of the Peruvian shrines, however, was Titicaca, an island on the lake of that name. The island of Coati, hard by, enjoyed an equal reverence. Terraced platforms on the former, reached by flights of steps, support two buildings provided for the use of pilgrims about to proceed to Coati. On Titicaca there are the ruins of an extensive palace which commands a splendid view of the surrounding barren country. A great bath or tank is situated half-way down a long range of terraces supported by cut stone masonry, and the pool, 40 feet long by 10, and 5 feet deep, has similar walls on three sides. Below this tank the water is made to irrigate terrace after terrace until it falls into the lake.

Coati

The island of Coati is about six miles distant. The principal building is on one of the loftiest of seven terraces, once radiant with flowers and shrubs, and filled with rich loam transported from a more fertile region. It is placed on three sides of a square, 183 feet long by 80, and is of stone laid in clay and coated with plaster. " It has," says Markham, " thirty-five chambers, only one of which is faced with hewn stones. The ornament on the façade consists of elaborate niches, which agreeably break the monotony of the wall, and above them runs a projecting cornice. The walls were painted yellow, and the niches red ; and there was a high-pitched roof, broken here and there by gables. The two largest chambers are 20 long by 12, and loftier than the rest, each with a great niche in the wall facing the entrance. These were probably the holy places or shrines of the temple. The beautiful series of terraces falls off from the esplanade of the temple to the shores of the lake."

Mysterious Chimu

The coast folk, of a different race from the Incas, had their centre of civilisation near the city of Truxillo, on the plain of Chimu. Here the ruins of a great city litter the plain for many acres. Arising from the mass of ruin, at intervals stand *huacas*, or artificial hills. The city was supplied with water by means of small canals, which also served to irrigate the gardens. The mounds alluded to were used for sepulture, and the largest, at Moche, is 800 feet long by 470 feet in breadth, and 200 feet in height. It is constructed of adobes. Besides serving the purpose of a cemetery, this mound probably supported a large temple on its summit.

The Palace

A vast palace occupied a commanding position. Its great hall was 100 feet long by 52 broad, and its walls were covered with a highly ornate series of arabesques in relief done in stucco, like the fretwork on the walls of Palenque. Another hall close at hand is ornamented in coloured stucco, and from it branch off many small rooms, which were evidently dormitories. From the first hall a long corridor leads to secret storehouses, where many vessels of gold and silver have been discovered hidden away, as if to secure them either from marauding bands or the gaze of the vulgar. All of these structures are hollowed out of a vast mound covering several acres, so that the entire building may be said to be partially subterranean in character. "About a hundred yards to the westward of this palace there was a sepulchral mound where many relics were discovered. The bodies were wrapped in cloths, woven in ornamental figures and patterns of different colours. On some of the cloths were sewn plates of silver, and they were edged with borders of feathers, the silver being occasionally cut in the shape of fishes. Among the ruins of the city there are great rectangular areas enclosed by massive walls, and containing courts, streets, dwellings, and reservoirs for water. The largest is about a mile south of the mound-palace, and is 550 yards long by 400. The outer wall is about 30 feet high, 10 feet thick at the base, with sides inclining toward each other. Some of the interior walls are highly ornamented in stuccoed patterns ; and in one part there is an edifice containing forty-five chambers or cells, in five rows of nine each, which is supposed to have been a prison. The enclosure also contained a reservoir 450 feet long by 195 broad, and 60 feet deep."

The Civilisation of Chimu

The ruins of Chimu are undoubtedly the outcome of a superior standard of civilisation. The buildings are elaborate, as are their internal arrangements. The extent of the city is great, and the art displayed in the manufacture of the utensils discovered within it and the taste evinced in the numerous wall-patterns show that a people of advanced culture inhabited it. The jeweller's work is in high relief, and the pottery and plaques found exhibit much artistic excellence.

Pachacamac

The famous ruins of the temple and city of Pachacamac, near the valley of Lurin, to the south of Lima, overlook the Pacific Ocean from a height of 500 feet. Four vast terraces still bear mighty perpendicular walls, at one time painted red. Here was found the only perfect Peruvian arch, built of large adobe bricks—a proof that the Peruvian mind did not stand still in matters architectural at least.

Irrigation Works

It was in works of irrigation, however, that the race exhibited its greatest engineering genius. In the valley of Nasca the Incas cut deep trenches to reinforce the irrigating power of a small river, and carried the system high up into the mountains, in order that the rainfall coming therefrom might be conducted into the needful channel. Lower down the valley the main watercourse is deflected into many branches, which irrigate each estate by feeding the small surface streams. This system adequately serves the fifteen estates of Nasca to-day! Another high-level canal for the irrigation of pasture-lands was led for more than a hundred and fifty miles along the eastern slope of the central cordillera.

A Singular Discovery

In Peru, as in Mexico, it is probable that the cross was employed as a symbol of the four winds. An account of the expedition of Fuentes to the valley of

Chichas recounts the discovery of a wooden cross as follows :[1]

" When the settlers who accompanied Fuentes in his glorious expedition approached the valley they found a wooden cross, hidden, as if purposely, in the most intricate part of the mountains. As there is not anything more flattering to the vanity of a credulous man than to be enabled to bring forward his testimony in the relation of a prodigy, the devotion of these good conquerors was kindled to such a degree by the discovery of this sacred memorial that they instantly hailed it as miraculous and divine. They accordingly carried it in procession to the town, and placed it in the church belonging to the convent of San Francisco, where it is still worshipped. It appears next to impossible that there should not, at that time, have been any individual among them sufficiently enlightened to combat such a persuasion, since, in reality, there was nothing miraculous in the finding of this cross, there having been other Christian settlers, before the arrival of Fuentes, in the same valley. The opinion, notwithstanding, that the discovery was altogether miraculous, instead of having been abandoned at the commencement, was confirmed still more and more with the progress of time. The Jesuits Antonio Ruiz and Pedro Lozano, in their respective histories of the missions of Paraguay, &c., undertook to demonstrate that the Apostle St. Thomas had been in America. This thesis, which was so novel, and so well calculated to draw the public attention, required, more than any other, the aid of the most powerful reasons, and of the most irrefragable documents, to be able to maintain itself, even in an hypothetical sense ; but nothing of all this was brought forward. Certain miserable con-

[1] Skinner's *State of Peru*, p. 313 (1805).

jectures, prepossession, and personal interest, supplied the place of truth and criticism. The form of a human foot, which they fancied they saw imprinted on the rock, and the different fables of this description invented by ignorance at every step, were the sole foundations on which all the relations on this subject were made to repose. The one touching the peregrinations of St. Thomas from Brazil to Quito must be deemed apocryphal, when it is considered that the above reverend fathers describe the Apostle with the staff in the hand, the black cassock girt about the waist, and all the other trappings which distinguish the missionaries of the society. The credit which these histories obtained at the commencement was equal to that bestowed on the cross of Tarija, which remained in the predicament of being the one St. Thomas had planted in person, in the continent of America."

The Chibchas

A people called the Chibchas dwelt at a very high point of the Andes range. They were brave and industrious, and possessed a culture of their own. They defended themselves against much stronger native races, but after the Spanish conquest their country was included in New Granada, and is now part of the United States of Colombia. Less experienced than the Peruvians or Aztecs, they could, however, weave and dye, carve and engrave, make roads, build temples, and work in stone, wood, and metals. They also worked in pottery and jewellery, making silver pendants and collars of shells and collars of precious stones. They were a wealthy folk, and their Spanish conquerors obtained much spoil. Little is known concerning them or their language, and there is not much of interest in the traditions relating to them.

Their mythology was simple. They believed the moon was the wife of Bochica, who represented the sun, and as she tried to destroy men Bochica only allowed her to give light during the night. When the aborigines were in a condition of barbarism Bochica taught them and civilised them. The legends about Bochica resemble in many points those about Quetzalcoatl or Manco Ccapac, as well as those relating to the founder of Buddhism and the first Inca of Peru. The Chibchas offered human sacrifices to their gods at certain intervals, and kept the wretched victim for some years in preparation for his doom. They venerated greatly the Lake of Quatavita, and are supposed to have flung their treasures into it when they were conquered. Although many attempts have been made to recover these, little of value has been found.

The Chibchas appear to have given allegiance to two leaders, one the Zippa, who lived at Bogota, the other the Zoque, who lived at Hunsa, now Tunja. These chiefs ruled supreme. Like the Incas, they could only have one lawful wife, and their sons did not succeed them—their power passed, as in some Central African tribes, to the eldest son of the sister.

When the Zippa died, sweet-smelling resin took the place of his internal parts, and the body was put in a wooden coffin, with sheets of gold for ornamentation. The coffin was hidden in an unknown sepulchre, and these tombs have never been discovered—at least, so say the Spaniards. Their weapons, garments, objects of daily use, even jars of *chicha*, were buried with these chiefs. It is very likely that a cave where rows of mummies richly dressed were found, and many jewels, was the secret burying-place of the Zippas and the Zoques. To these folk death meant only a continuation of the life on earth.

A Severe Legal Code

The laws of the Chibchas were severe—death was meted out to the murderer, and bodily punishment for stealing. A coward was made to look like a woman and do her work, while to an unfaithful wife was administered a dose of red pepper, which, if swallowed, released the culprit from the penalty of death and entitled her to an apology from her husband. The Chibchas made no use of cattle, and lived on honey. Their houses were built of clay, and were set in the midst of an enclosure guarded by watch-towers. The roofs were of a conical shape, covered with reed mats, and skilfully interlaced rushes were used to close the openings.

The Chibchas were skilful in working bronze, lead, copper, tin, gold, and silver, but not iron. The Saint-Germain Museum has many specimens of gold and silver articles made by these people. M. Uricaechea has still more uncommon specimens in his collection, such as two golden masks of the human face larger than life, and a great number of statuettes of men, and images of monkeys and frogs.

The Chibchas traded with what they made, exporting the rock salt they found in their own country and receiving in exchange cereals with which to cultivate their own poor soil. They also made curious little ornaments which might have passed for money, but they are not supposed to have understood coinage. They had few stone columns—only large granite rocks covered with huge figures of tigers and crocodiles. Humboldt mentions these, and two very high columns, covered with sculpture, at the junction of the Carare and Magdalena, greatly revered by the natives, were raised probably by the Chibchas.

A Strange Mnemonic System

On the arrival of the Spaniards the Peruvians were unacquainted with any system of writing or numeration. The only means of recording events they possessed was that provided by *quipos*, knotted pieces of string or hide of varying length and colour. According to the length or colour of these cords the significance of the record varied ; it was sometimes historical and sometimes mathematical. *Quipos* relating to the history of the Incas were carefully preserved by an officer called Quipo Camayol—literally, "The Guardian of the *Quipos*." The greater number were destroyed as monuments of idolatry by the fanatical Spanish monks who came over with the Conquistadores, but their loss is by no means important, as no study, however profound, could possibly unriddle the system upon which they were based. The Peruvians, however, long continued to use them in secret.

Practical Use of the Quipos

The Marquis de Nadaillac has placed on record a use to which the *quipos* were put in more modern times. He says : "A great revolt against the Spaniards was organised in 1792. As was found out later, the revolt had been organised by means of messengers carrying a piece of wood in which were enclosed threads the ends of which were formed of red, black, blue, or white fringes. The black thread had four knots, which signified that the messenger had started from Vladura, the residence of the chief of the conspiracy, four days after full moon. The white thread had ten knots, which signified that the revolt would break out ten days after the arrival of the messenger.

The person to whom the keeper was sent had in his turn to make a knot in the red thread if he agreed to join the confederates ; in the red and blue threads, on the contrary, if he refused." It was by means of these *quipos* that the Incas transmitted their instructions. On all the roads starting from the capital, at distances rarely exceeding five miles, rose *tambos*, or stations for the *chasquis* or couriers, who went from one post to another. The orders of the Inca thus became disseminated with great rapidity. Orders which emanated directly from the sovereign were marked with a red thread of the royal *llantu* (mantle), and nothing, as historians assure us, could equal the respect with which these messages were received.

The Incas as Craftsmen

The Incan Peruvians had made some progress in the metallurgic, ceramic, and textile arts. By washing the sands of the rivers of Caravaya they obtained large quantities of gold, and they extracted silver from the ore by means of blast-furnaces. Copper also was abundant, and was employed to manufacture bronze, of which most of their implements were made. Although it is difficult to know at what period their mining operations were carried on, it is evident that they could only have learned the art through long experience. Many proofs are to be found of their skill in jewellery, and amongst these are wonderful statuettes which they made from an amalgam of gold and mercury, afterwards exposed to great heat. A number of curious little ornaments made of various substances, with a little hole bored through them, were frequently found under the *huacas*—probably talismans. The finest handiwork of the Incas was undoubtedly in jewellery ; but unfortunately most of the examples of their work in this craft were melted down to assuage the insatiable avarice of the Spanish conquerors, and are therefore for ever lost to us. The spade and chisel employed in olden times by the Peruvians are much the same as the people use now, but some of their tools were clumsy. Their javelins, tomahawks, and other military arms were very futile weapons. Some found near the mines of Pasco were made of stone.

The spinning, weaving, and dyeing of the Peruvians were unequalled in aboriginal America, their cloths and tapestries being both graceful in design and strong in texture.

Stamps of bark or earthenware were employed to fix designs upon their woollen stuffs, and feathers were added to the garments made from these, the combination producing a gay effect much admired by the Spaniards. The British Museum possesses some good specimens of these manufactures.

Pottery

The Peruvians excelled in the potter's art. The pottery was baked in a kiln, and was varied in colour, red, black, and grey being the favourite shades. It was varnished outside, and the vases were moulded in two pieces and joined before heating. Much of the work is of great grace and elegance, and the shapes of animals were very skilfully imitated. Many drinking-cups of elegant design have been discovered, and some vases are of considerable size, measuring over three feet in height. A simple geometric pattern is usually employed for decoration, but sometimes rows of birds and insects figure in the ceramics. The pottery of the coast people is more rich and varied than that of the Inca race proper, and among its types we find vases moulded in the form of human faces, many of them exhibiting so

1. Vase of painted terra-cotta in form of a seated figure,
with busts on each side

2. Three black terra-cotta vases

Photo Mansell & Co.

(See page 280)

much character that we are forced to conclude that they are veritable portraits.   Fine stone dishes are often found, as well as platters of wood, and these frequently bear as ornament tasteful carvings representing serpents.   On several cups and vases are painted representations of battles between the Inca forces and the savages of the eastern forests using bows and arrows ; below wander the animals of the forest region, a brightly painted group.

The Archæological Museum of Madrid gives a representation of very varied kinds of Peruvian pottery, including some specimens modelled upon a series of plants, interesting to botanists.   The Louvre collections have one or two interesting examples of earthenware, as well as the Ethnographical Museum of St. Petersburg, and in all these collections there are types which are believed to be peculiar to the Old World.

The Trocadero Museum has a very curious specimen with two necks called the "Salvador."   A drawing on the vase represents a man with a tomahawk.   The Peruvians, like the Mexicans, also made musical instruments out of earthenware, and heavy ornaments, principally for the ear.

Historical Sketch of the Incan Peruvians

The Inca dominion, as the Spaniards found it, was instituted only about a century before the coming of the white man.   Before that time Inca sway held good over scattered portions of the country, but had not extended over the entire territory which in later times was connected with the Inca name.   That it was founded on the wreck of a more ancient power which once existed in the district of Chinchay-suyu there can be little doubt.   This power was wielded over a space bounded by the lake of Chinchay-cocha on the north and Abancay on the south, and extended to the Pacific at the valley of Chincha. It was constituted by an alliance of tribes under the leadership of the chief of Pucara, in the Huanca country. A branch of this confederacy, the Chanca, pushing southward in a general movement, encountered the Inca people or Colla-suyu, who, under their leader, Pachacutic, a young but determined chieftain, defeated the invaders in a decisive battle near Cuzco. In consequence of this defeat the Chanca deserted their former allies and made common cause with their victors. Together the armies made a determined attack on the Huanca alliance, which they broke up, and conquered the northern districts of the Chinchay-suyu. Thus Central Peru fell to the Inca arms.

The Inca Monarchs

Inca history, or rather tradition, as we must call it in the light of an unparalleled lack of original documentary evidence, spoke of a series of eleven monarchs from Manco Ccapac to Huaina Ccapac, who died shortly before the Spanish conquest. These had reigned for a collective period of nearly 350 years. The evidence that these chiefs had reigned was of the best, for their mummified bodies were preserved in the great Temple of the Sun at Cuzco, already described. There they received the same daily service as when in the flesh. Their private herds of llamas and slaves were still understood to belong to them, and food and drink were placed before them at stated intervals. Clothes were made for them, and they were carried about in palanquins as if for daily exercise. The descendants of each at periodical intervals feasted on the produce of their ancestor's private estate, and his mummy was set in the centre of the diners and treated as the principal guest.

The First Incas

After Manco Ccapac and his immediate successor, Sinchi Roca (Wise Chief), Lloque Yupanqui comes third in the series. He died while his son was still a child. Concerning Mayta Ccapac, who commenced his reign while yet a minor, but little is known. He was followed by Ccapac Yupanqui, who defeated the Conti-suyu, who had grown alarmed at the great power recently attained by Cuzco. The Inca and his men were attacked whilst about to offer sacrifice. A second attempt to sack Cuzco and divide its spoil and the women attached to the great Temple of the Sun like-wise ended in the total discomfiture of the jealous invaders. With Inca Roca, the next Inca, a new dynasty commences, but it is well-nigh impossible to trace the connection between it and the preceding one. Of the origin of Inca Roca nothing is related save that he claimed descent from Manco Ccapac. Roca, instead of waiting to be attacked in his own dominions, boldly confronted the Conti-suyu in their own territory, defeated them decisively at Pumatampu, and compelled them to yield him tribute. His successor, Yahuar-huaccac, initiated a similar campaign against the Colla-suyu people, against whom he had the assistance of the conquered Conti-suyu. But at a feast which he held in Cuzco before setting out he was attacked by his allies, and fled to the Coricancha, or Golden Temple of the Sun, for refuge, along with his wives. Resistance was unavailing, and the Inca and many of his favourites were slaughtered. The allied tribes which had over-run Central Peru now threatened Cuzco, and had they advanced with promptitude the Inca dynasty would have been wiped out and the city reduced to ruins. A strong man was at hand, however, who was capable of dealing with the extremely dangerous situation which had arisen. This was Viracocha, a chieftain chosen by the vote of the assembled warriors of Cuzco. By a prudent conciliation of the Conti-suyu and Colla-suyu he established a confederation which not only put an end to all threats of invasion, but so menaced the invaders that they were glad to return to their own territory and place it in a suitable state of defence.

Viracocha the Great

With Viracocha the Great, or "Godlike," the period of true Inca ascendancy commences. He was the real founder of the enlarged Inca dominion. He was elected Inca on his personal merits, and during a vigorous reign succeeded in making the influence of Cuzco felt in the contiguous southern regions. In his old age he retired to his country seats at Yucay and Xaquixahuana, and left the conduct of the realm to his son and successor, Urco-Inca, a weak-minded voluptuary, who neglected his royal duties, and was superseded by his younger brother, Pachacutic, a famous character in Inca history.

The Plain of Blood

The commencement of Pachacutic's reign witnessed one of the most sanguinary battles in the history of Peru. Hastu-huaraca, chief of the Antahuayllas, in the Chanca country, invaded the Inca territory, and encamped on the hills of Carmenca, which overlooks Cuzco. Pachacutic held a parley with him, but all to no purpose, for the powerful invader was determined to humble the Inca dynasty to the dust. Battle was speedily joined. The first day's fight was indecisive, but on the succeeding day Pachacutic won a great victory, the larger part of the invading force being left dead on the field of battle, and Hastu-huaraca retreating with five hundred followers only. The battle of Yahuar-pampa (Plain of Blood) was the turning-point in Peruvian history. The young Inca, formerly known as Yupanqui, was now called Pacha-cutic (He who changes the World). The warriors of the south made full submission to him, and came in crowds to offer him their services and seek his alliance and friendship, and he shortly found himself supreme in the territories over which his predecessors had exercised merely a nominal control.

The Conquest of Middle Peru

Hastu-huaraca, who had been commissioned by the allied tribesmen of Chinchay-suyu to reduce the Incas, now threw in his lot with them, and together conqueror and conquered proceeded to the liberation of the district of Chinchay-suyu from the tyranny of the Huanca alliance. The reduction of the southern portion of that territory was speedily accomplished. In the valley of Xauxa the invaders came upon the army of the Huanca, on which they inflicted a final defeat. The Inca spared and liberated the prisoners of war, who were numerous. Once more, at Tarma, were the Huanca beaten, after which all resistance appears to have been overcome. The city-state of Cuzco was now the dominant power throughout the whole of Central Peru, a territory 300 miles in length, whilst it exercised a kind of suzerainty over a district of equal extent toward the south-east, which it shortly converted into actual dominion.

Fusion of Races

This conquest of Central Peru led to the fusing of the Quichua-speaking tribes on the left bank of the Apurimac with the Aymara-speaking folk on the right bank, with the result that the more numerous Quichua speedily gained linguistic ascendancy over their brethren the Aymara. Subsequently to this the peoples of Southern and Central Peru, led by Inca headmen, swept in a great wave of migration over Cerro de Pasco, where they met with little or no resistance, and Pachacutic lived to be lord over a dominion extending for a thousand miles to the northward, and founder of a great Inca colony south of the equator almost identical in outline with the republic of Ecuador.

Two Branches of the Incas

These conquests, or rather race-movements, split up the Inca people into two separate portions, the respective centres of which were well-nigh a thousand miles apart. The centre of the northern district was at Tumipampa, Riopampa, and Quito at different periods. The political separation of these areas was only a question of time. Geographical conditions almost totally divided the two portions of the empire, a sparsely populated stretch of country 400 miles in extent lying between them (see map, p. 333.)

The Laws of Pachacutic

Pachacutic united to his fame as a warrior the reputation of a wise and liberal ruler. He built the great Temple of the Sun at Cuzco, probably on the site of a still older building, and established in its walls the convent in which five hundred maidens were set apart for the service of the god. He also, it is said, instituted the great rite of the Ccapac-cocha, at which maize, cloth, llamas, and children were sacrificed in honour of the sun-god. He devised a kind of census, by which governors were compelled periodically to render an account of the population under their

rule. This statement was made by means of *quipos*.
Agriculture was his peculiar care, and he was stringent
in the enforcement of laws regarding the tilling of the
soil, the foundation and upkeep of stores and granaries,
and the regulation of labour in general. As an architect
he took upon himself the task of personally designing
the principal buildings of the city of Cuzco, which were
rebuilt under his instructions and in accordance with
models moulded from clay by his own hands. He
appears to have had a passion for order, and to him we
may be justified in tracing the rigorous and almost
grandmotherly system under which the Peruvians
were living at the time of the arrival of their Spanish
conquerors. To Pachacutic, too, is assigned the raising
of the immense fortress of Sacsahuaman, already
described. He further instituted the order of knight-
hood known as Auqui, or "Warrior," entrance to
which was granted to suitable applicants at the great
feast of Ccapac Raymi, or Festival of the Sun. He
also named the succession of moons, and erected
the pillars on the hill of Carmenca by which the season
of solstice was found. In short, all law and order
which had a place in the Peruvian social economy were
attributed to him, and we may designate him the
Alfred of his race.

Tupac-Yupanqui

Pachacutic's son, Tupac-Yupanqui, for some time
before his father's death acted as his lieutenant. His
name signifies "Bright" or "Shining." His activity
extended to every portion of the Inca dominion, the
borders of which he enlarged, suppressing revolts, sub-
jugating tribes not wholly brought within the pale of
Inca influence, and generally completing the work so
ably begun by his father.

"The Gibbet"

A spirit of cruelty and excess such as was unknown to Pachacutic marked the military exploits of Tupac. In the valley of Huarco, near the Pacific coast, for example, he was repulsed by the natives, who were well supplied with food and stores of all sorts, and whose town was well fortified and very strongly situated. Tupac constructed an immense camp, or rather town, the outlines of which recalled those of his capital of Cuzco, on a hill opposite the city, and here he calmly sat down to watch the gradual starvation of the enemy. This siege continued for three years, until the wretched defenders, driven to despair through want of food, capitulated, relying on the assurance of their conqueror that they should become a part of the Inca nation and that their daughters should become the wives of Inca youths. The submission of their chiefs having been made, Tupac ordered a general massacre of the warriors and principal civilians. At the conquest the Spaniards could still see the immense heaps of bones which littered the spot where this heartless holocaust took place, and the name Huarco (The Gibbet) became indissolubly associated with the district.

Huaina Ccapac

Tupac died in 1493, and was succeeded by his son Huaina Ccapac (The Young Chief). Huaina was about twenty-two years of age at the time of his father's death, and although the late Inca had named Ccapac-Huari, his son by another wife, as his successor, the claims of Huaina were recognised. His reign was peaceful, and was marked by wise administrative improvements and engineering effort. At the same

288

time he was busily employed in holding the savage
peoples who surrounded his empire in check. He
favoured the northern colony, and rebuilt Tumipampa,
but resided at Quito. Here he dwelt for some years
with a favourite son by a wife of the lower class,
named Tupac-atau-huallpa (The Sun makes Good
Fortune). Huaina was the victim of an epidemic
raging in Peru at the time. He was greatly feared by
his subjects, and was the last Inca who held undisputed
sway over the entire dominion. Like Nezahualcoyotl
in Mexico, he attempted to set up the worship of one
god in Peru, to the detriment of all other *huacas*, or
sacred beings.

The Inca Civil War

On the death of Huaina his two sons, Huascar and
Atauhuallpa,[1] strove for the crown. Before his demise
Huaina had divided his dominion between his two
sons, but it was said that he had wrested Quito from a
certain chieftain whose daughter he had married, and
by whom he had Atauhuallpa, who was therefore rightful heir to that province. The other son, Huascar, or
Tupac-cusi-huallpa (The Sun makes Joy), was born to
his principal sister-wife—for, according to Inca custom,
the monarchs of Peru, like those of certain Egyptian
dynasties, filled with pride of race, and unwilling to
mingle their blood with that of plebeians, took spouses
from among their sisters. This is the story as given
by many Spanish chroniclers, but it has no foundation
in fact. Atauhuallpa was in reality the son of a woman
of the people, and Huascar was not the son of Huaina's
sister-wife, but of a wife of less intimate relationship.
Therefore both sons were on an equality as regards

[1] This is the name by which he is generally alluded to in Peruvian
history.

descent. Huascar, however, was nearer the throne by virtue of his mother's status, which was that of a royal princess, whereas the mother of Atauhuallpa was not officially recognised. Huascar by his excesses and his outrages on religion and public decency aroused the people to revolt against his power, and Atauhuallpa, discerning his opportunity in this *émeute*, made a determined attack on the royal forces, and succeeded in driving them slowly back, until at last Tumipampa was razed to the ground, and shortly afterwards the important southerly fortress of Caxamarca fell into the hands of the rebels.

A Dramatic Situation

Atauhuallpa remained at Caxamarca, and despatched the bulk of his forces into the enemy's country. These drove the warriors of Huascar back until the upper courses of the Apurimac were reached. Huascar fled from Cuzco, but was captured, and carried a prisoner with his mother, wife, and children to Atauhuallpa. Not many days afterwards news of the landing of the Spaniards was received by the rebel Inca. The downfall of the Peruvian Empire was at hand.

A Worthless Despotism

If the blessings of a well-regulated government were dispensed by the Incas, these benefits were assuredly counterbalanced by the degrading despotism which accompanied them. The political organisation of the Peruvian Empire was in every sense more complete than that of Mexico. But in a state where individual effort and liberty are entirely crushed even such an effective organisation as the Peruvian can avail the people little, and is merely a device for the support of a calculated tyranny.

CHAPTER VII : THE MYTHOLOGY OF PERU

The Religion of Ancient Peru

THE religion of the ancient Peruvians had obviously developed in a much shorter time than that of the Mexicans. The more ancient character inherent in it was displayed in the presence of deities many of which were little better than mere totems, and although a definite monotheism or worship of one god appears to have been reached, it was not by the efforts of the priestly caste that this was achieved, but rather by the will of the Inca Pachacutic, who seems to have been a monarch gifted with rare insight and ability—a man much after the type of the Mexican Nezahualcoyotl.

In Inca times the religion of the people was solely directed by the state, and regulated in such a manner that independent theological thought was permitted no outlet. But it must not be inferred from this that no change had ever come over the spirit of Peruvian religion. As a matter of fact sweeping changes had been effected, but these had been solely the work of the Inca race, the leaders of which had amalgamated the various faiths of the peoples whom they had conquered into one official belief.

Totemism

Garcilasso el Inca de la Vega, an early Spanish writer on matters Peruvian, states that tradition ran that in ante-Inca times every district, family, and village possessed its own god, each different from the others. These gods were usually such objects as trees, mountains, flowers, herbs, caves, large stones, pieces of jasper, and animals. The jaguar, puma, and bear were

MYTHS OF MEXICO AND PERU

worshipped for their strength and fierceness, the monkey and fox for their cunning, the condor for its size and because several tribes believed themselves to be descended from it. The screech-owl was worshipped for its beauty, and the common owl for its power of seeing in the dark. Serpents, particularly the larger and more dangerous varieties, were especially regarded with reverence.

Although Payne classes all these gods together as totems, it is plain that those of the first class—the flowers, herbs, caves, and pieces of jasper—are merely fetishes. A fetish is an object in which the savage believes to be resident a spirit which, by its magic, will assist him in his undertakings. A totem is an object or an animal, usually the latter, with which the people of a tribe believe themselves to be connected by ties of blood and from which they are descended. It later becomes the type or symbol of the tribe.

Paccariscas

Lakes, springs, rocks, mountains, precipices, and caves were all regarded by the various Peruvian tribes as *paccariscas*—places whence their ancestors had originally issued to the upper world. The *paccarisca* was usually saluted with the cry, "Thou art my birthplace, thou art my life-spring. Guard me from evil, O Paccarisca!" In the holy spot a spirit was supposed to dwell which served the tribe as a kind of oracle. Naturally the *paccarisca* was looked upon with extreme reverence. It became, indeed, a sort of life-centre for the tribe, from which they were very unwilling to be separated.

Worship of Stones

The worship of stones appears to have been almost as universal in ancient Peru as it was in ancient Pales-

292

tine. Man in his primitive state believes stones to be the framework of the earth, its bony structure. He considers himself to have emerged from some cave—in fact, from the entrails of the earth. Nearly all American creation-myths regard man as thus emanating from the bowels of the great terrestrial mother. Rocks which were thus chosen as *paccariscas* are found, among many other places, at Callca, in the valley of the Yucay, and at Titicaca there is a great mass of red sandstone on the top of a high ridge with almost inaccessible slopes and dark, gloomy recesses where the sun was thought to have hidden himself at the time of the great deluge which covered all the earth. The rock of Titicaca was, in fact, the great *paccarisca* of the sun itself.

We are thus not surprised to find that many standing stones were worshipped in Peru in aboriginal times. Thus Arriaga states that rocks of great size which bore some resemblance to the human figure were imagined to have been at one time gigantic men or spirits who, because they disobeyed the creative power, were turned into stone. According to another account they were said to have suffered this punishment for refusing to listen to the words of Thonapa, the son of the creator, who, like Quetzalcoatl or Manco Ccapac, had taken upon himself the guise of a wandering Indian, so that he might have an opportunity of bringing the arts of civilisation to the aborigines. At Tiahuanaco a certain group of stones was said to represent all that remained of the villagers of that place, who, instead of paying fitting attention to the wise counsel which Thonapa the Civiliser bestowed upon them, continued to dance and drink in scorn of the teachings he had brought to them.

Again, some stones were said to have become men,

as in the old Greek creation-legend of Deucalion and Pyrrha. In the legend of Ccapac Inca Pachacutic, when Cuzco was attacked in force by the Chancas an Indian erected stones to which he attached shields and weapons so that they should appear to represent so many warriors in hiding. Pachacutic, in great need of assistance, cried to them with such vehemence to come to his help that they became men, and rendered him splendid service.

Huacas

Whatever was sacred, of sacred origin, or of the nature of a relic the Peruvians designated a *huaca*, from the root *huacan*, to howl, native worship invariably taking the form of a kind of howl, or weird, dirge-like wailing. All objects of reverence were known as *huacas*, although those of a higher class were also alluded to as *viracochas*. The Peruvians had, naturally, many forms of *huaca*, the most popular of which were those of the fetish class which could be carried about by the individual. These were usually stones or pebbles, many of which were carved and painted, and some made to represent human beings. The llama and the ear of maize were perhaps the most usual forms of these sacred objects. Some of them had an agricultural significance. In order that irrigation might proceed favourably a *huaca* was placed at intervals in proximity to the *acequias*, or irrigation canals, which was supposed to prevent them leaking or otherwise failing to supply a sufficiency of moisture to the parched maize-fields. *Huacas* of this sort were known as *ccompas*, and were regarded as deities of great importance, as the food-supply of the community was thought to be wholly dependent upon their assistance. Other *huacas* of a similar kind were called *chichics* and *huancas*, and these
294

presided over the fortunes of the maize, and ensured that a sufficient supply of rain should be forthcoming. Great numbers of these agricultural fetishes were destroyed by the zealous commissary Hernandez de Avendaño.

The Mamas

Spirits which were supposed to be instrumental in forcing the growth of the maize or other plants were the *mamas*. We find a similar conception among many Brazilian tribes to-day, so that the idea appears to have been a widely accepted one in South American countries. The Peruvians called such agencies "mothers," adding to the generic name that of the plant or herb with which they were specially associated. Thus *acsumama* was the potato-mother, *quinuamama* the quinua-mother, *saramama* the maize-mother, and *cocamama* the mother of the coca-shrub. Of these the *saramama* was naturally the most important, governing as it did the principal source of the food-supply of the community. Sometimes an image of the *saramama* was carved in stone, in the shape of an ear of maize. The *saramama* was also worshipped in the form of a doll, or *huantaysara*, made out of stalks of maize, renewed at each harvest, much as the idols of the great corn-mother of Mexico were manufactured at each harvest-season. After having been made, the image was watched over for three nights, and then sacrifice was done to it. The priest or medicine-man of the tribe would then inquire of it whether or not it was capable of existing until that time in the next year. If its spirit replied in the affirmative it was permitted to remain where it was until the following harvest. If not it was removed, burnt, and another figure took its place, to which similar questions were put.

The Huamantantac

Connected with agriculture in some degree was the Huamantantac (He who causes the Cormorants to gather themselves together). This was the agency responsible for the gathering of sea-birds, resulting in the deposits of guano to be found along the Peruvian coast which are so valuable in the cultivation of the maize-plant. He was regarded as a most beneficent spirit, and was sacrificed to with exceeding fervour.

Huaris

The *huaris*, or "great ones," were the ancestors of the aristocrats of a tribe, and were regarded as specially favourable toward agricultural effort, possibly because the land had at one time belonged to them personally. They were sometimes alluded to as the "gods of strength," and were sacrificed to by libations of *chicha*. Ancestors in general were deeply revered, and had an agricultural significance, in that considerable tracts of land were tilled in order that they might be supplied with suitable food and drink offerings. As the number of ancestors increased more and more land was brought into cultivation, and the hapless people had their toil added to immeasurably by these constant demands upon them.

Huillcas

The *huillcas* were *huacas* which partook of the nature of oracles. Many of these were serpents, trees, and rivers, the noises made by which appeared to the primitive Peruvians—as, indeed, they do to primitive folk all over the world—to be of the quality of articulate speech. Both the Huillcamayu and the Apurimac rivers at Cuzco were *huillca* oracles of this kind, as their names, "Huillca-river" and "Great

Speaker," denote. These oracles often set the mandate of the Inca himself at defiance, occasionally supporting popular opinion against his policy.

The Oracles of the Andes

The Peruvian Indians of the Andes range within recent generations continued to adhere to the superstitions they had inherited from their fathers. A rare and interesting account of these says that they " admit an evil being, the inhabitant of the centre of the earth, whom they consider as the author of their misfortunes, and at the mention of whose name they tremble. The most shrewd among them take advantage of this belief to obtain respect, and represent themselves as his delegates. Under the denomination of *mohanes*, or *agoreros*, they are consulted even on the most trivial occasions. They preside over the intrigues of love, the health of the community, and the taking of the field. Whatever repeatedly occurs to defeat their prognostics, falls on themselves ; and they are wont to pay for their deceptions very dearly. They chew a species of vegetable called *piripiri*, and throw it into the air, accompanying this act by certain recitals and incantations, to injure some, to benefit others, to procure rain and the inundation of the rivers, or, on the other hand, to occasion settled weather, and a plentiful store of agricultural productions. Any such result, having been casually verified on a single occasion, suffices to confirm the Indians in their faith, although they may have been cheated a thousand times. Fully persuaded that they cannot resist the influence of the *piripiri*, as soon as they know that they have been solicited in love by its means, they fix their eyes on the impassioned object, and discover a thousand amiable traits, either real or fanciful, which indifference had before concealed from their view. But the principal power, efficacy, and it may be said misfortune of the *mohanes* consist in the cure of the sick. Every malady is ascribed to their enchantments, and means are instantly taken to ascertain by whom the mischief may have been wrought. For this purpose, the nearest relative takes a quantity of the juice of *floripondium*, and suddenly falls intoxicated by the violence of the plant. He is placed in a fit posture to prevent suffocation, and on his coming to himself, at the end of three days, the *mohane* who has the greatest resemblance to the sorcerer he saw in his visions is to undertake the cure, or if, in the interim, the sick man has perished, it is customary to subject him to the same fate. When not any sorcerer occurs in the visions, the first *mohane* they encounter has the misfortune to represent his image." [1]

Lake-Worship in Peru

At Lake Titicaca the Peruvians believed the inhabitants of the earth, animals as well as men, to have been fashioned by the creator, and the district was thus sacrosanct in their eyes. The people of the Collao called it Mamacota (Mother-water), because it furnished them with supplies of food. Two great idols were connected with this worship. One called Copacahuana was made of a bluish-green stone shaped like a fish with a human head, and was placed in a commanding position on the shores of the lake. On the arrival of the Spaniards so deeply rooted was the worship of this goddess that they could only suppress it by raising an image of the Virgin in place of the idol. The Christian emblem remains to this day. Mamacota was venerated as the giver of fish, with which the lake abounded. The other image, Copacati

[1] Skinner, *State of Peru*, p. 275.

(Serpent-stone), represented the element of water as embodied in the lake itself in the form of an image wreathed in serpents, which in America are nearly always symbolical of water.

The Lost Island

A strange legend is recounted of this lake-goddess. She was chiefly worshipped as the giver of rain, but Huaina Ccapac, who had modern ideas and journeyed through the country casting down *huacas*, had determined to raise on an island of Lake Titicaca a temple to Yatiri (The Ruler), the Aymara name of the god Pachacamac in his form of Pachayachachic. He commenced by raising the new shrine on the island of Titicaca itself. But the deity when called upon refused to vouchsafe any reply to his worshippers or priests. Huaina then commanded that the shrine should be transferred to the island of Apinguela. But the same thing happened there. He then inaugurated a temple on the island of Paapiti, and lavished upon it many sacrifices of llamas, children, and precious metals. But the offended tutelary goddess of the lake, irritated beyond endurance by this invasion of her ancient domain, lashed the watery waste into such a frenzy of storm that the island and the shrine which covered it disappeared beneath the waves and were never thereafter beheld by mortal eye.

The Thunder-God of Peru

The rain-and-thunder god of Peru was worshipped in various parts of the country under various names. Among the Collao he was known as Con, and in that part of the Inca dominions now known as Bolivia he was called Churoquella. Near the cordilleras of the coast he was probably known as Pariacaca, who expelled

the *huaca* of the district by dreadful tempests, hurling
rain and hail at him for three days and nights in such
quantities as to form the great lake of Pariacaca.
Burnt llamas were offered to him. But the Incas,
discontented with this local worship, which by no
means suited their system of central government,
determined to create one thunder-deity to whom all
the tribes in the empire must bow as the only god of
his class. We are not aware what his name was, but
we know from mythological evidence that he was a
mixture of all the other gods of thunder in the
Peruvian Empire, first because he invariably occupied
the third place in the triad of greater deities, the
creator, sun, and thunder, all of whom were more or
less amalgamations of provincial and metropolitan gods,
and secondly because a great image of him was erected
in the Coricancha at Cuzco, in which he was represented in human form, wearing a headdress which
concealed his face, symbolic of the clouds, which ever
veil the thunder-god's head. He had a special temple
of his own, moreover, and was assigned a share in the
sacred lands by the Inca Pachacutic. He was accompanied by a figure of his sister, who carried jars of water.
An unknown Quichuan poet composed on the myth
the following graceful little poem, which was translated
by the late Daniel Garrison Brinton, an enthusiastic
Americanist and professor of American archæology in
the University of Pennsylvania :

> Bounteous Princess,
> Lo, thy brother
> Breaks thy vessel
> Now in fragments.
> From the blow come
> Thunder, lightning,
> Strokes of lightning ;

THE THUNDER-GOD OF PERU

And thou, Princess,
Tak'st the water,
With it rainest,
And the hail or
Snow dispensest,
Viracocha,
World-constructor.

It will be observed that the translator here employs
the name Viracocha as if it were that of the deity. But
it was merely a general expression in use for a more
than usually sacred being. Brinton, commenting upon
the legend, says : "In this pretty waif that has floated
down to us from the wreck of a literature now for ever
lost there is more than one point to attract the notice
of the antiquary. He may find in it a hint to decipher
those names of divinities so common in Peruvian
legends, Contici and Illatici. Both mean 'the Thunder
Vase,' and both doubtless refer to the conception here
displayed of the phenomena of the thunderstorm."
Alluding to Peruvian thunder-myth elsewhere, he says
in an illuminating passage : "Throughout the realms
of the Incas the Peruvians venerated as maker of all
things and ruler of the firmament the god Ataguju.
The legend was that from him proceeded the first of
mortals, the man Guamansuri, who descended to the
earth and there wedded the sister of certain Guachimines, rayless ones or Darklings, who then possessed
it. They destroyed him, but their sister gave birth to
twin sons, Apocatequil and Piguerao. The former was
the more powerful. By touching the corpse of his
mother he brought her to life, he drove off and slew
the Guachimines, and, directed by Ataguju, released the
race of Indians from the soil by turning it up with a
spade of gold. For this reason they adored him as their
maker. He it was, they thought, who produced the

301

thunder and the lightning by hurling stones with his sling. And the thunderbolts that fall, said they, are his children. Few villages were willing to be without one or more of these. They were in appearance small, round stones, but had the admirable properties of securing fertility to the fields, protecting from lightning, and, by a transition easy to understand, were also adored as gods of fire as well material as of the passions, and were capable of kindling the dangerous flames of desire in the most frigid bosoms. Therefore they were in great esteem as love-charms. Apocatequil's statue was erected on the mountains, with that of his mother on one hand and his brother on the other. 'He was Prince of Evil, and the most respected god of the Peruvians. From Quito to Cuzco not an Indian but would give all he possessed to conciliate him. Five priests, two stewards, and a crowd of slaves served his image. And his chief temple was surrounded by a very considerable village, whose inhabitants had no other occupation but to wait on him.'" In memory of these brothers twins in Peru were always deemed sacred to the lightning.

There is an instance on record of how the *huillca* could refuse on occasion to recognise even royalty itself. Manco, the Inca who had been given the kingly power by Pizarro, offered a sacrifice to one of these oracular shrines. The oracle refused to recognise him, through the medium of its guardian priest, stating that Manco was not the rightful Inca. Manco therefore caused the oracle, which was in the shape of a rock, to be thrown down, whereupon its guardian spirit emerged in the form of a parrot and flew away. It is probable that the bird thus liberated had been taught by the priests to answer to the questions of those who came to consult the shrine. But we learn that on

Manco commanding that the parrot should be pursued it sought another rock, which opened to receive it, and the spirit of the *huillca* was transferred to this new abode.

The Great God Pachacamac

Later Peruvian mythology recognised only three gods of the first rank, the earth, the thunder, and the creative agency. Pachacamac, the great spirit of earth, derived his name from a word *pacha*, which may be best trans-lated as "things." In its sense of visible things it is equivalent to "world," applied to things which happen in succession it denotes "time," and to things connected with persons "property," especially clothes. The world of visible things is thus Mamapacha (Earth-Mother), under which name the ancient Peruvians worshipped the earth. Pachacamac, on the other hand, is not the earth itself, the soil, but the spirit which animates all things that emerge therefrom. From him proceed the spirits of the plants and animals which come from the earth. Pachamama is the mother-spirit of the mountains, rocks, and plains, Pachacamac the father-spirit of the grain-bearing plants, animals, birds, and man. In some localities Pachacamac and Pachamama were worshipped as divine mates. Possibly this practice was universal in early times, gradually lapsing into desuetude in later days. Pachamama was in another phase intended to denote the land imme-diately contiguous to a settlement, on which the inhabi-tants depended for their food-supply.

Peruvian Creation-Stories

It is easy to see how such a conception as Pacha-camac, the spirit of animated nature, would become one with the idea of a universal or even a partial creator.

That there was a pre-existing conception of a creative agency can be proved from the existence of the Peruvian name Conticsi-viracocha (He who gives Origin, or Beginning). This conception and that of Pachacamac must at some comparatively early period have clashed, and been amalgamated probably with ease when it was seen how nearly akin were the two ideas. Indeed, Pachacamac was alternatively known as Pacharurac, the "maker" of all things—sure proof of his amalgamation with the conception of the creative agency. As such he had his symbol in the great Coricancha at Cuzco, an oval plate of gold, suspended between those of the sun and the moon, and placed vertically, it may be hazarded with some probability, to represent in symbol that universal matrix from which emanated all things. Elsewhere in Cuzco the creator was represented by a stone statue in human form.

Pachayachachic

In later Inca days this idea of a creator assumed that of a direct ruler of the universe, known as Pachayachachic. This change was probably due to the influence of the Inca Pachacutic, who is known to have made several other doctrinal innovations in Peruvian theology. He commanded a great new temple to the creator-god to be built at the north angle of the city of Cuzco, in which he placed a statue of pure gold, of the size of a boy of ten years of age. The small size was to facilitate its removal, as Peruvian worship was nearly always carried out in the open air. In form it represented a man with his right arm elevated, the hand partially closed and the forefinger and thumb raised, as if in the act of uttering the creative word. To this god large possessions and revenues were assigned, for previously service rendered to him had been voluntary only.

Ideas of Creation

It is from aboriginal sources as preserved by the first Spanish colonists that we glean our knowledge of what the Incas believed the creative process to consist. By means of his word (*ñisca*) the creator, a spirit, powerful and opulent, made all things. We are provided with the formulæ of his very words by the Peruvian prayers still extant : " Let earth and heaven be," " Let a man be ; let a woman be," " Let there be day," " Let there be night," " Let the light shine." The sun is here regarded as the creative agency, and the ruling caste as the objects of a special act of creation.

Pacari Tampu

Pacari Tampu (House of the Dawn) was the place of origin, according to the later Inca theology, of four brothers and sisters who initiated the four Peruvian systems of worship. The eldest climbed a neighbouring mountain, and cast stones to the four points of the compass, thus indicating that he claimed all the land within sight. But his youngest brother succeeded in enticing him into a cave, which he sealed up with a great stone, thus imprisoning him for ever. He next persuaded his second brother to ascend a lofty mountain, from which he cast him, changing him into a stone in his descent. On beholding the fate of his brethren the third member of the quartette fled. It is obvious that we have here a legend concocted by the later Inca priesthood to account for the evolution of Peruvian religion in its different stages. The first brother would appear to represent the oldest religion in Peru, that of the *paccariscas*, the second that of a fetishistic stone-worship, the third perhaps that of Viracocha, and the last sun-worship pure and simple. There was, however, an "official" legend, which stated that the sun had three sons, Viracocha, Pachacamac, and Manco Ccapac. To the last the dominion of mankind was given, whilst the others were concerned with the workings of the universe. This politic arrangement placed all the power, temporal and spiritual, in the hands of the reputed descendants of Manco Ccapac—the Incas.

Worship of the Sea

The ancient Peruvians worshipped the sea as well as the earth, the folk inland regarding it as a menacing deity, whilst the people of the coast reverenced it as a god of benevolence, calling it Mama-cocha, or Mother-sea, as it yielded them subsistence in the form of fish, on which they chiefly lived. They worshipped the whale, fairly common on that coast, because of its enormous size, and various districts regarded with adoration the species of fish most abundant there. This worship can have partaken in no sense of the nature of totemism, as the system forbade that the totem animal should be eaten. It was imagined that the prototype of each variety of fish dwelt in the upper world, just as many tribes of North American Indians believe that the eponymous ancestors of certain animals dwell at the four points of the compass or in the sky above them. This great fish-god engendered the others of his species, and sent them into the waters of the deep that they might exist there until taken for the use of man. Birds, too, had their eponymous counterparts among the stars, as had animals. Indeed, among many of the South American races, ancient and modern, the constellations were called after certain beasts and birds.

Viracocha

The Aymara-Quichua race worshipped Viracocha as a great culture hero. They did not offer him sacrifices or tribute, as they thought that he, being creator and possessor of all things, needed nothing from men, so they only gave him worship. After him they idolised the sun. They believed, indeed, that Viracocha had made both sun and moon, after emerging from Lake Titicaca, and that then he made the earth and peopled it. On his travels westward from the lake he was sometimes assailed by men, but he revenged himself by sending terrible storms upon them and destroying their property, so they humbled themselves and acknowledged him as their lord. He forgave them and taught them everything, obtaining from them the name of Pachayachachic. In the end he disappeared in the western ocean. He either created or there were born with him four beings who, according to mythical beliefs, civilised Peru. To them he assigned the four quarters of the earth, and they are thus known as the four winds, north, south, east, and west. One legend avers they came from the cave Pacari, the Lodging of the Dawn.

Sun-Worship in Peru

The name " Inca " means " People of the Sun," which luminary the Incas regarded as their creator. But they did not worship him totemically—that is, they did not claim him as a progenitor, although they regarded him as possessing the attributes of a man. And here we may observe a difference between Mexican and Peruvian sun-worship. For whereas the Nahua primarily regarded the orb as the abode of the Man of the Sun, who came to earth in the shape of Quet coatl, the Peruvians looked upon the sun itself as the deity. The Inca race did not identify their ancestors as children of the sun until a comparatively late date. Sun-worship was introduced by the Inca Pachacutic, who averred that the sun appeared to him in a dream and addressed him as his child. Until that time the worship of the sun had always been strictly subordinated to that of the creator, and the deity appeared only as second in the trinity of creator, sun, and thunder. But permanent provision was made for sacrifices to the sun before the other deities were so recognised, and as the conquests of the Incas grew wider and that provision extended to the new territories they came to be known as "the Lands of the Sun," the natives observing the dedication of a part of the country to the luminary, and concluding therefrom that it applied to the whole. The material reality of the sun would enormously assist his cult among a people who were too barbarous to appreciate an unseen god, and this colonial conception reacting upon the mother-land would undoubtedly inspire the military class with a resolve to strengthen a worship so popular in the conquered provinces, and of which they were in great measure the protagonists and missionaries.

The Sun's Possessions

In every Peruvian village the sun had considerable possessions. His estates resembled those of a territorial chieftain, and consisted of a dwelling-house, a *charm*   of land, flocks of llamas and pacos, women dedicated to his service. The soil within the solar enclosure de-the inhabitants of the neighbouring their toil being stored in the house. The Women of the Sun prepared the daily food and drink of the luminary, which consisted of maize and *chicha*. They also spun wool and wove it into fine stuff, which was burned in order that it might ascend to the celestial regions, where the deity could make use of it. Each village reserved a portion of its solar produce for the great festival at Cuzco, and it was carried thither on the backs of llamas which were destined for sacrifice.

Inca Occupation of Titicaca

The Rock of Titicaca, the renowned place of the sun's origin, naturally became an important centre of his worship. The date at which the worship of the sun originated at this famous rock is extremely remote, but we may safely assume that it was long before the conquest of the Collao by the Apu-Ccapac-Inca Pachacutic, and that reverence for the luminary as a war-god by the Colla chiefs was noticed by Tupac, who in suppressing the revolt concluded that the local observance at the rock had some relationship to the disturbance. It is, however, certain that Tupac proceeded after the reconquest to establish at this natural centre of sun-worship solar rites on a new basis, with the evident intention of securing on behalf of the Incas of Cuzco such exclusive benefit as might accrue from the complete possession of the sun's *paccarisca*. According to a native account, a venerable *colla* (or hermit), consecrated to the service of the sun, had proceeded on foot from Titicaca to Cuzco for the purpose of commending this ancient seat of sun-worship to the notice of Tupac. The consequence was that Apu-Ccapac-Inca, after visiting the island and inquiring into the ancient local customs, re-established them in a more regular form. His accounts can hardly be accepted in face of the facts which have been gathered. Rather did it naturally

follow that Titicaca became subservient to Tupac after
the revolt of the Collao had been quelled. Henceforth
the worship of the sun at the place of his origin was
entrusted to Incas resident in the place, and was celebrated with Inca rites. The island was converted into
a solar estate and the aboriginal inhabitants removed.
The land was cultivated and the slopes of the hills
levelled, maize was sown and the soil consecrated, the
grain being regarded as the gift of the sun. This work
produced considerable change in the island. Where
once was waste and idleness there was now fertility
and industry. The harvests were skilfully apportioned,
so much being reserved for sacrificial purposes, the
remainder being sent to Cuzco, partly to be sown in
the *chacras,* or estates of the sun, throughout Peru,
partly to be preserved in the granary of the Inca and
the *huacas* as a symbol that there would be abundant
crops in the future and that the grain already stored
would be preserved. A building of the Women
of the Sun was erected about a mile from the rock,
so that the produce might be available for sacrifices.
For their maintenance, tribute of potatoes, ocas, and
quinua was levied upon the inhabitants of the villages
on the shores of the lake, and of maize upon the people
of the neighbouring valleys.

Pilgrimages to Titicaca

Titicaca at the time of the conquest was probably
more frequented than Pachacamac itself. These two
places were held to be the cardinal shrines of the two
great *huacas,* the creator and the sun respectively. A
special reason for pilgrimage to Titicaca was to sacrifice
to the sun, as the source of physical energy and the
giver of long life ; and he was especially worshipped
by the aged, who believed he had preserved their lives.

Then followed the migration of pilgrims to Titicaca, for whose shelter houses were built at Capacahuana, and large stores of maize were provided for their use. The ceremonial connected with the sacred rites of the rock was rigorously observed. The pilgrim ere embarking on the raft which conveyed him to the island must first confess his sins to a *huillac* (a speaker to an object of worship) ; then further confessions were required at each of the three sculptured doors which had successively to be passed before reaching the sacred rock. The first door (Puma-puncu) was surmounted by the figure of a puma ; the others (Quenti-puncu and Pillco-puncu) were ornamented with feathers of the different species of birds commonly sacrificed to the sun. Having passed the last portal, the traveller beheld at a distance of two hundred paces the sacred rock itself, the summit glittering with gold-leaf. He was permitted to proceed no further, for only the officials were allowed entry into it. The pilgrim on departing received a few grains of the sacred maize grown on the island. These he kept with care and placed with his own store, believing they would preserve his stock. The confidence the Indian placed in the virtue of the Titicaca maize may be judged from the prevalent belief that the possessor of a single grain would not suffer from starvation during the whole of his life.

Sacrifices to the New Sun

The Intip-Raymi, or Great Festival of the Sun, was celebrated by the Incas at Cuzco at the winter solstice. In connection with it the Tarpuntaita-cuma, or sacrificing Incas, were charged with a remarkable duty, the worshippers journeying eastward to meet one of these functionaries on his way. On the principal hill-tops between Cuzco and Huillcanuta, on the road to the rock of Titicaca, burnt offerings of llamas, coca, and maize were made at the feast to greet the arrival of the young sun from his ancient birthplace. Molina has enumerated more than twenty of these places of sacrifice. The striking picture of the celebration of the solar sacrifice on these bleak mountains in the depth of the Peruvian winter has, it seems, no parallel in the religious rites of the ancient Americans. Quitting their thatched houses at early dawn, the worshippers left the valley below, carrying the sacrificial knife and brazier, and conducting the white llama, heavily laden with fuel, maize, and coca leaves, wrapped in fine cloth, to the spot where the sacrifice was to be made. When sunrise appeared the pile was lighted. The victim was slain and thrown upon it. The scene then presented a striking contrast to the bleak surrounding wilderness. As the flames grew in strength and the smoke rose higher and thicker the clear atmosphere was gradually illuminated from the east. When the sun advanced above the horizon the sacrifice was at its height. But for the crackling of the flames and the murmur of a babbling stream on its way down the hill to join the river below, the silence had hitherto been unbroken. As the sun rose the Incas marched slowly round the burning mass, plucking the wool from the scorched carcase, and chanting monotonously : "O Creator, Sun and Thunder, be for ever young! Multiply the people ; let them ever be in peace !"

The Citoc Raymi

The most picturesque if not the most important solar festival was that of the Citoc Raymi (Gradually Increasing Sun), held in June, when nine days were given up to the ceremonial. A rigorous fast was observed for three days previous to the event, during which no

Conducting the White Llama to the Sacrifice
William Sewell
(See page 312)

fire must be kindled. On the fourth day the Inca, accompanied by the people *en masse*, proceeded to the great square of Cuzco to hail the rising sun, which they awaited in silence. On its appearance they greeted it with a joyous tumult, and, joining in procession, marched to the Golden Temple of the Sun, where llamas were sacrificed, and a new fire was kindled by means of an arched mirror, followed by sacrificial offerings of grain, flowers, animals, and aromatic gums. This festival may be taken as typical of all the seasonal celebrations. The Inca calendar was purely agricultural in its basis, and marked in its great festivals the renewal or abandonment of the labours of the field. Its astronomical observations were not more advanced than those of the calendars of many American races otherwise inferior in civilisation.

Human Sacrifice in Peru

Writers ignorant of their subject have often dwelt upon the absence of human sacrifice in ancient Peru, and have not hesitated to draw comparisons between Mexico and the empire of the Incas in this respect, usually not complimentary to the former. Such statements are contradicted by the clearest evidence. Human sacrifice was certainly not nearly so prevalent in Peru, but that it was regular and by no means rare is well authenticated. Female victims to the sun were taken from the great class of Acllacuna (Selected Ones), a general tribute of female children regularly levied throughout the Inca Empire. Beautiful girls were taken from their parents at the age of eight by the Inca officials, and were handed over to certain female trainers called *mamacuna* (mothers). These matrons systematically trained their *protégées* in housewifery and ritual. Residences or convents called *aclla-huasi*

313

(houses of the Selected) were provided for them in the principal cities.

Methods of Medicine-Men

A quaint account of the methods of the medicine-men of the Indians of the Peruvian Andes probably illustrates the manner in which the superstitions of a barbarian people evolve into a more stately ritual.

"It cannot be denied," it states, "that the *mohanes* [priests] have, by practice and tradition, acquired a knowledge of many plants and poisons, with which they effect surprising cures on the one hand, and do much mischief on the other, but the mania of ascribing the whole to a preternatural virtue occasions them to blend with their practice a thousand charms and superstitions. The most customary method of cure is to place two hammocks close to each other, either in the dwelling, or in the open air : in one of them the patient lies extended, and in the other the *mohane*, or *agorero*. The latter, in contact with the sick man, begins by rocking himself, and then proceeds, by a strain in falsetto, to call on the birds, quadrupeds, and fishes to give health to the patient. From time to time he rises on his seat, and makes a thousand extravagant gestures over the sick man, to whom he applies his powders and herbs, or sucks the wounded or diseased parts. If the malady augments, the *agorero*, having been joined by many of the people, chants a short hymn, addressed to the soul of the patient, with this burden: 'Thou must not go, thou must not go.' In repeating this he is joined by the people, until at length a terrible clamour is raised, and augmented in proportion as the sick man becomes still fainter and fainter, to the end that it may reach his ears. When all the charms are unavailing, and death approaches, the *mohane* leaps from his hammock, and betakes him-self to flight, amid the multitude of sticks, stones, and clods of earth which are showered on him. Successively all those who belong to the nation assemble, and, dividing themselves into bands, each of them (if he who is in his last agonies is a warrior) approaches him, saying : 'Whither goest thou ? Why dost thou leave us ? With whom shall we proceed to the *aucas* [the enemies] ?' They then relate to him the heroical deeds he has performed, the number of those he has slain, and the pleasures he leaves behind him. This is practised in different tones : while some raise the voice, it is lowered by others ; and the poor sick man is obliged to support these importunities without a murmur, until the first symptoms of approaching dis-solution manifest themselves. Then it is that he is surrounded by a multitude of females, some of whom forcibly close the mouth and eyes, others envelop him in the hammock, oppressing him with the whole of their weight, and causing him to expire before his time, and others, lastly, run to extinguish the candle, and dissipate the smoke, that the soul, not being able to perceive the hole through which it may escape, may remain entangled in the structure of the roof. That this may be speedily effected, and to prevent its return to the interior of the dwelling, they surround the entrances with filth, by the stench of which it may be expelled.

Death by Suffocation

"As soon as the dying man is suffocated by the closing of the mouth, nostrils, &c., and wrapt up in the covering of his bed, the most circumspect Indian, whether male or female, takes him in the arms in the best manner possible, and gives a *gentle* shriek, which echoes to the bitter lamentations of the immediate relatives, and to the cries of a thousand old women collected for the occasion. As long as this dismal howl subsists, the latter are subjected to a constant fatigue, raising the palm of the hand to wipe away the tears, and lowering it to dry it on the ground. The result of this alternate action is, that a circle of earth, which gives them a most hideous appearance, is collected about the eyelids and brows, and they do not wash themselves until the mourning is over. These first clamours conclude by several good pots of *masato*, to assuage the thirst of sorrow, and the company next proceed to make a great clatter among the utensils of the deceased : some break the kettles, and others the earthen pots, while others, again, burn the apparel, to the end that his memory may be the sooner forgotten. If the defunct has been a *cacique*, or powerful warrior, his exequies are performed after the manner of the Romans : they last for many days, all the people weeping in concert for a considerable space of time, at daybreak, at noon, in the evening, and at midnight. When the appointed hour arrives, the mournful music begins in front of the house of the wife and relatives, the heroical deeds of the deceased being chanted to the sound of instruments. All the inhabitants of the vicinity unite in chorus from within their houses, some chirping like birds, others howling like tigers, and the greater part of them chattering like monkeys, or croaking like frogs. They constantly leave off by having recourse to the *masato*, and by the destruction of whatever the deceased may have left behind him, the burning of his dwelling being that which concludes the ceremonies. Among some of the Indians, the nearest relatives cut off their hair as a token of their grief, agreeably to the practice of the Moabites, and other nations. . . .

THE VISION OF YUPANQUI

The Obsequies of a Chief

"On the day of decease, they put the body, with its insignia, into a large earthen vessel, or painted jar, which they bury in one of the angles of the quarter, laying over it a covering of potter's clay, and throwing in earth until the grave is on a level with the surface of the ground. When the obsequies are over, they forbear to pay a visit to it, and lose every recollection of the name of the warrior. The Roamaynas disenterre their dead, as soon as they think that the fleshy parts have been consumed, and having washed the bones form the skeleton, which they place in a coffin of potter's clay, adorned with various symbols of death, like the hieroglyphics on the wrappers of the Egyptian mummies. In this state the skeleton is carried home, to the end that the survivors may bear the deceased in respectful memory, and not in imitation of those extraordinary voluptuaries of antiquity, who introduced into their most splendid festivals a spectacle of this nature, which, by reminding them of their dissolution, might stimulate them to taste, before it should overtake them, all the impure pleasures the human passions could afford them. A space of time of about a year being elapsed, the bones are once more inhumed, and the individual to whom they belonged forgotten for ever." [1]

Peruvian Myths

Peru is not so rich in myths as Mexico, but the following legends well illustrate the mythological ideas of the Inca race :

The Vision of Yupanqui

The Inca Yupanqui before he succeeded to the sovereignty is said to have gone to visit his father,

[1] Skinner, *State of Peru*, pp. 271 *et seq.*

Viracocha Inca. On his way he arrived at a fountain
called Susur-pugaio. There he saw a piece of crystal
fall into the fountain, and in this crystal he saw the
figure of an Indian, with three bright rays as of the
sun coming from the back of his head. He wore a
hau,u, or royal fringe, across the forehead like the Inca.
Serpents wound round his arms and over his shoulders.
He had ear-pieces in his ears like the Incas, and was
also dressed like them. There was the head of a lion
between his legs, and another lion was about his
shoulders. Inca Yupanqui took fright at this strange
figure, and was running away when a voice called to
him by name telling him not to be afraid, because it
was his father, the sun, whom he beheld, and that he
would conquer many nations, but he must remember
his father in his sacrifices and raise revenues for him,
and pay him great reverence. Then the figure vanished,
but the crystal remained, and the Inca afterwards saw
all he wished in it. When he became king he had a
statue of the sun made, resembling the figure as closely
as possible, and ordered all the tribes he had conquered
to build splendid temples and worship the new deity
instead of the creator.

The Bird Bride

The Canaris Indians are named from the province
of Canaribamba, in Quito, and they have several myths
regarding their origin. One recounts that at the deluge
two brothers fled to a very high mountain called
Huacaquan, and as the waters rose the hill ascended
simultaneously, so that they escaped drowning. When
the flood was over they had to find food in the valleys,
and they built a tiny house and lived on herbs and
roots. They were surprised one day when they went
home to find food already prepared for them and *chicha*

to drink. This continued for ten days. Then the elder brother decided to hide himself and discover who brought the food. Very soon two birds, one Aqua, the other Torito (otherwise *quacamayo* birds), appeared dressed as Canaris, and wearing their hair fastened in the same way. The larger bird removed the *llicella*, or mantle the Indians wear, and the man saw that they had beautiful faces and discovered that the bird-like beings were in reality women. When he came out the bird-women were very angry and flew away. When the younger brother came home and found no food he was annoyed, and determined to hide until the bird-women returned. After ten days the *quacamayos* appeared again on their old mission, and while they were busy the watcher contrived to close the door, and so prevented the younger bird from escaping. She lived with the brothers for a long time, and became the mother of six sons and daughters, from whom all the Canaris proceed. Hence the tribe look upon the *quacamayo* birds with reverence, and use their feathers at their festivals.

Thonapa

Some myths tell of a divine personage called Thonapa, who appears to have been a hero-god or civilising agent like Quetzalcoatl. He seems to have devoted his life to preaching to the people in the various villages, beginning in the provinces of Colla-suya. When he came to Yamquisupa he was treated so badly that he would not remain there. He slept in the open air, clad only in a long shirt and a mantle, and carried a book. He cursed the village. It was soon immersed in water, and is now a lake. There was an idol in the form of a woman to which the people offered sacrifice at the top of a high hill, Cachapucara. This idol Thonapa detested, so he burnt it, and also destroyed the hill. On another occasion Thonapa cursed a large assembly of people who were holding a great banquet to celebrate a wedding, because they refused to listen to his preaching. They were all changed into stones, which are visible to this day. Wandering through Peru, Thonapa came to the mountain of Caravaya, and after raising a very large cross he put it on his shoulders and took it to the hill Carapucu, where he preached so fervently that he shed tears. A chief's daughter got some of the water on her head, and the Indians, imagining that he was washing his head (a ritual offence), took him prisoner near the Lake of Carapucu. Very early the next morning a beautiful youth appeared to Thonapa, and told him not to fear, for he was sent from the divine guardian who watched over him. He released Thonapa, who escaped, though he was well guarded. He went down into the lake, his mantle keeping him above the water as a boat would have done. After Thonapa had escaped from the barbarians he remained on the rock of Titicaca, afterwards going to the town of Tiya-manacu, where again he cursed the people and turned them into stones. They were too bent upon amusement to listen to his preaching. He then followed the river Chacamarca till it reached the sea, and, like Quetzalcoatl, disappeared. This is good evidence that he was a solar deity, or "man of the sun," who, his civilising labours completed, betook himself to the house of his father.

A Myth of Manco Ccapac Inca

When Manco Ccapac Inca was born a staff which had been given to his father turned into gold. He had seven brothers and sisters, and at his father's death he assembled all his people in order to see how much he

" A beautiful youth appeared to Thonapa "
William Sewell
(See page 320)

"He sang the song of *Chamayhuarisca*"

William Sewell

(See page 321)

could venture in making fresh conquests. He and his brothers supplied themselves with rich clothing, new arms, and the golden staff called *tapac-yauri* (royal sceptre). He had also two cups of gold from which Thonapa had drunk, called *tapacusi*. They proceeded to the highest point in the country, a mountain where the sun rose, and Manco Ccapac saw several rainbows. which he interpreted as a sign of good fortune, Delighted with the favouring symbols, he sang the song of *Chamayhuarisca* (The Song of Joy). Manco Ccapac wondered why a brother who had accompanied him did not return, and sent one of his sisters in search of him, but she also did not come back, so he went himself, and found both nearly dead beside a *huaca*. They said they could not move, as the *huaca*, a stone, retarded them. In a great rage Manco struck this stone with his *tapac-yauri*. It spoke, and said that had it not been for his wonderful golden staff he would have had no power over it. It added that his brother and sister had sinned, and therefore must remain with it (the *huaca*) in the lower regions, but that Manco was to be " greatly honoured." The sad fate of his brother and sister troubled Manco exceedingly, but on going back to the place where he first saw the rainbows he got comfort from them and strength to bear his grief.

Coniraya Viracocha

Coniraya Viracocha was a tricky nature spirit who declared he was the creator, but who frequently appeared attired as a poor ragged Indian. He was an adept at deceiving people. A beautiful woman, Cavillaca, who was greatly admired, was one day weaving a mantle at the foot of a *lucma* tree. Coniraya, changing himself into a beautiful bird, climbed the tree,

took some of his generative seed, made it into a ripe
lucma, and dropped it near the beautiful virgin, who
saw and ate the fruit.   Some time afterwards a son was
born to Cavillaca.   When the child was older she wished
that the *huacas* and gods should meet and declare who
was the father of the boy.   All dressed as finely as
possible, hoping to be chosen as her husband.   Coniraya
was there, dressed like a beggar, and Cavillaca never
even looked at him.   The maiden addressed the
assembly, but as no one immediately answered her
speech she let the child go, saying he would be sure
to crawl to his father.   The infant went straight up to
Coniraya, sitting in his rags, and laughed up to him.
Cavillaca, extremely angry at the idea of being associated
with such a poor, dirty creature, fled to the sea-
shore.   Coniraya then put on magnificent attire and
followed her to show her how handsome he was, but
still thinking of him in his ragged condition she would
not look back.   She went into the sea at Pachacamac
and was changed into a rock.   Coniraya, still following
her, met a condor, and asked if it had seen a woman.
On the condor replying that it had seen her quite near,
Coniraya blessed it, and said whoever killed it would be
killed himself.   He then met a fox, who said he would
never meet Cavillaca, so Coniraya told him he would
always retain his disagreeable odour, and on account of
it he would never be able to go abroad except at night,
and that he would be hated by every one.   Next came
a lion, who told Coniraya he was very near Cavillaca,
so the lover said he should have the power of punishing
wrongdoers, and that whoever killed him would wear
the skin without cutting off the head, and by preserving
the teeth and eyes would make him appear still alive ;
his skin would be worn at festivals, and thus he would
be honoured after death.   Then another fox who gave

bad news was cursed, and a falcon who said Cavillaca was near was told he would be highly esteemed, and that whoever killed him would also wear his skin at festivals. The parrots, giving bad news, were to cry so loud that they would be heard far away, and their cries would betray them to enemies. Thus Coniraya blessed the animals which gave him news he liked, and cursed those which gave the opposite. When at last he came to the sea he found Cavillaca and the child turned into stone, and there he encountered two beautiful young daughters of Pachacamac, who guarded a great serpent. He made love to the elder sister, but the younger one flew away in the form of a wild pigeon. At that time there were no fishes in the sea, but a certain goddess had reared a few in a small pond, and Coniraya emptied these into the ocean and thus peopled it. The angry deity tried to outwit Coniraya and kill him, but he was too wise and escaped. He returned to Huarochiri, and played tricks as before on the villagers.

Coniraya slightly approximates to the Jurupari of the Uapès Indians of Brazil, especially as regards his impish qualities.[1]

The Llama's Warning

An old Peruvian myth relates how the world was nearly left without an inhabitant. A man took his llama to a fine place for feeding, but the beast moaned and would not eat, and on its master questioning it, it said there was little wonder it was sad, because in five days the sea would rise and engulf the earth. The man, alarmed, asked if there was no way of escape, and the llama advised him to go to the top of a high mountain, Villa-coto, taking food for five days. When

[1] See Spence, article " Brazil " in *Encyclopdia of Religion and Ethics* vol. ii.

they reached the summit of the hill all kinds of birds and animals were already there. When the sea rose the water came so near that it washed the tail of a fox, and that is why foxes' tails are black! After five days the water fell, leaving only this one man alive, and from him the Peruvians believed the present human race to be descended.

The Myth of Huathiacuri

After the deluge the Indians chose the bravest and richest man as leader. This period they called Purunpacha (the time without a king). On a high mountain-top appeared five large eggs, from one of which Paricaca, father of Huathiacuri, later emerged. Huathiacuri, who was so poor that he had not means to cook his food properly, learned much wisdom from his father, and the following story shows how this assisted him. A certain man had built a most curious house, the roof being made of yellow and red birds' feathers. He was very rich, possessing many llamas, and was greatly esteemed on account of his wealth. So proud did he become that he aspired to be the creator himself; but when he became very ill and could not cure himself his divinity seemed doubtful. Just at this time Huathiacuri was travelling about, and one day he saw two foxes meet and listened to their conversation. From this he heard about the rich man and learned the cause of his illness, and forthwith he determined to go on to find him. On arriving at the curious house he met a lovely young girl, one of the rich man's daughters. She told him about her father's illness, and Huathiacuri, charmed with her, said he would cure her father if she would only give him her love. He looked so ragged and dirty that she refused, but she took him to her father and informed

'' The younger one flew away ''
William Sewell
(See page 323)

" His wife at first indignantly denied the accusation "
William Sewell
(See page 325)

him that Huathiacuri said he could cure him. Her father consented to give him an opportunity to do so. Huathiacuri began his cure by telling the sick man that his wife had been unfaithful, and that there were two serpents hovering above his house to devour it, and a toad with two heads under his grinding-stone. His wife at first indignantly denied the accusation, but on Huathiacuri reminding her of some details, and the serpents and toad being discovered, she confessed her guilt. The reptiles were killed, the man recovered, and the daughter was married to Huathiacuri.

Huathiacuri's poverty and raggedness displeased the girl's brother-in-law, who suggested to the bridegroom a contest in dancing and drinking. Huathiacuri went to seek his father's advice, and the old man told him to accept the challenge and return to him. Paricaca then sent him to a mountain, where he was changed into a dead llama. Next morning a fox and its vixen carrying a jar of *chicha* came, the fox having a flute of many pipes. When they saw the dead llama they laid down their things and went toward it to have a feast, but Huathiacuri then resumed his human form and gave a loud cry that frightened away the foxes, whereupon he took possession of the jar and flute. By the aid of these, which were magically endowed, he beat his brother-in-law in dancing and drinking.

Then the brother-in-law proposed a contest to prove who was the handsomer when dressed in festal attire. By the aid of Paricaca Huathiacuri found a red lion-skin, which gave him the appearance of having a rainbow round his head, and he again won.

The next trial was to see who could build a house the quickest and best. The brother-in-law got all his men to help, and had his house nearly finished before the other had his foundation laid. But here again

Paricaca's wisdom proved of service, for Huathiacuri got animals and birds of all kinds to help him during the night, and by morning the building was finished except the roof. His brother-in-law got many llamas to come with straw for his roof, but Huathiacuri ordered an animal to stand where its loud screams frightened the llamas away, and the straw was lost. Once more Huathiacuri won the day. At last Paricaca advised Huathiacuri to end this conflict, and he asked his brother-in-law to see who could dance best in a blue shirt with white cotton round the loins. The rich man as usual appeared first, but when Huathiacuri came in he made a very loud noise and frightened him, and he began to run away. As he ran Huathiacuri turned him into a deer. His wife, who had followed him, was turned into a stone, with her head on the ground and her feet in the air, because she had given her husband such bad advice.

The four remaining eggs on the mountain-top then opened, and four falcons issued, which turned into four great warriors. These warriors performed many miracles, one of which consisted in raising a storm which swept away the rich Indian's house in a flood to the sea.

Paricaca

Having assisted in the performance of several miracles, Paricaca set out determined to do great deeds. He went to find Caruyuchu Huayallo, to whom children were sacrificed. He came one day to a village where a festival was being celebrated, and as he was in very poor clothes no one took any notice of him or offered him anything, till a young girl, taking pity on him, brought him *chicha* to drink. In gratitude Paricaca told her to seek a place of safety for herself, as the

316

village would be destroyed after five days, but she was to tell no one of this. Annoyed at the inhospitality of the people, Paricaca then went to a hill-top and sent down a fearful storm and flood, and the whole village was destroyed. Then he came to another village, now San Lorenzo. He saw a very beautiful girl, Choque Suso, crying bitterly. Asking her why she wept, she said the maize crop was dying for want of water. Paricaca at once fell in love with this girl, and after first damming up the little water there was, and thus leaving none for the crop, he told her he would give her plenty of water if she would only return his love. She said he must get water not only for her own crop but for all the other farms before she could consent. He noticed a small rill, from which, by opening a dam, he thought he might get a sufficient supply of water for the farms. He then got the assistance of the birds in the hills, and animals such as snakes, lizards, and so on, in removing any obstacles in the way, and they widened the channel so that the water irrigated all the land. The fox with his usual cunning managed to obtain the post of engineer, and carried the canal to near the site of the church of San Lorenzo. Paricaca, having accomplished what he had promised, begged Choque Suso to keep her word, which she willingly did, but she proposed living at the summit of some rocks called Yanacaca. There the lovers stayed very happily, at the head of the channel called Cocochallo, the making of which had united them ; and as Choque Suso wished to remain there always, Paricaca eventually turned her into a stone.

In all likelihood this myth was intended to account for the invention of irrigation among the early Peruvians, and from being a local legend probably spread over the length and breadth of the country.

Conclusion

The advance in civilisation attained by the peoples of America must be regarded as among the most striking phenomena in the history of mankind, especially if it be viewed as an example of what can be achieved by isolated races occupying a peculiar environment. It cannot be too strongly emphasised that the cultures and mythologies of old Mexico and Peru were evolved without foreign assistance or intervention, that, in fact, they were distinctively and solely the fruit of American aboriginal thought evolved upon American soil. An absorbing chapter in the story of human advancement is provided by these peoples, whose architecture, arts, graphic and plastic, laws and religions prove them to have been the equals of most of the Asiatic nations of antiquity, and the superiors of the primitive races of Europe, who entered into the heritage of civilisation through the gateway of the East. The aborigines of ancient America had evolved for themselves a system of writing which at the period of their discovery was approaching the alphabetic type, a mathematical system unique and by no means despicable, and an architectural science in some respects superior to any of which the Old World could boast. Their legal codes were reasonable and founded upon justice ; and if their religions were tainted with cruelty, it was a cruelty which they regarded as inevitable, and as the doom placed upon them by sanguinary and insatiable deities and not by any human agency.

In comparing the myths of the American races with the deathless stories of Olympus or the scarcely less classic tales of India, frequent resemblances and analogies cannot fail to present themselves, and these

328

" He saw a very beautiful girl crying bitterly "

William Sewell

(See page 327)

CONCLUSION

are of value as illustrating the circumstance that in every quarter of the globe the mind of man has shaped for itself a system of faith based upon similar principles. But in the perusal of the myths and beliefs of Mexico and Peru we are also struck with the strangeness and remoteness alike of their subject-matter and the type of thought which they present. The result of centuries of isolation is evident in a profound contrast of " atmosphere." It seems almost as if we stood for a space upon the dim shores of another planet, spectators of the doings of a race of whose modes of thought and feeling we were entirely ignorant.

For generations these stories have been hidden, along with the memory of the gods and folk of whom they tell, beneath a thick dust of neglect, displaced here and there only by the efforts of antiquarians working singly and unaided. Nowadays many well-equipped students are striving to add to our knowledge of the civilisations of Mexico and Peru. To the mythical stories of these peoples, alas! we cannot add. The greater part of them perished in the flames of the Spanish *autos-de-fé*. But for those which have survived we must be grateful, as affording so many casements through which we may catch the glitter and gleam of civilisations more remote and bizarre than those of the Orient, shapes dim yet gigantic, misty yet many-coloured, the ghosts of peoples and beliefs not the least splendid and solemn in the roll of dead nations and vanished faiths.

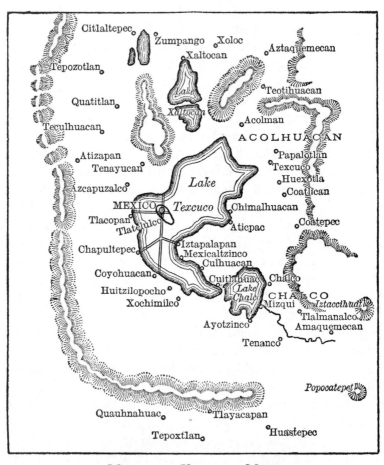

MAP OF THE VALLEY OF MEXICO
*From the author's " Civilization of Ancient Mexico," by
permission of the Cambridge University Press*

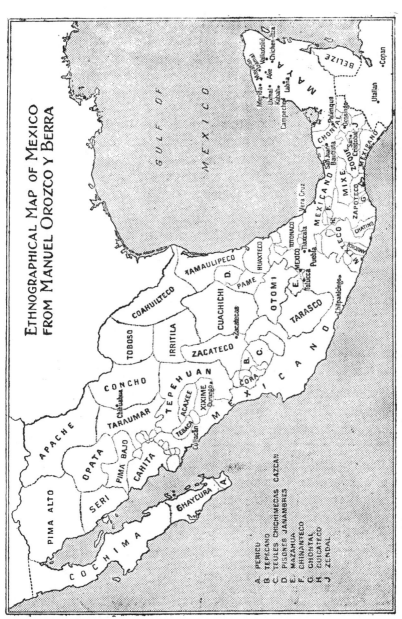

ETHNOGRAPHICAL MAP OF MEXICO
FROM MANUEL OROZCO Y BERRA

A. PERICU
B. TEPACANO
C. TEULES CHICHIMECAS CAZCAN
D. PISONES JANAMBRES
E. MAZAHUA
F. CHINANTECO
G. CHONTAL
H. EUIZATECO
J. ZENDAL

The names of the smaller areas are shown in the margin, with indicators A, B, C, &c.

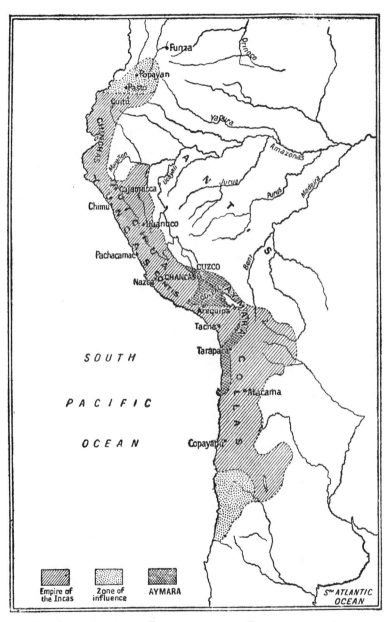

Funza

Popayan
Pasto
Quito

Yapura

Amazonas

Marañon

Ucayali

Cajamarca

Chimu

Jurua

Purus

Madeira

Huanuco

Pachacamac

CUZCO

Nazca CHANCAS

Beni

Arequipa

Tacna

SOUTH

Tarapaca

COLLA

PACIFIC

Atacama

OCEAN

Copayapu

Empire of
the Incas

Zone of
influence

AYMARA

Sth ATLANTIC
OCEAN

DISTRIBUTION OF THE RACES UNDER THE EMPIRE OF THE INCAS

BIBLIOGRAPHY

THE following bibliography is not intended to be exhaustive, but merely to indicate to those who desire to follow up the matter provided in the preceding pages such works as will best repay their attention.

Mexico

Acosta, José de : *Historia Natural y Moral de las Yndias.* Seville, 1580.

Alzate y Ramirez : *Descripcion de las Antiguedades de Xochicalco.* 1791.

Bancroft, H. H. : *Native Races of the Pacific States of America.* 1875. A compilation of historical matter relating to aboriginal America, given almost without comment. Useful to beginners.

Boturini Benaduci, L. : *Idea de una Nueva Historia General de la America Septentrional.* Madrid, 1746. Contains a number of valuable original manuscripts.

Bourbourg, Abbé Brasseur de : *Histoire des Nations Civilisées du Mexique et de l'Amérique Centrale.* Paris, 1857–59. The Abbé possessed much knowledge of the peoples of Central America and their ancient history, but had a leaning toward the marvellous which renders his works of doubtful value.

Charnay, Désiré : *Ancient Cities of the New World.* London, 1887. This translation from the French is readable and interesting, and is of assistance to beginners. It is, however, of little avail as a serious work of reference, and has been superseded.

Chevalier, M. : *Le Mexique Ancien et Moderne.* Paris, 1886.

Clavigero, Abbé : *Storia Antica del Messico.* Cesena, 1780. English translation, London, 1787. Described in text.

Diaz, Bernal : *Historia Verdadera de la Conquista de Nueva España.* 1837. An eye-witness's account of the conquest of Mexico.

Enock, C. Reginald : *Mexico, its Ancient and Modern Civilisation,* &c. London, 1909.

Gomara, F. L. de : *Historia General de las Yndias.* Madrid, 1749.

Herrera, Antonio de : *Historia General de los Hechos de los Castellanos en las Islas y Tierra Firme del Mar Oceano.* 4 vols. Madrid, 1601

BIBLIOGRAPHY

HUMBOLDT, ALEX. VON : *Vues des Cordillères.* Paris, 1816. English translation by Mrs. Williams.

IXTLILXOCHITL, F. DE ALVA : *Historia Chichimeca; Relaciones.* Edited by A. Chavero. Mexico, 1891–92.

KINGSBOROUGH, LORD : *Antiquities of Mexico.* London, 1830.

LUMHOLTZ, C. : *Unknown Mexico.* 1903.

MACNUTT, F. C.: *Letters of Cortés to Charles V.* London, 1908.

NADAILLAC, MARQUIS DE : *Prehistoric America.* Translation. London, 1885.

NOLL, A. H. : *A Short History of Mexico.* Chicago, 1903.

NUTTALL, ZELIA : *The Fundamental Principles of Old and New World Civilisations.* 1901.

PAYNE, E. J. : *History of the New World called America.* London, 1892–99. By far the best and most exhaustive work in English upon the subject. It is, however, unfinished.

PEÑAFIEL, F.: *Monumentos del Arte Mexicano Antiguo.* Berlin, 1890.

PRESCOTT, W. H. : *History of the Conquest of Mexico.* Of romantic interest only. Prescott did not study Mexican history for more than two years, and his work is now quite superseded from a historical point of view. Its narrative charm, however, is unassailable.

SAHAGUN, BERNARDINO DE : *Historia General de las Cosas de Nueva España.* Mexico, 1829.

SELER, E. : *Mexico and Guatemala.* Berlin, 1896.

SERRA, JUSTO (Editor) : *Mexico, its Social Evolution,* &c. 2 vols. Mexico, 1904.

SPENCE, LEWIS : *The Civilization of Ancient Mexico.* A digest of the strictly verifiable matter of Mexican history and antiquities. All tradition is eliminated, the author's aim being to present the beginner and the serious student with a series of unembellished facts.

STARR, F. : *The Indians of Southern Mexico.* 1899.

THOMAS, CYRUS, AND MAGEE, W. J. : *The History of North America.* 1908.

TORQUEMADA, JUAN DE : *Monarquia Indiana.* Madrid, 1723.

Bulletin 28 of the Bureau of American Ethnology contains trans-

BIBLIOGRAPHY

lations of valuable essays by the German scholars Seler, Schellhas Förstemann, &c.

Many of the above works deal with Central America as well as with Mexico proper.

Central America

COGOLLUDO, D. LOPEZ : *Historia de Yucathan.* 1688. Very scarce.

DIEGO DE LANDA : *Relacion de Cosas de Yucatan.* Paris, 1836. Translation by Brasseur.

DUPAIX, COLONEL : *Antiquités Mexicaines.* Paris, 1834-36.

MAUDSLAY, A. P. : *Biologia Centrali-Americana.* Publication proceeding. Contains many excellent sketches of ruins, &c.

SPENCE, LEWIS : *The Popol Vuh.* London, 1908.

Peru

ENOCK, C. R. : *Peru : its Former and Present Civilisation,* &c. London 1908.

MARKHAM, SIR CLEMENTS R. : *History of Peru.* Chicago, 1892.

PRESCOTT, W. H. : *History of the Conquest of Peru.* 3 vols. Philadelphia, 1868.

SQUIER, E. G. : *Peru : Incidents of Travei and Exploration in the Land of the Incas.* London, 1877.

TSCHUDI, J. J. VON : *Reisen durch Südamerika.* 5 vols. Leipsic, 1866-'68. *Travels in Peru.* London, 1847.

VEGA, GARCILASSO EL INCA DE LA : *Royal Commentaries oj the Incas,* 1609. Hakluyt Society's Publications.

In seeking the original sources of Peruvian history we must refer to the early Spanish historians who visited the country, either at the period of the conquest or immediately subsequent to it. From those Spaniards who wrote at a time not far distant from that event we have gained much valuable knowledge concerning the contemporary condition of Peru, and a description of the principal works of these pioneers will materially assist the reader who is bent on pursuing the study of Peruvian antiquities.

Pedro de Cieza de Leon composed a geographical account of Peru in 1554, devoting the latter part of his chronicle to the subject of the Inca civilisation. This work has been translated into English

BIBLIOGRAPHY

by Sir Clements R. Markham, and published by the Hakluyt Society.

Juan José de Betanzos, who was well acquainted with the Quichua language, and who married an Inca princess, wrote an account of the Incas in 1551, which was edited and printed by Señor Jimenes de la Espada in 1880.

Polo de Ondegardo, a lawyer and politician, wrote his two *Relaciones* in 1561 and 1571, making valuable reports on the laws and system of administration of the Incas. One of these works has been translated by Sir Clements R. Markham, and printed by the Hakluyt Society.

Augustin de Zarate, accountant, who arrived in Peru with Blasco Nuñez Vela, the first Viceroy, is the author of the *Provincia del Peru*, which was published at Antwerp in 1555.

Fernando de Santillan, judge of the Linia Audience, contributed an interesting *Relacion* in 1550, edited and printed in 1879 by Señor Jimenes de la Espada.

Juan de Matienzo, a lawyer contemporary with Ondegardo, was the author of the valuable work *Gobierno de el Peru*, not yet translated.

Christoval de Molina, priest of Cuzco, wrote an interesting story of Inca ceremonial and religion between 1570 and 1584, which has been published by the Hakluyt Society. The translator is Sir C. R. Markham.

Miguel Cavello Balboa, of Quito, gives us the only particulars we possess of Indian coast history, and the most valuable information on the war between Huascar and Atauhuallpa, in his splendid *Miscellanea Austral*, 1576, translated into French in 1840 by Ternaux-Compans.

A Jesuit priest, José de Acosta, compiled a *Natural History of the Indies*, which was published for the first time in 1588. An English translation of the work is provided by the Hakluyt Society.

Fernando Montesinos in his *Memorias Antiguas Historiales del Peru* and *Anales Memorias Nuevas del Peru* quotes a long line of sovereigns who preceded the Incas. These works were translated into French in 1840.

Relacion de los Costombras Antiguas de los Naturales del Peru, written by an anonymous Jesuit, records an account of Inca civilisation. The work was published in Spain in 1879. Another Jesuit, Francisco de Avila, wrote on the superstitions of the Indians of Huarochiri and their gods. His work was translated into English and published by the Hakluyt Society.

338

BIBLIOGRAPHY

Pablo José de Arriaga, a priest who policed the country, destroying the false gods, compiled in 1621 *Extirpacion de la Idolatria del Peru*, describing the downfall of the ancient Inca religion.

Antonio de la Calancha compiled an interesting history of the Incas in his work on the Order of St. Augustine in Peru (1638-1653).

In his *Historia de Copacabana y de su Milagrosa Imagen* (1620) Alonzo Ramos Gavilan disclosed much information concerning the colonists during the time of the Inca rule.

A valuable history of the Incas is provided by Garcilasso el Inca de la Vega in his *Commentarios Reales*. The works of previous authors are reviewed, and extracts are given from the compilations of the Jesuit Blas Valera, whose writings are lost. The English translation is published by the Hakluyt Society.

Relacion de Antiguedades deste Reyno del Peru, by Pachacuti Yamqui Salcamayhua, an Indian of the Collao, was translated into English by Sir C. R. Markham, and published by the Hakluyt Society.

The *Historia del Reino del Quinto*, compiled by Juan de Velasco, was translated into French by Ternaux-Compans in 1840.

Antonio de Herrera gives a brief account of the history and civilisation of the Inca people in his *General History of the Indies*.

In his *History of America* Robertson was the first to compile a thorough account of the Incas. Prescott, however, in 1848 eclipsed his work by his own fascinating account. Sir Arthur Helps has also given a *résumé* of Inca progress in his *Spanish Conquest* (1855).

The Peruvian Sebastian Lorente published in 1860 a history of ancient Peru, which presents the subject more broadly than the narratives of the American and English authors, and as the result of many years of further research he contributed a series of essays to the *Revista Peruana*.

One of the best works dealing with the antiquities of the Inca period is *Antiguedades Peruanas*, by Don Mariano Rivero (English translation by Dr. Hawkes, 1853). The compilation on Peru by E. G. Squier (1877), and a similar narrative by C. Weiner (Paris, 1880), both of which stand in accuracy above the others, are also worthy of mention.

The work of Reiss and Stubel, narrating their excavations at Ancon, is richly presented in three volumes, with 119 plates.

The works of Sir Clements Markham are the best guide to English scholars on the subject.

INDEX AND GLOSSARY

NOTE ON THE PRONUNCIATION OF THE MEXICAN, MAYAN, AND PERUVIAN LANGUAGES

MEXICAN

As the Spanish alphabet was that first employed to represent Mexican or Nahuatl phonology, so Mexican words and names must be pronounced, for the most part, according to the Castilian system. An exception is the letter *x*, which in Spanish is sometimes written as *j* and pronounced as *h* aspirate ; and in Nahuatl sometimes as in English, at other times as *sh* or *s*. Thus the word " Mexico " is pronounced by the aboriginal Mexican with the hard *x*, but by the Spaniard as " May-hee-co." The name of the native author Ixtlilxochitl is pronounced " Ishtlilshotshitl," the *ch* being articulated as *tsh*, for euphony. Xochicalco is " So-chi-cal-co." The vowel sounds are pronounced as in French or Italian. The *tl* sound is pronounced with almost a click of the tongue.

MAYAN

The Maya alphabet consists of twenty-two letters, of which *ə*. *ch, k, pp, th, tz* are peculiar to the language, and cannot be properly pronounced by Europeans. It is deficient in the letters *d, f, g, j, q, r, s*. The remaining letters are sounded as in Spanish. The letter *x* occurring at the beginning of a word is pronounced *ex*. For example, Xbalanque is pronounced " Exbalanke." The frequent occurrence of elisions in spoken Maya renders its pronunciation a matter of great difficulty, and the few grammars on the language agree as to the hopelessness of conveying any true idea of the exact articulation of the language by means of written directions. Norman in his work entitled *Rambles in Yucatan* remarks : " This perhaps accounts for the disappearance of all grammars and vocabularies of the Maya tongue from the peninsula of Yucatan, the priests finding it much easier to learn the language directly from the Indian than to acquire it from books."

PERUVIAN

The two languages spoken in Peru in ancient times were the Quichua, or Inca, and the Aymara. These still survive. The former was the language of the Inca rulers of the country, but both sprang from one common linguistic stock. As these languages were first reduced to writing by means of a European alphabet, their pronunciation presents but little difficulty, the words practically being pronounced as they are written, having regard to the " Continental " pronunciation of the vowels. In Quichua the same sound is given to the intermediate *c* before a consonant and to the final *c*, as in " chacra " and " Pachacamac." The general accent is most frequently on the penultimate syllable

INDEX AND GLOSSARY

A

AAC, PRINCE. In the story of Queen Móo, 240, 244–245, 246

ACALAN. District in Guatemala ; race-movements and, 150

ACLLACUNA (Selected Ones). Body of maidens from whom victims for sacrifice were taken in Peru, 313

ACLLA-HUASI. Houses in which the Acllacuna lived, 313

ACOLHUACAN. District in Mexico, 26

ACOLHUANS (or ACOLHUAQUE) (People of the Broad Shoulder). Mexican race, 26 ; said to have founded Mexico, 26 ; a pure Nahua race, perhaps the Toltecs, 26 ; their supremacy, 48

ACOLHUAQUE. See Acolhuans

ACOSTA, JOSÉ DE. Work on Mexican lore, 58

ACSUMAMA. Guardian spirit of the potato plant in Peru, 295

ACXITL. Toltec king, son of Huemac II, 17, 19

ACXOPIL. Ruler of the Kiche, 158–159

AGOREROS (or MOHANES). Members of Peruvian tribes who claimed power as oracles, 297–298, 314

AHUIZOTL. Mexican king, 30

AH-ZOTZILS. A Maya tribe, 172

AKAB-SIB (Writing in the Dark). A bas-relief at El Castillo, Chichen-Itza, 190

AKÉ. Maya ruins at, 186–187

AMERICA. Superficial resemblance between peoples, customs, and art-forms of Asia and, 1 ; civilisation, native origin of, 1–2, 3, 328 ; animal and plant life peculiar to, 2 ; man, origin of, in, 2 ; geographical connection between Asia and, 3 ; traditions of intercourse between Asia and, 3 ; Chinese Fu-Sang and, 3 ; possible Chinese and Japanese visits to,

3–4 ; Coronado's expedition to, 4 ; legends of intercourse between Europe and, 4 ; " Great Ireland " probably the same as, 4 ; St. Brandan's voyage and, 4 ; reached by early Norsemen, 5 ; the legend of Madoc and, 5–6 ; early belief in, respecting incursions from the east, 6 ; prophecy of Chilan Balam re coming of white men to, 8

AMERICA, CENTRAL. Indigenous origin of civilisation of, 1 ; legend of Toltec migration to, 20

ANAHUAC (By the Water). Native name of the Mexican plateau, 18. See Mexico

ANCESTOR-WORSHIP in Peru, 296

ANDEANS. The prehistoric civilisation of, 249–250 ; architectural remains of, 250

ANTAHUAYLLAS. Peruvian tribe, 284

ANTILIA. Legends of, have no connection with American myth, 6

ANTI-SUYU. One of the four racial divisions of ancient Peru, 255

APINGUELA. Island on Lake Titicaca ; Huaina Ccapac and the lake-goddess and, 299

APOCATEQUIL. Peruvian thunder-god, the " Prince of Evil " ; in a creation-myth, 301–302

APU-CCAPAC (Sovereign Chief). Title of the Inca rulers, 248

" APU - OLLANTA." A drama-legend of the Incas, 251–253

APURIMAC (Great Speaker). River in Peru ; regarded as an oracle, 296

AQUA. A bird-maiden; in the myth of origin of the Canaris, 319

ARARA (Fire-bird). Same as Kinich-ahau, which see

ARCHITECTURE. I. Of the Nahua, 31–34. II. Of the Maya, 149–150, 178–198 ; the most individual expression of the people, 178 ; Yucatan exhibits the most perfect specimens, and the decadent phase, 178 ;

INDEX AND GLOSSARY

INDEX AND GLOSSARY

INDEX AND GLOSSARY

INDEX AND GLOSSARY

INDEX AND GLOSSARY

348

INDEX AND GLOSSARY

INDEX AND GLOSSARY

represented, 73; associated with the gladiatorial stone, 73; as Mexitli, 74; as serpent-god of lightning, associated with the summer, 74; in connection with Tlaloc, 74; the Toxcatl festival of, 74; the priesthood of, 75; in connection with the legend of the sacrificed princess, 124

HUN-APU (Master, or Magician). A hero-god, twin with Xbalanque; in a Kiche myth, 211–219; in the myth in the second book of the *Popol Vuh*, 220, 223–227; mentioned, 237

HUN-CAMB. One of the rulers of Xibalba, the Kiche Hades, 220, 221, 224

HUNABKU. God of the Maya, representing divine unity, 171

HUNAC EEL. Ruler of the Cocomes, 155

HUNBATZ. Son of Hunhun-Apu, 220, 222, 223

HUNCHOUBN. Son of Hunhun-Apu, 220, 222, 223

HUNHUN-APU. Son of Xpiyacoc and Xmucane; in the myth in the second book of the *Popol Vuh*, 220–222, 224, 225, 227

HUNPICTOK (Commander-in-Chief of Eight Thousand Flints). The palace of, at Itzamal, 187–188

HUNSA. City at which the Zoque of the Chibchas lived, 276

HURAKAN (The One-legged). Maya god of lightning; prototype of Tlaloc, 76, 78; the mustachioed image of, at Itzamal, 188; = the mighty wind, in the Kiche story of the creation, 209; and the creation of man in the second book of the *Popol Vuh*, 229–230; probably same as Nahua Tezcatlipoca, 237; his sub-gods, 237

I

ICUTEMAL. Ruler of the Kiche, 159

ILHUICATLAN (In the Sky). Column in temple at Mexico, connected with the worship of the planet Venus, 96

ILLATICI (The Thunder Vase). Peruvian deity representing the thunderstorm, 301

INCA ROCA. Sixth Inca, 283

INCAS (People of the Sun). The Peruvian ruling race; a composite people, 254; place of origin, 254; inferior to the Mexicans in general culture, 248; mythology of, 255–258, 317–327; character of their civilisation, 259; no personal freedom, 260; age of marriage, 260; their system of mummification, 262–264; severity of their legal code, 264; social system, 264–265; calendar, 265–266; religious festivals, 267; architecture, 268–269; architectural remains, 270–273; irrigation works, 273; possessed no system of writing, 278; the *quipos*, 278–279; as craftsmen, 279–281; the pottery of, 280–281; period and extent of their dominion, 281–282; fusion of the constituent peoples, 285–286; splitting of the race, 286; their despotism, 290; religion of, 291; sun-worship of, 307–313

INCAS. The rulers of Peru, 282–290; the Inca the representative of the sun, 260; unlimited power of, 260; the moon the mythic mother of the dynasty, 262

INTI-HUASI. Building sacred to the sun in Peruvian villages, 308

INTIHUATANA. Inca device for marking the date of the sun-festivals, 265

INTIP RAYMI (Great Feast of the Sun). Peruvian festival, 267, 311–312

INTIPAMPA (Field of the Sun). Garden in which the Coricancha of Cuzco stood, 260–261

INDEX AND GLOSSARY

INDEX AND GLOSSARY

INDEX AND GLOSSARY

composition originally, 237–238. *The first book :* The creation, 209 ; the downfall of man, 209–210 ; story of Vukub-Cakix, 210–213 ; the undoing of Zipacna, 213–216 ; the overthrow of Cabrakan, 216–219 ; the creation-story probably the result of the fusion of several myths, 235. *The second book :* Hunhun-Apu and Vukub-Hunapu descend to the Underworld, 220–221; Hunhun-Apu and Xquiq, 222 ; birth and exploits of Hun-Apu and Xbalanque, 223–224 ; the hero-brothers in Xibalba, and the discomfiture of the Lords of Hell, 225–227 ; the conception in this book common to other mythologies, 228 ; the savage dread of death probably responsible for the conception of its vanquishment, 228 ; other sources of the myth, 228. *The third book :* Man is created, 229 ; woman is created, 230 ; gods are vouchsafed to man, 230 ; Tohil provides fire, 230–231 ; the race is confounded in speech and migrates, 231 ; the sun appears, 231 ; death of the first men, 232 ; resemblance of the myth to those of other American peoples, 232 ; similarity of the migration-story to others, 233–234 ; probable origin of the migration-myth, 234–235. *The fourth book,* 238–239

POTOSI. Peruvian city, 248

POWEL. *History of Wales,* cited, 5

POYAUHTECATL, MOUNT. In Quetzalcoatl myth, 65

PPAPP-HOL-CHAC (The House of Heads and Lightnings). Ruin at Itzamal, 187

PRIESTHOOD, MEXICAN, 114–117 ; power of, 114 ; beneficent ministrations of, 115 ; revenues of, 115 ; education conducted by, 115–116 ; orders of, 116 ; rigorous existence of, 116–117

PUCARA. Peruvian fortress-city ; leader in the Huanca alliance, 282

PUEBLO INDIANS. Probably related to Nahua, 24

PULQUE. The universal Mexican beverage, 45

PULQUE-GODS, 104–105

PUMA-PUNCU. Door to be passed before reaching Rock of Titicaca, 311

PUMA-SNAKE. Mixtec deer-god ; in creation-myth, 120

PUMATAMPU. Place in Peru ; Inca Roca defeats the Conti-suyu at, 283

PURUNPACHA. The period after the deluge when there was no king, in Peru, 324

PYRAMID OF SACRIFICE. Ruin at Uxmal, 194

Q

QUÄAQUA. Sun-god of the Salish Indians, 83

QUACAMAYO BIRDS. In a myth of the Canaris Indians, 319

QUAQUIUTL. Indian tribe, 83

QUATLAPANQUI (The Head-splitter). A *pulque*-god, 104

QUATAVITA, THE LAKE OF. The Chibchas and, 276

QUAUHQUAUHTINCHAN (House of the Eagles). Sacrifice to the sun in, 99

QUAUHTITLAN. Place mentioned in legend of Quetzalcoatl's journey from Tollan, 64

QUAUHXICALLI (Cup of the Eagles). Mexican sacrificial stone, 99, 100

QUAUITLEUA. Festival of Tlaloc, 77

QUAUITLICAC. In myth of Huitzilopochtli's origin, 71, 72

QUEMADA. Place in Mexico ; cyclopean ruins at, 32

QUENTI-PUNCU. Door to be passed before reaching Rock of Titicaca, 311

QUETZALCOATL (" Feathered Serpent " or " Feathered Staff ")

INDEX AND GLOSSARY

Telpochtli, 66; as usually depicted, 66; Aztec conception of, as wind-god, 66; as Yoalli Ehecatl, 66; extent and development of the cult of, 67–68; as Moneneque, 67; and the Teotleco festival, 68–69; the Toxcatl festival of, 69–70, 74; in the character of Tlazolteotl, 107, 108

TEZCOTZINCO. The villa of Nezahualcoyotl, 133–136

TEZCUCO. I. Chichimec city, 26, 47; rivalry with Azcapozalco, 49; its hegemony, 49; conquered by Tecpanecs, 51; allied with Aztecs, 52; Tezcatlipoca the tribal god, 59; the story of Nezahualcoyotl, the prince of, 125–128. II. Lake, 26; in legend the foundation of Mexico, 28; the cities upon, 47, 49–50

TEZOZOMOC, F. DE A. On Mexican mythology, 58

THEOZAPOTLAN. Mexican city, 203

THLINGIT. Indian tribe, 83

THOMAS, PROFESSOR C. Research on Maya writing, 162; on God L, 176

THOMAS, ST. The Apostle; Cortés believed to be, 7; associated with the Maya cross, 187, 275; and the wooden cross found in the valley of the Chichas, 274

THONAPA. Son of the creator in Peruvian myth; in connection with stone-worship, 293; myths of, 319–320

THUNDER-GOD, Peruvian, 299–302

TIAHUANACO. Prehistoric city of the Andeans, 249–250; the great doorway at, 249; in a legend of Manco Ccapac, 256; in Inca creation-myth, 258; and legend of Thonapa the Civiliser, 293

TIÇOTZICATZIN. In the story of Princess Papan, 140

TIKAL. Maya city; architectural remains at, 196

TITICACA. I. Lake, 249; settlements of the Quichua-Aymara on the shores of, 254; Manco Ccapac and Mama Oullo Huaca descend to earth near, 256; regarded by Peruvians as place where men and animals were created, 298; called Mamacota by people of the Collao, 298; idols connected with, 298–299. II. Island on Lake Titicaca; the most sacred of the Peruvian shrines, 270; ruined palace on, 270; sacred rock on, the paccarisca of the sun, 293, 309; sun-worship and the Rock of Titicaca, 309–311; the Inca Tupac and the Rock, 309–310; effect on the island of the Inca worship of the Rock, 310; pilgrimage to, 310–311; Thonapa on, 320

TITLACAHUAN. Same as Tezcatlipoca, which see

TITLACAHUAN-TEZCATLIPOCA, 123

TIYA-MANACU. Town in Peru; Thonapa at, 320

TLACAHUEPAN. Mexican deity; plots against Quetzalcoatl, 60; and the legend of the amusing infant and the pestilence, 63–64

TLACHTLI. National ball-game of the Nahua and Maya, 33, 220, 224, 227

TLACOPAN. Mexican city, 26, 50; Aztecs allied with, 52

TLAELQUANI (Filth-eater). A name of Tlazolteotl, which see

TLALHUICOLE. Tlascalan warrior; the story of, 136–138

TLALOC. The Mexican rain-god, or god of waters, 29, 75; and the foundation of Mexico, 29; in association with Huitzilopochtli, 74; as usually represented, 74–76; espoused to Chalchihuitlicue, 75; Tlalocs his offspring, 75; Kiche god Hurakan his prototype, 76; manifestations of, 76; festivals of, 77; human sacrifice in connection with, 76–77; and Atamalqualiztli festival, 77–78; similarities to, in other mythologies, 78

INDEX AND GLOSSARY

INDEX AND GLOSSARY

TOTEC (Our Great Chief). A sungod, 101–102; his feast, the chief solar festival, 101–102

TOTEMISM. Among the primitive Peruvians, 291–292

TOTONACS. Aboriginal Mexican race, 23; and the sun, 82

TOUEYO. Tezcatlipoca's disguise, 61–63

TOVEYO. Toltec sorcerer; and the magic drum, 16

TOXCATL. Festival; of Tezcatlipoca, 69–70; of Huitzilopochtli, 74

TOXILMOLPILIA. Mexican calendar ceremony; and the native dread of the last day, 41

TROANO CODEX. Maya manuscript, 160; Dr. Le Plongeon and the reference to Queen Móo in, 246

TUCUMAN (World's End). Name given by the Quichua-Aymara to their land of origin, 254

TULAN (or TULAN-ZUIVA). City; the starting-point of the Kiche migrations, 157–158, 231; the Kiche arrive at, and receive their gods, 230; parallel with the Mexican Chicomoztoc, 230; the Kiche confounded in their speech at, 231

TUMIPAMPA. Sometime centre of the northern district of Peru, 286, 289, 290

TUPAC-ATAU-HUALLPA (The Sun makes Good Fortune). Son of Huaina Ccapac, 289

TUPAC-YUPANQUI (Bright). Tenth Inca, son of Pachacutic, 252–253, 287–288; achievements as ruler, 287; and the Huarcans, 288; and the Rock of Titicaca, 309–310

TUTUL XIUS. Ruling caste among the Itzaes; found Ziyan Caan and Chichen-Itza, 153; expelled from Chichen-Itza by Cocomes, 153; settle in Potonchan, build Uxmal, and regain power, 154; again overthrown, and found Mani, 155; finally

assist in conquering the Cocomes, 156

TZITZIMIMES. Demons attendant on Mictlan, 96

TZOMPANTITLAN. Place mentioned in the myth of Huitzilopochtli's origin, 71

TZOMPANTLI (Pyramid of Skulls). Minor temple of Huitzilopochtli, 31

TZUNUNIHA (House of the Water). One of the first women of the *Popol Vuh* myth, 230

TZUTUHILS. A Maya people of Guatemala, 158, 159

U

UAYAYAB. Demon who presided over the *nemontemi* (unlucky days), 177; God N identified with, 177

UEMAC. Tezcatlipoca and the daughter of, 61–63

UITZLAMPA. Place in Mexico; in myth of Huitzilopochtli's origin, 72

URCO-INCA. Inca superseded by Pachacutic, 284

URICAECHEA, M. His collection of Chibcha antiquities, 277

UXMAL. Mexican city, founded by Tutul Xius, 154; abandoned, 155; ruins at, 191–194; primitive type of its architecture, 194

V

VATICAN MSS., 37; description of the journey of the soul in, 37–38

VEGA, GARCILASSO EL INCA DE LA. *Hist. des Incas*, cited, 7; on the gods of the early Peruvians, 291

VENUS. The planet; worship of, 96–97; the only star worshipped by Mexicans, 96; Camaxtli identified with, 111; temple of, at Cuzco, 262

VERA CRUZ. Quetzalcoatl lands at, 6

VERAPAZ. District in Guatemala, 158

INDEX AND GLOSSARY

365

leaders, 91–92 ; Xolotl has affinities with, 95 ; God A thought to resemble, 174

XIUHTECUTLI (Lord of the Year). A name of the Mexican fire-god, 95

XIUMALPILLI. In Mexican calendar, 40

XIYAN CAAN. City in Yucatan, 153

XMUCANE (Female Vigour). The mother-god in the Kiche story of the creation in the *Popol Vuh*, 209 ; in the Vukub-Cakix myth, 212–213 ; in the myth in the second book of the *Popol Vuh*, 220–225 ; equivalent to the Mexican Omeciuatl, 236

XOCHICALCO (The Hill of Flowers). A *teocalli* near Tezcuco, 33–34

XOCHIMILCOS. Aztec tribe, 233

XOCHIPILLI. A name of Macuilxochitl, *which see*

XOCHITLA. A flower-garden near Tollan ; the legend of Tezcatlipoca and, 63

XOCHITONAL. Monster in the Mexican Other-world, 38

XOCHIYAYOTL (The War of Flowers). Campaign for the capture of victims for sacrifice, 98–99, 100

XOLOTL. I. King of the Chichimecs, 20 ; Teotihuacan rebuilt by, 33. II. A sun-god, 93–94 ; of southern origin and foreign to Mexico, 93 ; probably identical with Nanahuatl, 93 ; representative of human sacrifice, 93 ; has affinities with Xipe, 93 ; representations of, 94

XPIYACOC. The father god in the *Popol Vuh* story of the creation, 209 ; in the Vukub-Cakix myth, 212–213 ; in the myth in the second book of the *Popol Vuh*, 220 ; equivalent to the Mexican Ometecutli, 236

XQUIQ (Blood). A princess of Xibalba, daughter of Cuchumaquiq ; in *Popol Vuh* myth, 222

XULU. A sorcerer mentioned in *Popol Vuh* myth, 227

Y

YACATECUTLI. Tutelar god of travellers of the merchant class in Mexico, 114 ; the Maya Ekchuah probably parallel with, 177

YAHUARHUACCAC. Seventh Inca, 283

YAHUAR-PAMPA (Plain of Blood). Battle of, 285

YAMQUISUPA. Village ; Thonapa and, 319

YANACACA. Rocks ; in a myth of Paricaca, 327

YAOTZIN (The Enemy). A manifestation of Tezcatlipoca, 66

YATIRI (The Ruler). Aymara name of Pachacamac in his form of Pachayachachic ; Huaina Ccapac and, 299

YEAR. The Mexican, 39, 40

YETL. God of natives of British Columbia, 12 ; probably cognate with Quetzalcoatl, 12, 83

YMA SUMAC (How Beautiful). Daughter of Curi-Coyllur ; in the drama *Apu-Ollanta*, 252–253

YOALLI EHECATL (The Night Wind). A manifestation of Tezcatlipoca, 66

YOHUALTICITL. A name of Metztli, *which see*

YOLCUAT. Form of Quetzalcoatl, 84

YOPI. Indian tribe ; Xipe adopted from, 92

YUCATAN. Settlement of the Maya in, 151–152 ; architectural remains in, 178

YUCAY. Inca ruins at, 269

YUM KAAX (Lord of the Harvest Fields). Maya deity ; God E probably identical with, 174

YUNCA. Name given to the tropical and lowland districts of Peru, 255

366

INDEX AND GLOSSARY

A CATALOG OF SELECTED DOVER
BOOKS IN ALL FIELDS OF INTEREST

CONCERNING THE SPIRITUAL IN ART, Wassily Kandinsky. Pioneering work by father of abstract art. Thoughts on color theory, nature of art. Analysis of earlier masters. 12 illustrations. 80pp. of text. 5⅜ x 8½. 23411-8

ANIMALS: 1,419 Copyright-Free Illustrations of Mammals, Birds, Fish, Insects, etc., Jim Harter (ed.). Clear wood engravings present, in extremely lifelike poses, over 1,000 species of animals. One of the most extensive pictorial sourcebooks of its kind. Captions. Index. 284pp. 9 x 12. 23766-4

CELTIC ART: The Methods of Construction, George Bain. Simple geometric techniques for making Celtic interlacements, spirals, Kells-type initials, animals, humans, etc. Over 500 illustrations. 160pp. 9 x 12. (Available in U.S. only.) 22923-8

AN ATLAS OF ANATOMY FOR ARTISTS, Fritz Schider. Most thorough reference work on art anatomy in the world. Hundreds of illustrations, including selections from works by Vesalius, Leonardo, Goya, Ingres, Michelangelo, others. 593 illustrations. 192pp. 7⅛ x 10¼. 20241-0

CELTIC HAND STROKE-BY-STROKE (Irish Half-Uncial from "The Book of Kells"): An Arthur Baker Calligraphy Manual, Arthur Baker. Complete guide to creating each letter of the alphabet in distinctive Celtic manner. Covers hand position, strokes, pens, inks, paper, more. Illustrated. 48pp. 8¼ x 11. 24336-2

EASY ORIGAMI, John Montroll. Charming collection of 32 projects (hat, cup, pelican, piano, swan, many more) specially designed for the novice origami hobbyist. Clearly illustrated easy-to-follow instructions insure that even beginning papercrafters will achieve successful results. 48pp. 8¼ x 11. 27298-2

THE COMPLETE BOOK OF BIRDHOUSE CONSTRUCTION FOR WOOD-WORKERS, Scott D. Campbell. Detailed instructions, illustrations, tables. Also data on bird habitat and instinct patterns. Bibliography. 3 tables. 63 illustrations in 15 figures. 48pp. 5¼ x 8½. 24407-5

BLOOMINGDALE'S ILLUSTRATED 1886 CATALOG: Fashions, Dry Goods and Housewares, Bloomingdale Brothers. Famed merchants' extremely rare catalog depicting about 1,700 products: clothing, housewares, firearms, dry goods, jewelry, more. Invaluable for dating, identifying vintage items. Also, copyright-free graphics for artists, designers. Co-published with Henry Ford Museum & Greenfield Village. 160pp. 8¼ x 11. 25780-0

HISTORIC COSTUME IN PICTURES, Braun & Schneider. Over 1,450 costumed figures in clearly detailed engravings—from dawn of civilization to end of 19th century. Captions. Many folk costumes. 256pp. 8⅜ x 11¾. 23150-X

STICKLEY CRAFTSMAN FURNITURE CATALOGS, Gustav Stickley and L. & J. G. Stickley. Beautiful, functional furniture in two authentic catalogs from 1910. 594 illustrations, including 277 photos, show settles, rockers, armchairs, reclining chairs, bookcases, desks, tables. 183pp. 6½ x 9¼. 23838-5

AMERICAN LOCOMOTIVES IN HISTORIC PHOTOGRAPHS: 1858 to 1949, Ron Ziel (ed.). A rare collection of 126 meticulously detailed official photographs, called "builder portraits," of American locomotives that majestically chronicle the rise of steam locomotive power in America. Introduction. Detailed captions. xi+ 129pp. 9 x 12. 27393-8

AMERICA'S LIGHTHOUSES: An Illustrated History, Francis Ross Holland, Jr. Delightfully written, profusely illustrated fact-filled survey of over 200 American lighthouses since 1716. History, anecdotes, technological advances, more. 240pp. 8 x 10¾. 25576-X

TOWARDS A NEW ARCHITECTURE, Le Corbusier. Pioneering manifesto by founder of "International School." Technical and aesthetic theories, views of industry, economics, relation of form to function, "mass-production split" and much more. Profusely illustrated. 320pp. 6⅛ x 9¼. (Available in U.S. only.) 25023-7

HOW THE OTHER HALF LIVES, Jacob Riis. Famous journalistic record, exposing poverty and degradation of New York slums around 1900, by major social reformer. 100 striking and influential photographs. 233pp. 10 x 7⅞. 22012-5

FRUIT KEY AND TWIG KEY TO TREES AND SHRUBS, William M. Harlow. One of the handiest and most widely used identification aids. Fruit key covers 120 deciduous and evergreen species; twig key 160 deciduous species. Easily used. Over 300 photographs. 126pp. 5⅜ x 8½. 20511-8

COMMON BIRD SONGS, Dr. Donald J. Borror. Songs of 60 most common U.S. birds: robins, sparrows, cardinals, bluejays, finches, more–arranged in order of increasing complexity. Up to 9 variations of songs of each species.
Cassette and manual 99911-4

ORCHIDS AS HOUSE PLANTS, Rebecca Tyson Northen. Grow cattleyas and many other kinds of orchids–in a window, in a case, or under artificial light. 63 illustrations. 148pp. 5⅜ x 8½. 23261-1

MONSTER MAZES, Dave Phillips. Masterful mazes at four levels of difficulty. Avoid deadly perils and evil creatures to find magical treasures. Solutions for all 32 exciting illustrated puzzles. 48pp. 8¼ x 11. 26005-4

MOZART'S DON GIOVANNI (DOVER OPERA LIBRETTO SERIES), Wolfgang Amadeus Mozart. Introduced and translated by Ellen H. Bleiler. Standard Italian libretto, with complete English translation. Convenient and thoroughly portable–an ideal companion for reading along with a recording or the performance itself. Introduction. List of characters. Plot summary. 121pp. 5¼ x 8½. 24944-1

TECHNICAL MANUAL AND DICTIONARY OF CLASSICAL BALLET, Gail Grant. Defines, explains, comments on steps, movements, poses and concepts. 15-page pictorial section. Basic book for student, viewer. 127pp. 5⅜ x 8½. 21843-0

THE CLARINET AND CLARINET PLAYING, David Pino. Lively, comprehensive work features suggestions about technique, musicianship, and musical interpretation, as well as guidelines for teaching, making your own reeds, and preparing for public performance. Includes an intriguing look at clarinet history. "A godsend," *The Clarinet,* Journal of the International Clarinet Society. Appendixes. 7 illus. 320pp. 5⅜ x 8½. 40270-3

HOLLYWOOD GLAMOR PORTRAITS, John Kobal (ed.). 145 photos from 1926-49. Harlow, Gable, Bogart, Bacall; 94 stars in all. Full background on photographers, technical aspects. 160pp. 8⅜ x 11¼. 23352-9

THE ANNOTATED CASEY AT THE BAT: A Collection of Ballads about the Mighty Casey/Third, Revised Edition, Martin Gardner (ed.). Amusing sequels and parodies of one of America's best-loved poems: Casey's Revenge, Why Casey Whiffed, Casey's Sister at the Bat, others. 256pp. 5⅜ x 8½. 28598-7

THE RAVEN AND OTHER FAVORITE POEMS, Edgar Allan Poe. Over 40 of the author's most memorable poems: "The Bells," "Ulalume," "Israfel," "To Helen," "The Conqueror Worm," "Eldorado," "Annabel Lee," many more. Alphabetic lists of titles and first lines. 64pp. 5$\frac{3}{16}$ x 8¼. 26685-0

PERSONAL MEMOIRS OF U. S. GRANT, Ulysses Simpson Grant. Intelligent, deeply moving firsthand account of Civil War campaigns, considered by many the finest military memoirs ever written. Includes letters, historic photographs, maps and more. 528pp. 6⅛ x 9¼. 28587-1

ANCIENT EGYPTIAN MATERIALS AND INDUSTRIES, A. Lucas and J. Harris. Fascinating, comprehensive, thoroughly documented text describes this ancient civilization's vast resources and the processes that incorporated them in daily life, including the use of animal products, building materials, cosmetics, perfumes and incense, fibers, glazed ware, glass and its manufacture, materials used in the mummification process, and much more. 544pp. 6⅛ x 9¼. (Available in U.S. only.) 40446-3

RUSSIAN STORIES/RUSSKIE RASSKAZY: A Dual-Language Book, edited by Gleb Struve. Twelve tales by such masters as Chekhov, Tolstoy, Dostoevsky, Pushkin, others. Excellent word-for-word English translations on facing pages, plus teaching and study aids, Russian/English vocabulary, biographical/critical introductions, more. 416pp. 5⅜ x 8½. 26244-8

PHILADELPHIA THEN AND NOW: 60 Sites Photographed in the Past and Present, Kenneth Finkel and Susan Oyama. Rare photographs of City Hall, Logan Square, Independence Hall, Betsy Ross House, other landmarks juxtaposed with contemporary views. Captures changing face of historic city. Introduction. Captions. 128pp. 8¼ x 11. 25790-8

AIA ARCHITECTURAL GUIDE TO NASSAU AND SUFFOLK COUNTIES, LONG ISLAND, The American Institute of Architects, Long Island Chapter, and the Society for the Preservation of Long Island Antiquities. Comprehensive, well-researched and generously illustrated volume brings to life over three centuries of Long Island's great architectural heritage. More than 240 photographs with authoritative, extensively detailed captions. 176pp. 8¼ x 11. 26946-9

NORTH AMERICAN INDIAN LIFE: Customs and Traditions of 23 Tribes, Elsie Clews Parsons (ed.). 27 fictionalized essays by noted anthropologists examine religion, customs, government, additional facets of life among the Winnebago, Crow, Zuni, Eskimo, other tribes. 480pp. 6⅛ x 9¼. 27377-6

CATALOG OF DOVER BOOKS

FRANK LLOYD WRIGHT'S DANA HOUSE, Donald Hoffmann. Pictorial essay of residential masterpiece with over 160 interior and exterior photos, plans, elevations, sketches and studies. 128pp. 9¼ x 10¾. 29120-0

THE MALE AND FEMALE FIGURE IN MOTION: 60 Classic Photographic Sequences, Eadweard Muybridge. 60 true-action photographs of men and women walking, running, climbing, bending, turning, etc., reproduced from rare 19th-century masterpiece. vi + 121pp. 9 x 12. 24745-7

1001 QUESTIONS ANSWERED ABOUT THE SEASHORE, N. J. Berrill and Jacquelyn Berrill. Queries answered about dolphins, sea snails, sponges, starfish, fishes, shore birds, many others. Covers appearance, breeding, growth, feeding, much more. 305pp. 5¼ x 8¼. 23366-9

ATTRACTING BIRDS TO YOUR YARD, William J. Weber. Easy-to-follow guide offers advice on how to attract the greatest diversity of birds: birdhouses, feeders, water and waterers, much more. 96pp. 5³⁄₁₆ x 8¼. 28927-3

MEDICINAL AND OTHER USES OF NORTH AMERICAN PLANTS: A Historical Survey with Special Reference to the Eastern Indian Tribes, Charlotte Erichsen-Brown. Chronological historical citations document 500 years of usage of plants, trees, shrubs native to eastern Canada, northeastern U.S. Also complete identifying information. 343 illustrations. 544pp. 6½ x 9¼. 25951-X

STORYBOOK MAZES, Dave Phillips. 23 stories and mazes on two-page spreads: Wizard of Oz, Treasure Island, Robin Hood, etc. Solutions. 64pp. 8¼ x 11. 23628-5

AMERICAN NEGRO SONGS: 230 Folk Songs and Spirituals, Religious and Secular, John W. Work. This authoritative study traces the African influences of songs sung and played by black Americans at work, in church, and as entertainment. The author discusses the lyric significance of such songs as "Swing Low, Sweet Chariot," "John Henry," and others and offers the words and music for 230 songs. Bibliography. Index of Song Titles. 272pp. 6½ x 9¼. 40271-1

MOVIE-STAR PORTRAITS OF THE FORTIES, John Kobal (ed.). 163 glamor, studio photos of 106 stars of the 1940s: Rita Hayworth, Ava Gardner, Marlon Brando, Clark Gable, many more. 176pp. 8⅜ x 11¼. 23546-7

BENCHLEY LOST AND FOUND, Robert Benchley. Finest humor from early 30s, about pet peeves, child psychologists, post office and others. Mostly unavailable elsewhere. 73 illustrations by Peter Arno and others. 183pp. 5⅜ x 8½. 22410-4

YEKL and THE IMPORTED BRIDEGROOM AND OTHER STORIES OF YIDDISH NEW YORK, Abraham Cahan. Film Hester Street based on *Yekl* (1896). Novel, other stories among first about Jewish immigrants on N.Y.'s East Side. 240pp. 5⅜ x 8½. 22427-9

SELECTED POEMS, Walt Whitman. Generous sampling from *Leaves of Grass*. Twenty-four poems include "I Hear America Singing," "Song of the Open Road," "I Sing the Body Electric," "When Lilacs Last in the Dooryard Bloom'd," "O Captain! My Captain!"–all reprinted from an authoritative edition. Lists of titles and first lines. 128pp. 5³⁄₁₆ x 8¼. 26878-0

THE BEST TALES OF HOFFMANN, E. T. A. Hoffmann. 10 of Hoffmann's most important stories: "Nutcracker and the King of Mice," "The Golden Flowerpot," etc. 458pp. 5⅜ x 8½. 21793-0

FROM FETISH TO GOD IN ANCIENT EGYPT, E. A. Wallis Budge. Rich detailed survey of Egyptian conception of "God" and gods, magic, cult of animals, Osiris, more. Also, superb English translations of hymns and legends. 240 illustrations. 545pp. 5⅜ x 8½. 25803-3

FRENCH STORIES/CONTES FRANÇAIS: A Dual-Language Book, Wallace Fowlie. Ten stories by French masters, Voltaire to Camus: "Micromegas" by Voltaire; "The Atheist's Mass" by Balzac; "Minuet" by de Maupassant; "The Guest" by Camus, six more. Excellent English translations on facing pages. Also French-English vocabulary list, exercises, more. 352pp. 5⅜ x 8½. 26443-2

CHICAGO AT THE TURN OF THE CENTURY IN PHOTOGRAPHS: 122 Historic Views from the Collections of the Chicago Historical Society, Larry A. Viskochil. Rare large-format prints offer detailed views of City Hall, State Street, the Loop, Hull House, Union Station, many other landmarks, circa 1904-1913. Introduction. Captions. Maps. 144pp. 9⅜ x 12¼. 24656-6

OLD BROOKLYN IN EARLY PHOTOGRAPHS, 1865-1929, William Lee Younger. Luna Park, Gravesend race track, construction of Grand Army Plaza, moving of Hotel Brighton, etc. 157 previously unpublished photographs. 165pp. 8⅞ x 11¾. 23587-4

THE MYTHS OF THE NORTH AMERICAN INDIANS, Lewis Spence. Rich anthology of the myths and legends of the Algonquins, Iroquois, Pawnees and Sioux, prefaced by an extensive historical and ethnological commentary. 36 illustrations. 480pp. 5⅜ x 8½. 25967-6

AN ENCYCLOPEDIA OF BATTLES: Accounts of Over 1,560 Battles from 1479 B.C. to the Present, David Eggenberger. Essential details of every major battle in recorded history from the first battle of Megiddo in 1479 B.C. to Grenada in 1984. List of Battle Maps. New Appendix covering the years 1967-1984. Index. 99 illustrations. 544pp. 6½ x 9¼. 24913-1

SAILING ALONE AROUND THE WORLD, Captain Joshua Slocum. First man to sail around the world, alone, in small boat. One of great feats of seamanship told in delightful manner. 67 illustrations. 294pp. 5⅜ x 8½. 20326-3

ANARCHISM AND OTHER ESSAYS, Emma Goldman. Powerful, penetrating, prophetic essays on direct action, role of minorities, prison reform, puritan hypocrisy, violence, etc. 271pp. 5⅜ x 8½. 22484-8

MYTHS OF THE HINDUS AND BUDDHISTS, Ananda K. Coomaraswamy and Sister Nivedita. Great stories of the epics; deeds of Krishna, Shiva, taken from puranas, Vedas, folk tales; etc. 32 illustrations. 400pp. 5⅜ x 8½. 21759-0

THE TRAUMA OF BIRTH, Otto Rank. Rank's controversial thesis that anxiety neurosis is caused by profound psychological trauma which occurs at birth. 256pp. 5⅜ x 8½. 27974-X

A THEOLOGICO-POLITICAL TREATISE, Benedict Spinoza. Also contains unfinished Political Treatise. Great classic on religious liberty, theory of government on common consent. R. Elwes translation. Total of 421pp. 5⅜ x 8½. 20249-6

MY BONDAGE AND MY FREEDOM, Frederick Douglass. Born a slave, Douglass became outspoken force in antislavery movement. The best of Douglass' autobiographies. Graphic description of slave life. 464pp. 5⅜ x 8½. 22457-0

FOLLOWING THE EQUATOR: A Journey Around the World, Mark Twain. Fascinating humorous account of 1897 voyage to Hawaii, Australia, India, New Zealand, etc. Ironic, bemused reports on peoples, customs, climate, flora and fauna, politics, much more. 197 illustrations. 720pp. 5⅜ x 8½. 26113-1

THE PEOPLE CALLED SHAKERS, Edward D. Andrews. Definitive study of Shakers: origins, beliefs, practices, dances, social organization, furniture and crafts, etc. 33 illustrations. 351pp. 5⅜ x 8½. 21081-2

THE MYTHS OF GREECE AND ROME, H. A. Guerber. A classic of mythology, generously illustrated, long prized for its simple, graphic, accurate retelling of the principal myths of Greece and Rome, and for its commentary on their origins and significance. With 64 illustrations by Michelangelo, Raphael, Titian, Rubens, Canova, Bernini and others. 480pp. 5⅜ x 8½. 27584-1

PSYCHOLOGY OF MUSIC, Carl E. Seashore. Classic work discusses music as a medium from psychological viewpoint. Clear treatment of physical acoustics, auditory apparatus, sound perception, development of musical skills, nature of musical feeling, host of other topics. 88 figures. 408pp. 5⅜ x 8½. 21851-1

THE PHILOSOPHY OF HISTORY, Georg W. Hegel. Great classic of Western thought develops concept that history is not chance but rational process, the evolution of freedom. 457pp. 5⅜ x 8½. 20112-0

THE BOOK OF TEA, Kakuzo Okakura. Minor classic of the Orient: entertaining, charming explanation, interpretation of traditional Japanese culture in terms of tea ceremony. 94pp. 5⅜ x 8½. 20070-1

LIFE IN ANCIENT EGYPT, Adolf Erman. Fullest, most thorough, detailed older account with much not in more recent books, domestic life, religion, magic, medicine, commerce, much more. Many illustrations reproduce tomb paintings, carvings, hieroglyphs, etc. 597pp. 5⅜ x 8½. 22632-8

SUNDIALS, Their Theory and Construction, Albert Waugh. Far and away the best, most thorough coverage of ideas, mathematics concerned, types, construction, adjusting anywhere. Simple, nontechnical treatment allows even children to build several of these dials. Over 100 illustrations. 230pp. 5⅜ x 8½. 22947-5

THEORETICAL HYDRODYNAMICS, L. M. Milne-Thomson. Classic exposition of the mathematical theory of fluid motion, applicable to both hydrodynamics and aerodynamics. Over 600 exercises. 768pp. 6⅛ x 9¼. 68970-0

SONGS OF EXPERIENCE: Facsimile Reproduction with 26 Plates in Full Color, William Blake. 26 full-color plates from a rare 1826 edition. Includes "The Tyger," "London," "Holy Thursday," and other poems. Printed text of poems. 48pp. 5¼ x 7. 24636-1

OLD-TIME VIGNETTES IN FULL COLOR, Carol Belanger Grafton (ed.). Over 390 charming, often sentimental illustrations, selected from archives of Victorian graphics–pretty women posing, children playing, food, flowers, kittens and puppies, smiling cherubs, birds and butterflies, much more. All copyright-free. 48pp. 9¼ x 12¼. 27269-9

CATALOG OF DOVER BOOKS

PERSPECTIVE FOR ARTISTS, Rex Vicat Cole. Depth, perspective of sky and sea, shadows, much more, not usually covered. 391 diagrams, 81 reproductions of drawings and paintings. 279pp. 5⅜ x 8½.   22487-2

DRAWING THE LIVING FIGURE, Joseph Sheppard. Innovative approach to artistic anatomy focuses on specifics of surface anatomy, rather than muscles and bones. Over 170 drawings of live models in front, back and side views, and in widely varying poses. Accompanying diagrams. 177 illustrations. Introduction. Index. 144pp. 8⅜ x11¼.   26723-7

GOTHIC AND OLD ENGLISH ALPHABETS: 100 Complete Fonts, Dan X. Solo. Add power, elegance to posters, signs, other graphics with 100 stunning copyright-free alphabets: Blackstone, Dolbey, Germania, 97 more–including many lower-case, numerals, punctuation marks. 104pp. 8⅛ x 11.   24695-7

HOW TO DO BEADWORK, Mary White. Fundamental book on craft from simple projects to five-bead chains and woven works. 106 illustrations. 142pp. 5⅜ x 8.
                                        20697-1

THE BOOK OF WOOD CARVING, Charles Marshall Sayers. Finest book for beginners discusses fundamentals and offers 34 designs. "Absolutely first rate . . . well thought out and well executed."–E. J. Tangerman. 118pp. 7¾ x 10⅝.   23654-4

ILLUSTRATED CATALOG OF CIVIL WAR MILITARY GOODS: Union Army Weapons, Insignia, Uniform Accessories, and Other Equipment, Schuyler, Hartley, and Graham. Rare, profusely illustrated 1846 catalog includes Union Army uniform and dress regulations, arms and ammunition, coats, insignia, flags, swords, rifles, etc. 226 illustrations. 160pp. 9 x 12.   24939-5

WOMEN'S FASHIONS OF THE EARLY 1900s: An Unabridged Republication of "New York Fashions, 1909," National Cloak & Suit Co. Rare catalog of mail-order fashions documents women's and children's clothing styles shortly after the turn of the century. Captions offer full descriptions, prices. Invaluable resource for fashion, costume historians. Approximately 725 illustrations. 128pp. 8⅜ x 11¼.   27276-1

THE 1912 AND 1915 GUSTAV STICKLEY FURNITURE CATALOGS, Gustav Stickley. With over 200 detailed illustrations and descriptions, these two catalogs are essential reading and reference materials and identification guides for Stickley furniture. Captions cite materials, dimensions and prices. 112pp. 6½ x 9¼.   26676-1

EARLY AMERICAN LOCOMOTIVES, John H. White, Jr. Finest locomotive engravings from early 19th century: historical (1804–74), main-line (after 1870), special, foreign, etc. 147 plates. 142pp. 11⅜ x 8¼.   22772-3

THE TALL SHIPS OF TODAY IN PHOTOGRAPHS, Frank O. Braynard. Lavishly illustrated tribute to nearly 100 majestic contemporary sailing vessels: Amerigo Vespucci, Clearwater, Constitution, Eagle, Mayflower, Sea Cloud, Victory, many more. Authoritative captions provide statistics, background on each ship. 190 black-and-white photographs and illustrations. Introduction. 128pp. 8⅞ x 11¾.
                                        27163-3

LITTLE BOOK OF EARLY AMERICAN CRAFTS AND TRADES, Peter Stockham (ed.). 1807 children's book explains crafts and trades: baker, hatter, cooper, potter, and many others. 23 copperplate illustrations. 140pp. 4⅝ x 6.   23336-7

VICTORIAN FASHIONS AND COSTUMES FROM HARPER'S BAZAR, 1867–1898, Stella Blum (ed.). Day costumes, evening wear, sports clothes, shoes, hats, other accessories in over 1,000 detailed engravings. 320pp. 9⅜ x 12¼.   22990-4

GUSTAV STICKLEY, THE CRAFTSMAN, Mary Ann Smith. Superb study surveys broad scope of Stickley's achievement, especially in architecture. Design philosophy, rise and fall of the Craftsman empire, descriptions and floor plans for many Craftsman houses, more. 86 black-and-white halftones. 31 line illustrations. Introduction 208pp. 6½ x 9¼.   27210-9

THE LONG ISLAND RAIL ROAD IN EARLY PHOTOGRAPHS, Ron Ziel. Over 220 rare photos, informative text document origin (1844) and development of rail service on Long Island. Vintage views of early trains, locomotives, stations, passengers, crews, much more. Captions. 8⅞ x 11¾.   26301-0

VOYAGE OF THE LIBERDADE, Joshua Slocum. Great 19th-century mariner's thrilling, first-hand account of the wreck of his ship off South America, the 35-foot boat he built from the wreckage, and its remarkable voyage home. 128pp. 5⅜ x 8½.
40022-0

TEN BOOKS ON ARCHITECTURE, Vitruvius. The most important book ever written on architecture. Early Roman aesthetics, technology, classical orders, site selection, all other aspects. Morgan translation. 331pp. 5⅜ x 8½.   20645-9

THE HUMAN FIGURE IN MOTION, Eadweard Muybridge. More than 4,500 stopped-action photos, in action series, showing undraped men, women, children jumping, lying down, throwing, sitting, wrestling, carrying, etc. 390pp. 7⅞ x 10⅝.
20204-6 Clothbd.

TREES OF THE EASTERN AND CENTRAL UNITED STATES AND CANADA, William M. Harlow. Best one-volume guide to 140 trees. Full descriptions, woodlore, range, etc. Over 600 illustrations. Handy size. 288pp. 4½ x 6⅜.   20395-6

SONGS OF WESTERN BIRDS, Dr. Donald J. Borror. Complete song and call repertoire of 60 western species, including flycatchers, juncoes, cactus wrens, many more–includes fully illustrated booklet.   Cassette and manual 99913-0

GROWING AND USING HERBS AND SPICES, Milo Miloradovich. Versatile handbook provides all the information needed for cultivation and use of all the herbs and spices available in North America. 4 illustrations. Index. Glossary. 236pp. 5⅜ x 8½.
25058-X

BIG BOOK OF MAZES AND LABYRINTHS, Walter Shepherd. 50 mazes and labyrinths in all–classical, solid, ripple, and more–in one great volume. Perfect inexpensive puzzler for clever youngsters. Full solutions. 112pp. 8⅛ x 11.   22951-3

PIANO TUNING, J. Cree Fischer. Clearest, best book for beginner, amateur. Simple repairs, raising dropped notes, tuning by easy method of flattened fifths. No previous skills needed. 4 illustrations. 201pp. 5⅜ x 8½. 23267-0

HINTS TO SINGERS, Lillian Nordica. Selecting the right teacher, developing confidence, overcoming stage fright, and many other important skills receive thoughtful discussion in this indispensible guide, written by a world-famous diva of four decades' experience. 96pp. 5⅜ x 8½. 40094-8

THE COMPLETE NONSENSE OF EDWARD LEAR, Edward Lear. All nonsense limericks, zany alphabets, Owl and Pussycat, songs, nonsense botany, etc., illustrated by Lear. Total of 320pp. 5⅜ x 8½. (Available in U.S. only.) 20167-8

VICTORIAN PARLOUR POETRY: An Annotated Anthology, Michael R. Turner. 117 gems by Longfellow, Tennyson, Browning, many lesser-known poets. "The Village Blacksmith," "Curfew Must Not Ring Tonight," "Only a Baby Small," dozens more, often difficult to find elsewhere. Index of poets, titles, first lines. xxiii + 325pp. 5⅜ x 8¼. 27044-0

DUBLINERS, James Joyce. Fifteen stories offer vivid, tightly focused observations of the lives of Dublin's poorer classes. At least one, "The Dead," is considered a masterpiece. Reprinted complete and unabridged from standard edition. 160pp. 5³⁄₁₆ x 8¼. 26870-5

GREAT WEIRD TALES: 14 Stories by Lovecraft, Blackwood, Machen and Others, S. T. Joshi (ed.). 14 spellbinding tales, including "The Sin Eater," by Fiona McLeod, "The Eye Above the Mantel," by Frank Belknap Long, as well as renowned works by R. H. Barlow, Lord Dunsany, Arthur Machen, W. C. Morrow and eight other masters of the genre. 256pp. 5⅜ x 8½. (Available in U.S. only.) 40436-6

THE BOOK OF THE SACRED MAGIC OF ABRAMELIN THE MAGE, translated by S. MacGregor Mathers. Medieval manuscript of ceremonial magic. Basic document in Aleister Crowley, Golden Dawn groups. 268pp. 5⅜ x 8½. 23211-5

NEW RUSSIAN-ENGLISH AND ENGLISH-RUSSIAN DICTIONARY, M. A. O'Brien. This is a remarkably handy Russian dictionary, containing a surprising amount of information, including over 70,000 entries. 366pp. 4½ x 6⅛. 20208-9

HISTORIC HOMES OF THE AMERICAN PRESIDENTS, Second, Revised Edition, Irvin Haas. A traveler's guide to American Presidential homes, most open to the public, depicting and describing homes occupied by every American President from George Washington to George Bush. With visiting hours, admission charges, travel routes. 175 photographs. Index. 160pp. 8¼ x 11. 26751-2

NEW YORK IN THE FORTIES, Andreas Feininger. 162 brilliant photographs by the well-known photographer, formerly with *Life* magazine. Commuters, shoppers, Times Square at night, much else from city at its peak. Captions by John von Hartz. 181pp. 9¼ x 10¾. 23585-8

INDIAN SIGN LANGUAGE, William Tomkins. Over 525 signs developed by Sioux and other tribes. Written instructions and diagrams. Also 290 pictographs. 111pp. 6⅛ x 9¼. 22029-X

CATALOG OF DOVER BOOKS

ANATOMY: A Complete Guide for Artists, Joseph Sheppard. A master of figure drawing shows artists how to render human anatomy convincingly. Over 460 illustrations. 224pp. 8⅜ x 11¼. 27279-6

MEDIEVAL CALLIGRAPHY: Its History and Technique, Marc Drogin. Spirited history, comprehensive instruction manual covers 13 styles (ca. 4th century through 15th). Excellent photographs; directions for duplicating medieval techniques with modern tools. 224pp. 8⅜ x 11¼. 26142-5

DRIED FLOWERS: How to Prepare Them, Sarah Whitlock and Martha Rankin. Complete instructions on how to use silica gel, meal and borax, perlite aggregate, sand and borax, glycerine and water to create attractive permanent flower arrangements. 12 illustrations. 32pp. 5⅜ x 8½. 21802-3

EASY-TO-MAKE BIRD FEEDERS FOR WOODWORKERS, Scott D. Campbell. Detailed, simple-to-use guide for designing, constructing, caring for and using feeders. Text, illustrations for 12 classic and contemporary designs. 96pp. 5⅜ x 8½. 25847-5

SCOTTISH WONDER TALES FROM MYTH AND LEGEND, Donald A. Mackenzie. 16 lively tales tell of giants rumbling down mountainsides, of a magic wand that turns stone pillars into warriors, of gods and goddesses, evil hags, powerful forces and more. 240pp. 5⅜ x 8½. 29677-6

THE HISTORY OF UNDERCLOTHES, C. Willett Cunnington and Phyllis Cunnington. Fascinating, well-documented survey covering six centuries of English undergarments, enhanced with over 100 illustrations: 12th-century laced-up bodice, footed long drawers (1795), 19th-century bustles, 19th-century corsets for men, Victorian "bust improvers," much more. 272pp. 5⅜ x 8¼. 27124-2

ARTS AND CRAFTS FURNITURE: The Complete Brooks Catalog of 1912, Brooks Manufacturing Co. Photos and detailed descriptions of more than 150 now very collectible furniture designs from the Arts and Crafts movement depict davenports, settees, buffets, desks, tables, chairs, bedsteads, dressers and more, all built of solid, quarter-sawed oak. Invaluable for students and enthusiasts of antiques, Americana and the decorative arts. 80pp. 6½ x 9¼. 27471-3

WILBUR AND ORVILLE: A Biography of the Wright Brothers, Fred Howard. Definitive, crisply written study tells the full story of the brothers' lives and work. A vividly written biography, unparalleled in scope and color, that also captures the spirit of an extraordinary era. 560pp. 6⅛ x 9¼. 40297-5

THE ARTS OF THE SAILOR: Knotting, Splicing and Ropework, Hervey Garrett Smith. Indispensable shipboard reference covers tools, basic knots and useful hitches; handsewing and canvas work, more. Over 100 illustrations. Delightful reading for sea lovers. 256pp. 5⅜ x 8½. 26440-8

FRANK LLOYD WRIGHT'S FALLINGWATER: The House and Its History, Second, Revised Edition, Donald Hoffmann. A total revision–both in text and illustrations–of the standard document on Fallingwater, the boldest, most personal architectural statement of Wright's mature years, updated with valuable new material from the recently opened Frank Lloyd Wright Archives. "Fascinating"–*The New York Times*. 116 illustrations. 128pp. 9¼ x 10¾. 27430-6

CATALOG OF DOVER BOOKS

PHOTOGRAPHIC SKETCHBOOK OF THE CIVIL WAR, Alexander Gardner. 100 photos taken on field during the Civil War. Famous shots of Manassas Harper's Ferry, Lincoln, Richmond, slave pens, etc. 244pp. 10⅝ x 8¼. 22731-6

FIVE ACRES AND INDEPENDENCE, Maurice G. Kains. Great back-to-the-land classic explains basics of self-sufficient farming. The one book to get. 95 illustrations. 397pp. 5⅜ x 8½. 20974-1

SONGS OF EASTERN BIRDS, Dr. Donald J. Borror. Songs and calls of 60 species most common to eastern U.S.: warblers, woodpeckers, flycatchers, thrushes, larks, many more in high-quality recording. Cassette and manual 99912-2

A MODERN HERBAL, Margaret Grieve. Much the fullest, most exact, most useful compilation of herbal material. Gigantic alphabetical encyclopedia, from aconite to zedoary, gives botanical information, medical properties, folklore, economic uses, much else. Indispensable to serious reader. 161 illustrations. 888pp. 6½ x 9¼. 2-vol. set. (Available in U.S. only.) Vol. I: 22798-7 Vol. II: 22799-5

HIDDEN TREASURE MAZE BOOK, Dave Phillips. Solve 34 challenging mazes accompanied by heroic tales of adventure. Evil dragons, people-eating plants, bloodthirsty giants, many more dangerous adversaries lurk at every twist and turn. 34 mazes, stories, solutions. 48pp. 8¼ x 11. 24566-7

LETTERS OF W. A. MOZART, Wolfgang A. Mozart. Remarkable letters show bawdy wit, humor, imagination, musical insights, contemporary musical world; includes some letters from Leopold Mozart. 276pp. 5⅜ x 8½. 22859-2

BASIC PRINCIPLES OF CLASSICAL BALLET, Agrippina Vaganova. Great Russian theoretician, teacher explains methods for teaching classical ballet. 118 illustrations. 175pp. 5⅜ x 8½. 22036-2

THE JUMPING FROG, Mark Twain. Revenge edition. The original story of The Celebrated Jumping Frog of Calaveras County, a hapless French translation, and Twain's hilarious "retranslation" from the French. 12 illustrations. 66pp. 5⅜ x 8½. 22686-7

BEST REMEMBERED POEMS, Martin Gardner (ed.). The 126 poems in this superb collection of 19th- and 20th-century British and American verse range from Shelley's "To a Skylark" to the impassioned "Renascence" of Edna St. Vincent Millay and to Edward Lear's whimsical "The Owl and the Pussycat." 224pp. 5⅜ x 8½. 27165-X

COMPLETE SONNETS, William Shakespeare. Over 150 exquisite poems deal with love, friendship, the tyranny of time, beauty's evanescence, death and other themes in language of remarkable power, precision and beauty. Glossary of archaic terms. 80pp. 5³⁄₁₆ x 8¼. 26686-9

THE BATTLES THAT CHANGED HISTORY, Fletcher Pratt. Eminent historian profiles 16 crucial conflicts, ancient to modern, that changed the course of civilization. 352pp. 5⅜ x 8½. 41129-X

THE WIT AND HUMOR OF OSCAR WILDE, Alvin Redman (ed.). More than 1,000 ripostes, paradoxes, wisecracks: Work is the curse of the drinking classes; I can resist everything except temptation; etc. 258pp. 5⅜ x 8½. 20602-5

SHAKESPEARE LEXICON AND QUOTATION DICTIONARY, Alexander Schmidt. Full definitions, locations, shades of meaning in every word in plays and poems. More than 50,000 exact quotations. 1,485pp. 6½ x 9¼. 2-vol. set.
Vol. 1: 22726-X
Vol. 2: 22727-8

SELECTED POEMS, Emily Dickinson. Over 100 best-known, best-loved poems by one of America's foremost poets, reprinted from authoritative early editions. No comparable edition at this price. Index of first lines. 64pp. 5³⁄₁₆ x 8¼. 26466-1

THE INSIDIOUS DR. FU-MANCHU, Sax Rohmer. The first of the popular mystery series introduces a pair of English detectives to their archnemesis, the diabolical Dr. Fu-Manchu. Flavorful atmosphere, fast-paced action, and colorful characters enliven this classic of the genre. 208pp. 5³⁄₁₆ x 8¼. 29898-1

THE MALLEUS MALEFICARUM OF KRAMER AND SPRENGER, translated by Montague Summers. Full text of most important witchhunter's "bible," used by both Catholics and Protestants. 278pp. 6⅝ x 10. 22802-9

SPANISH STORIES/CUENTOS ESPAÑOLES: A Dual-Language Book, Angel Flores (ed.). Unique format offers 13 great stories in Spanish by Cervantes, Borges, others. Faithful English translations on facing pages. 352pp. 5⅜ x 8½. 25399-6

GARDEN CITY, LONG ISLAND, IN EARLY PHOTOGRAPHS, 1869–1919, Mildred H. Smith. Handsome treasury of 118 vintage pictures, accompanied by carefully researched captions, document the Garden City Hotel fire (1899), the Vanderbilt Cup Race (1908), the first airmail flight departing from the Nassau Boulevard Aerodrome (1911), and much more. 96pp. 8⅞ x 11¾. 40669-5

OLD QUEENS, N.Y., IN EARLY PHOTOGRAPHS, Vincent F. Seyfried and William Asadorian. Over 160 rare photographs of Maspeth, Jamaica, Jackson Heights, and other areas. Vintage views of DeWitt Clinton mansion, 1939 World's Fair and more. Captions. 192pp. 8⅞ x 11. 26358-4

CAPTURED BY THE INDIANS: 15 Firsthand Accounts, 1750-1870, Frederick Drimmer. Astounding true historical accounts of grisly torture, bloody conflicts, relentless pursuits, miraculous escapes and more, by people who lived to tell the tale. 384pp. 5⅜ x 8½. 24901-8

THE WORLD'S GREAT SPEECHES (Fourth Enlarged Edition), Lewis Copeland, Lawrence W. Lamm, and Stephen J. McKenna. Nearly 300 speeches provide public speakers with a wealth of updated quotes and inspiration–from Pericles' funeral oration and William Jennings Bryan's "Cross of Gold Speech" to Malcolm X's powerful words on the Black Revolution and Earl of Spenser's tribute to his sister, Diana, Princess of Wales. 944pp. 5⅜ x 8⅜. 40903-1

THE BOOK OF THE SWORD, Sir Richard F. Burton. Great Victorian scholar/adventurer's eloquent, erudite history of the "queen of weapons"–from prehistory to early Roman Empire. Evolution and development of early swords, variations (sabre, broadsword, cutlass, scimitar, etc.), much more. 336pp. 6⅛ x 9¼.
25434-8

AUTOBIOGRAPHY: The Story of My Experiments with Truth, Mohandas K. Gandhi. Boyhood, legal studies, purification, the growth of the Satyagraha (nonviolent protest) movement. Critical, inspiring work of the man responsible for the freedom of India. 480pp. 5⅜ x 8½. (Available in U.S. only.) 24593-4

CELTIC MYTHS AND LEGENDS, T. W. Rolleston. Masterful retelling of Irish and Welsh stories and tales. Cuchulain, King Arthur, Deirdre, the Grail, many more. First paperback edition. 58 full-page illustrations. 512pp. 5⅜ x 8½. 26507-2

THE PRINCIPLES OF PSYCHOLOGY, William James. Famous long course complete, unabridged. Stream of thought, time perception, memory, experimental methods; great work decades ahead of its time. 94 figures. 1,391pp. 5⅜ x 8½. 2-vol. set. Vol. I: 20381-6 Vol. II: 20382-4

THE WORLD AS WILL AND REPRESENTATION, Arthur Schopenhauer. Definitive English translation of Schopenhauer's life work, correcting more than 1,000 errors, omissions in earlier translations. Translated by E. F. J. Payne. Total of 1,269pp. 5⅜ x 8½. 2-vol. set. Vol. 1: 21761-2 Vol. 2: 21762-0

MAGIC AND MYSTERY IN TIBET, Madame Alexandra David-Neel. Experiences among lamas, magicians, sages, sorcerers, Bonpa wizards. A true psychic discovery. 32 illustrations. 321pp. 5⅜ x 8½. (Available in U.S. only.) 22682-4

THE EGYPTIAN BOOK OF THE DEAD, E. A. Wallis Budge. Complete reproduction of Ani's papyrus, finest ever found. Full hieroglyphic text, interlinear transliteration, word-for-word translation, smooth translation. 533pp. 6½ x 9¼. 21866-X

MATHEMATICS FOR THE NONMATHEMATICIAN, Morris Kline. Detailed, college-level treatment of mathematics in cultural and historical context, with numerous exercises. Recommended Reading Lists. Tables. Numerous figures. 641pp. 5⅜ x 8½. 24823-2

PROBABILISTIC METHODS IN THE THEORY OF STRUCTURES, Isaac Elishakoff. Well-written introduction covers the elements of the theory of probability from two or more random variables, the reliability of such multivariable structures, the theory of random function, Monte Carlo methods of treating problems incapable of exact solution, and more. Examples. 502pp. 5⅜ x 8½. 40691-1

THE RIME OF THE ANCIENT MARINER, Gustave Doré, S. T. Coleridge. Doré's finest work; 34 plates capture moods, subtleties of poem. Flawless full-size reproductions printed on facing pages with authoritative text of poem. "Beautiful. Simply beautiful."–*Publisher's Weekly*. 77pp. 9¼ x 12. 22305-1

NORTH AMERICAN INDIAN DESIGNS FOR ARTISTS AND CRAFTSPEOPLE, Eva Wilson. Over 360 authentic copyright-free designs adapted from Navajo blankets, Hopi pottery, Sioux buffalo hides, more. Geometrics, symbolic figures, plant and animal motifs, etc. 128pp. 8⅜ x 11. (Not for sale in the United Kingdom.) 25341-4

SCULPTURE: Principles and Practice, Louis Slobodkin. Step-by-step approach to clay, plaster, metals, stone; classical and modern. 253 drawings, photos. 255pp. 8⅛ x 11. 22960-2

THE INFLUENCE OF SEA POWER UPON HISTORY, 1660–1783, A. T. Mahan. Influential classic of naval history and tactics still used as text in war colleges. First paperback edition. 4 maps. 24 battle plans. 640pp. 5⅜ x 8½. 25509-3

CATALOG OF DOVER BOOKS

THE STORY OF THE TITANIC AS TOLD BY ITS SURVIVORS, Jack Winocour (ed.). What it was really like. Panic, despair, shocking inefficiency, and a little heroism. More thrilling than any fictional account. 26 illustrations. 320pp. 5⅜ x 8½. 20610-6

FAIRY AND FOLK TALES OF THE IRISH PEASANTRY, William Butler Yeats (ed.). Treasury of 64 tales from the twilight world of Celtic myth and legend: "The Soul Cages," "The Kildare Pooka," "King O'Toole and his Goose," many more. Introduction and Notes by W. B. Yeats. 352pp. 5⅜ x 8½. 26941-8

BUDDHIST MAHAYANA TEXTS, E. B. Cowell and others (eds.). Superb, accurate translations of basic documents in Mahayana Buddhism, highly important in history of religions. The Buddha-karita of Asvaghosha, Larger Sukhavativyuha, more. 448pp. 5⅜ x 8½. 25552-2

ONE TWO THREE . . . INFINITY: Facts and Speculations of Science, George Gamow. Great physicist's fascinating, readable overview of contemporary science: number theory, relativity, fourth dimension, entropy, genes, atomic structure, much more. 128 illustrations. Index. 352pp. 5⅜ x 8½. 25664-2

EXPERIMENTATION AND MEASUREMENT, W. J. Youden. Introductory manual explains laws of measurement in simple terms and offers tips for achieving accuracy and minimizing errors. Mathematics of measurement, use of instruments, experimenting with machines. 1994 edition. Foreword. Preface. Introduction. Epilogue. Selected Readings. Glossary. Index. Tables and figures. 128pp. 5⅜ x 8½. 40451-X

DALÍ ON MODERN ART: The Cuckolds of Antiquated Modern Art, Salvador Dalí. Influential painter skewers modern art and its practitioners. Outrageous evaluations of Picasso, Cézanne, Turner, more. 15 renderings of paintings discussed. 44 calligraphic decorations by Dalí. 96pp. 5⅜ x 8½. (Available in U.S. only.) 29220-7

ANTIQUE PLAYING CARDS: A Pictorial History, Henry René D'Allemagne. Over 900 elaborate, decorative images from rare playing cards (14th–20th centuries): Bacchus, death, dancing dogs, hunting scenes, royal coats of arms, players cheating, much more. 96pp. 9¼ x 12¼. 29265-7

MAKING FURNITURE MASTERPIECES: 30 Projects with Measured Drawings, Franklin H. Gottshall. Step-by-step instructions, illustrations for constructing handsome, useful pieces, among them a Sheraton desk, Chippendale chair, Spanish desk, Queen Anne table and a William and Mary dressing mirror. 224pp. 8⅛ x 11¼. 29338-6

THE FOSSIL BOOK: A Record of Prehistoric Life, Patricia V. Rich et al. Profusely illustrated definitive guide covers everything from single-celled organisms and dinosaurs to birds and mammals and the interplay between climate and man. Over 1,500 illustrations. 760pp. 7½ x 10⅛. 29371-8

Paperbound unless otherwise indicated. Available at your book dealer, online at **www.doverpublications.com**, or by writing to Dept. GI, Dover Publications, Inc., 31 East 2nd Street, Mineola, NY 11501. For current price information or for free catalogues (please indicate field of interest), write to Dover Publications or log on to **www.doverpublications.com** and see every Dover book in print. Dover publishes more than 500 books each year on science, elementary and advanced mathematics, biology, music, art, literary history, social sciences, and other areas.